TOO FAT
TOO SLUTTY
TOO LOUD

TOO FAT
TOO SLUTTY
TOO LOUD

THE RISE AND REIGN OF
THE UNRULY WOMAN

ANNE HELEN PETERSEN

SCRIBNER

LONDON NEW YORK TORONTO SYDNEY NEW DELHI

First published in the USA by Plume, an imprint of Penguin Random House LLC, 2017
First published in Great Britain by Scribner, an imprint of Simon & Schuster UK Ltd, 2017
A CBS COMPANY

1 3 5 7 9 10 8 6 4 2

Simon & Schuster UK Ltd
1st Floor
222 Gray's Inn Road
London WC1X 8HB

www.simonandschuster.co.uk
www.simonandschuster.com.au
www.simonandschuster.co.in

Simon & Schuster Australia, Sydney
Simon & Schuster India, New Delhi

A CIP catalogue record for this book
is available from the British Library

Hardback ISBN: 978-1-4711-7176-5
eBook ISBN: 978-1-4711-7177-2
Export Trade Paperback ISBN: 978-1-4711-7190-1

Printed and bound by CPI Group (UK) Ltd, Croydon CR0 4YY

Simon & Schuster UK Ltd are committed to sourcing paper
that is made from wood grown in sustainable forests and support the Forest
Stewardship Council, the leading international forest certification organisation.
Our books displaying the FSC logo are printed on FSC certified paper.

For my unruly mother

Contents

Introduction ix

1. Too Strong ✦ Serena Williams 1

2. Too Fat ✦ Melissa McCarthy 27

3. Too Gross ✦ Abbi Jacobson and Ilana Glazer 51

4. Too Slutty ✦ Nicki Minaj 73

5. Too Old ✦ Madonna 95

6. Too Pregnant ✦ Kim Kardashian 111

CONTENTS

7. TOO SHRILL ✦ HILLARY CLINTON 135

8. TOO QUEER ✦ CAITLYN JENNER 163

9. TOO LOUD ✦ JENNIFER WEINER 185

10. TOO NAKED ✦ LENA DUNHAM 211

CONCLUSION 231

Acknowledgments 235

Notes 237

INTRODUCTION

On November 8, 2016, I woke up early and said, to no one in particular, "I'm so excited to vote for our first female president!" I wasn't alone in this sentiment: the entire city of New York seemed to vibrate with anticipation that day. Walking back from my polling place, I saw a mom with her three young daughters, all dressed in Hillary Clinton pantsuits. At the corner of Clinton and President Streets in Brooklyn, dozens of people were taking selfies. On the subway, a stranger saw my voting sticker and said, "Thank you for doing your civic duty!" Some sites predicted as small as a 1 percent chance of Trump winning. The day's outcome seemed assured.

Fast-forward twelve hours. I'm sitting at the BuzzFeed office in Manhattan, where the tone has taken an abrupt turn from excitement to panic. During the month leading up to the election, I had spoken to hundreds of women at Trump rallies—many of whom overflowed with hatred for Clinton. They joined the shouts to "lock her up" that echoed through the rallies; they wore shirts emblazoned with "Monica Sucks, Hillary Swallows." Statistically, these women were a minority. But they had tapped into a larger reservoir of dislike, distrust, and repulsion that, as the election results flowing into the office were gradually making clear, had mobilized against Clinton.

I cease my frantic refreshing of Twitter and stare blankly ahead. A plastic cup of white wine grows warm beside me. Donald Trump's win becomes probable, then certain. My phone lights up.

"I'm so sorry to do this," my editor says, "but we need you to write something."

I had expected a relaxing, joyful rest of the week. I was exhausted from weeks reporting on the road. I could have cried. But instead, I opened up a new document, typing: *This Is How Much America Hates Women.*

Not all women, of course. Just women like Fox anchor Megyn Kelly, who'd questioned Trump about his history with women during the primary debates. Women like former Miss Universe Alicia Machado, who'd dared to gain weight. Women like Elizabeth Warren, who simply won't shut up, or Rosie O'Donnell, with whom Trump had feuded for years. Women like the dozen who've accused him of sexual impropriety and/or assault, and Clinton herself, whom he'd referred to as a "nasty woman."

In other words, *unruly* women—the type who incite Trump's ire, and whom millions of voters have decided they can degrade and dismiss, simply because they question, interrogate, or otherwise challenge the status quo. Of course, there have been unruly women for as long as there have been boundaries of what constitutes acceptable "feminine" behavior: women who, in some way, step outside the boundaries of good womanhood, who end up being labeled too fat, too loud, too slutty, too whatever characteristic women are supposed to keep under control. The hatred directed toward the unruly women of the 2016 campaign is simply an extension of the anxiety that's accumulated around this type of woman for centuries.

Which is why Trump's defeat would've felt like such a victory for unruly women everywhere: a mandate that this type of demeaning, dehumanizing behavior toward women is simply not acceptable, particularly from the president of the United States. Instead, Trump's victory signals the beginning of a backlash that has been quietly brewing for years, as unruly women of various forms have come to dominate the cultural landscape.

And while the unruly woman is under threat, she isn't going anywhere: Clinton, after all, won the popular vote by nearly three million votes, and the election has mobilized untold numbers of women to protect their rights and those of others. Trump's America feels unsafe for so many; the future of the nation seems uncertain. But unruliness—in its many manifestations, small and large, in action, in representation, in language—feels more important, more *necessary,* than ever.

◆ ◆ ◆

Unruly women surround us in our everyday lives, yet such figures become most powerful in celebrity form, where they become even more layered and fraught with contradiction. The next ten chapters thus examine female celebrities, from Serena Williams to Lena Dunham, who have been conceived of as unruly in some capacity. And while each chapter is named for the celebrity's dominant mode of unruliness—too slutty, too gross, too queer—each of these women is unruly in multiple, compounding ways: Serena Williams is too strong, but she's also too masculine, too rude, too fashionable, too black; Lena Dunham is too naked, but she's also too loud, too aggressive, too powerful, too revealing, too *much*.

I've filled the book with women who occupy all different corners of the mainstream, from the literary world to Hollywood, from HBO to the tennis court. It includes several women of color, but the prevalence of straight white women serves to highlight an ugly truth: that the difference between cute, acceptable unruliness and unruliness that results in ire is often as simple as the color of a woman's skin, whom she prefers to sleep with, and her proximity to traditional femininity. When a black woman talks too loud or too honestly, she becomes "troubling" or "angry" or "out of control"; a queer woman who talks about sex suddenly becomes proof that all gay people are intrinsically promiscuous. It's one thing to be a young, cherub-faced, straight woman doing and saying things that make people uncomfortable. It's quite another—and far riskier—to do those same things in a body that is not white, not straight, not slender, not young, or not American.

Each chapter starts with the thesis of a particular woman's unruliness—Melissa McCarthy's status as "too fat," for example—and unravels the way this behavior has been historically framed as an affliction at odds with proper femininity. The more you analyze what makes these behaviors transgressive, the easier it is to see what they're threatening: what it means to be a woman, of course, but also entrenched understandings of women's passive role in society.

While the book centers around highly visible women, it also reveals the expectations surrounding every woman's behavior—and why talking too loudly, acting too promiscuously, or exposing too much skin is so incredibly threatening to the status quo.

That threat is part of why talking about any of the women in this book opens the floodgates to controversy. Whether the discussion takes place on Facebook or at happy hour, mentioning these women is the quickest way to escalate the conversation, alienate friends, offend elders, and turn off dates. Their bodies, words, and actions have become a locus for the type of inflammatory rhetoric usually reserved only for political figures. It's as if each of these women is constantly igniting the line of acceptable behavior: you don't know where it is until she steps over it, at which point it bursts into flames.

Celebrities are our most visible and binding embodiments of ideology at work: the way we pinpoint and police representations of everything from blackness to queerness, from femininity to pregnancy. Which is why the success of these unruly women is inextricable from the confluence of attitudes toward women in the 2010s: the public reembrace of feminism set against a backdrop of increased legislation of women's bodies, the persistence of the income gap, the policing of how women's bodies should look and act in public, and the election of Trump. Through this lens, unruliness can be viewed as an amplification of anger about a climate that publicly embraces equality but does little to enact change. It's no wonder we have such mixed feelings about these women: they're constant reminders of the chasm between what we think we believe and how we actually behave.

✦ ✦ ✦

This is far from the first time the unruly woman has taken on such outsized importance in the American imagination. Anne Boleyn, Marie Antoinette, Simone de Beauvoir, Virginia Woolf, Mae West, Elizabeth Taylor, Eleanor Roosevelt, Jane Fonda—all were unruly in some capacity, and that unruliness is part of the reason their names live on. The most potent manifestation in recent history, however, dates to the early nineties, when Roseanne Barr became the unruly woman par excellence: her show, *Roseanne*, dominated the television landscape, overtaking *The Cosby Show* as the top-rated program on television in 1989. For the next six years, it remained in the top five Nielsen programs—an unprecedented feat for a show that not only focused on a working-class family, but also introduced and interrogated queer and feminist issues.

Roseanne boldly challenged the image of middle-class respectability proffered by sitcoms like *The Cosby Show*, *Growing Pains*, *Family Ties*, and *Family Matters*. The family's house was messy and claustrophobic; money was always tight, and Roseanne and her husband, Dan, played by John Goodman, were always exhausted from work. Their kids could be rude or obscene, and the parents often responded in kind.

In her groundbreaking work *The Unruly Woman*, Kathleen Rowe Karlyn points to the ways in which Barr used her stardom to highlight the vast gap between the progressive aspirations of Second Wave Feminism and the lived reality of providing for a working-class family in the wake of Reaganism.[1] That Roseanne chose a working-class mother as the avatar of her rebellion is significant: the fiscal constraints of her situation meant that her options for rebellion manifested in the volume of her voice, the expanse of her body, the clutter of her living room, and the overarching refusal to make a working-class home be simply a less expensive version of a bourgeois one.

Outside of *Roseanne*, Barr cultivated an equally unruly celebrity image: there was her public courting of and marriage to fellow comedian Tom Arnold, and her 1990 rendition of the national anthem at a baseball game, so off-key and flippant it prompted President George H. W. Bush to decry it as "disgraceful." She was, as my mother put it, not in "good taste"—which is part of why, as a ten-year-old girl, I wasn't allowed to watch *Roseanne* even as I witnessed equally ribald humor on shows like *Home Improvement*.

Karlyn points to a "profound ambivalence" around Roseanne— even though she was the star of one of the most popular shows on television, even if the readers of *People* magazine voted her their "Top Female Star," she was still a subject of slight disgust.[2] *Esquire* manifested this split attitude when it featured her in its pages by writing two pieces: one in favor, the other against. On the cover of *Vanity Fair*, she was declared "Roseanne on Top"—but the accompanying image showed her pinning Arnold to the ground, her breasts overflowing, her mouth in a devious cackle. Her power was abundant, but it had to be distorted—made frightening—for public consumption. Roseanne was figured as just barely in control of herself, her body, her behavior, which made it all the easier to frame her as dangerously *out* of control (and a threat to America) when she dared to sing the national anthem off-key. It would take more than a decade for a woman with a similarly unruly energy to reach something close to her level of stardom again.

What happened to Roseanne should be instructive. It's tempting to think of unruly women as radicals transgressing and usurping societal norms—and while they do make rebellion and disobedience imaginable or palatable, their actions can also serve to fortify dominant norms. Take the example of Dixie Chick Natalie Maines, who became the outspoken spokesperson for a feminist, liberal, progressive wing of country in the mid-2000s. By transgressing the boundaries of their genre, the Dixie Chicks endeared themselves to certain fans, but they also alienated themselves from the very root of their stardom. Today, articles about slightly transgressive country stars like Kacey Musgraves hold up the Dixie Chicks as a cautionary tale. The Dixie Chicks may have crossed the line, but they didn't break it down; instead, the line has been built up stronger than before.

It's a common narrative for the unruly woman. It happened to Mae West, the ribald comedian of the 1930s whose full figure sparked a trend against "reducing," only to have her witty, and self-authored, brand of humor censored to the point of banality and obscurity over the course of the decade. It struck Jane Fonda amidst her activism in Vietnam; it beset Roseanne in the 1990s; it afflicted Rosie O'Donnell after the demise of her talk show in the 2000s, and it has already begun to happen to many of the women featured in this book: unruliness can spark a firestorm, but it can also scorch the very ground on which they tread.

Roseanne, Jane Fonda, and Mae West were all divisive figures, but it wasn't as simple as camps for and against: they could spark feelings of fascination and repulsion at the same time, a sentiment that should sound familiar to fans of many of the women in this book. There are all sorts of things that attract our

curiosity but which societal norms tell us we should reject—
things that trespass the unspoken yet often rigid borders of good
taste. Scholars have a term for objects, peoples, and ideas that
inspire these feelings of attraction and rejection: "abject." By
strict definition, "abject" refers to things that are horrendously
bad, unpleasant, or degrading—things that, as the word's Latin
roots, *abijicere* (to reject) and *jacere* (to throw), suggest, must be
repudiated and cast aside.

Instead of hiding their abjection, unruly women amplify it:
Madonna asserts her body as sexual past the age when it can be;
Abbi Jacobson and Ilana Glazer talk openly about shit and periods;
Kim Kardashian refuses to hide her pregnant body. Others do so
by troubling the distinction between borders: Serena Williams's
body is muscular like a man's and curvy like a woman's, while
Nicki Minaj and Hillary Clinton trespass into male-dominated
cultural spheres. If a defining characteristic of the abject is the
command to throw it out, these women refuse it—which, of course,
renders them all the more compelling.

✦ ✦ ✦

Every few decades, an unruly female celebrity inflames the popular consciousness. What distinguishes our current cultural moment, then, is how thoroughly unruly women have come to
dominate the zeitgeist: *Girls* and *Broad City* have inspired more
conversation over the last three years than any other thirty-
minute shows. Melissa McCarthy is one of the most reliable box
office draws in Hollywood today. Lena Dunham's book, *Not That
Kind of Girl*, reached number two on *The New York Times* bestseller list; her newsletter, *Lenny*, boasts more than half a million

subscribers. Nicki Minaj's third album, *The Pinkprint*, debuted at number two on the *Billboard* charts; the video for "Anaconda" has been viewed 650 million times. Serena Williams has won twenty-three grand slams. The *20/20* special focused on Caitlyn Jenner's transition garnered a staggering 20.7 million viewers.[3] Jennifer Weiner's books have sold more than thirteen million copies worldwide. Kim Kardashian took in more than $51 million in 2016.[4] And Clinton, remember, won the popular vote by more than 2.8 million.

Yet for all these women's visibility and profitability, they compete against a far more palatable—and, in many cases, more successful—form of femininity: the lifestyle supermom. Exemplified by Reese Witherspoon, Jessica Alba, Blake Lively, Gwyneth Paltrow, and Ivanka Trump, these women rarely trend on Twitter, but they've built tremendously successful brands by embracing the "new domesticity," defined by consumption, maternity, and a sort of twenty-first-century gentility. They have slim, disciplined bodies and adorable pregnancies; they never wear the wrong thing or speak negatively or make themselves abrasive in any way. Importantly, these celebrities are also all white—or, in the case of Jessica Alba, careful to elide any connotations of ethnicity—and straight.

By transforming themselves into brands, filling their online stores with goods and clothing and accessories, they imply that every woman can have the same sort of contentment: all they need to do is buy a dress, purchase some chemical-free baby wipes, and follow a complicated recipe for a vegan smoothie, and they can have the same bronzed glow of contentment as these celebs. You can see their influence across Pinterest and the mommy-blogosphere, where many women reproduce the rhetoric of self-care and affirmation even as they police the bodies, parenting choices, consumption habits, and lifestyle decisions of both themselves and others.

The women I've chosen for case studies in this book function as implicit and explicit alternatives to the "new domesticity." Yet at the same time, they've also all made themselves amenable to popular consumption. Some, like Kardashian, generally abide by social standards, but her unruly performance of pregnancy, and the backlash against it, highlights just how readily the tide of public acceptance can turn. Others, like Kardashian's stepparent, Caitlyn Jenner, belong to a category that's only very recently become societally sanctioned and even legally protected—yet every step that Jenner makes is carefully calculated so as to assuage anxieties about her transformation. Melissa McCarthy calls out the assumptions people make about fat people but never gets truly mad; Hillary Clinton is incredibly mindful to modulate her voice so as to never appear angry in public.

There are hundreds of women in the public sphere who don't exercise such careful modulation—women who are relegated to niche corners of pop culture because they've been figured as too big, queer, loud, smart, sexual, or otherwise abject for mainstream audiences. Women like Lea DeLaria, the first openly gay comic to appear on late-night television all the way back in 1993, who has struggled to find higher-profile roles than her supporting bit on *Orange Is the New Black*. Or Mo'Nique, who was outspoken about her refusal to participate in the Oscar campaign for her performance in *Precious*—and found herself a Hollywood outcast. Or even Kim Novak, once considered one of the most beautiful stars in Hollywood, whose plastic surgery–facilitated attempts to maintain her youthful face have rendered her an object of severe ridicule.

Women like DeLaria, Mo'Nique, and Novak might be briefly defended in think pieces, but they're nevertheless excluded from salable stardom: they're simply too much for the broad, middling, easily offended audience so necessary for a mainstream stardom. The rejection of these women makes it clear: there's still a firm line of acceptable female behavior. And while it might, in this moment, be cool and profitable to toe it, to find oneself on the other side is tantamount to career suicide.

In the end, all of the unruly women in this book have made concessions in order to have their work approved and disseminated by the mainstream. By focusing on unruliness that's made its way into the mainstream, this book considers the costs and benefits of smoothing one's sharp edges just enough to make it onto the cover of *Vanity Fair* or into the pages of *GQ*, multiplexes across America, or the White House—and the implication that unruliness is still largely the provenance of women who are white and straight.

✦ ✦ ✦

Someone might look at a picture of me, or read my résumé, and wonder what interest I would have in unruliness: I'm white, I'm blonde, I'm not fat. I grew up middle-class in a midsize town. I got straight As. I was a cheerleader for seven years. The only time I got in trouble in high school was for skipping A.P. English to go to the premiere of *Star Wars*. I'm straight and cisgender. I attended a good college and went on to pursue a PhD. I've received one speeding ticket. But so much of that amenability—that need to please, that lack of acting out—stemmed from a posture of fear.

My mother was a weirdo, non-makeup-wearing mathematician, so the fear certainly didn't come from her. But I was always cripplingly terrified of what people thought of me: my classmates, the boys I liked and even the ones I didn't, random people on the street, the teachers whose approval I craved. That fear was so overwhelming that I allowed it to temper and otherwise silence the parts of myself that gave me joy. I stopped raising my hand as much in class. I disciplined my body through various forms of over-exercise and disordered eating, not because I liked running, but because I was mortified by the thought of getting fat. I didn't believe God would forsake me if I lost my virginity, but I kept it out of anxiety that I'd be labeled a slut. I didn't drink because who knew what embarrassing thing I might say or do while drunk. I was happy, ostensibly, but every move was motivated by fear. Part of this fear was derived from living in a rural town where gossip and small-mindedness made other ways of being unthinkable, but part of it was entirely my own devising.

I spent the bulk of my adolescent life internalizing the fact that girls who crossed that invisible line would become pariahs: excised from their communities and families, unable to find work or companionship. I was wrong, of course, but it took finding my own group of weird, confident, *too much* friends for me to lean into my own difference, my own modes of unruliness. It's taken many years for those behaviors to blossom, and many internal checks remain stubbornly difficult to slough. Just because you spend years analyzing unruliness doesn't mean you're not subject to the trenchant cultural imperative to shun, shame, and reject it.

Which is precisely why I wanted to write this book: these unruly women are so magnetic, but that magnetism is countered, at every point, by ideologies that train both men and women to distance themselves from those behaviors in our own lives. Put differently, it's one thing to admire such abrasiveness and disrespect for the status quo in someone else; it's quite another to take that risk in one's own life.

That's why the threat of a backlash feels so real. These female celebrities may be popular, but does their stardom contribute to an actual sea change of "acceptable" behaviors and bodies and ways of being for women today? None of these chapters offers a clear answer, in part because that answer is less dependent on the women themselves and more on the way we, as cultural consumers, decide to talk and think about them. Not as women "acting out" and, as such, in need of censoring, but as endlessly deserving of our consideration: both critical and compassionate.

My hope is that this book unites the enthralling, infuriating, and exhilarating conversations that swirl around these women, but also incites new and more expansive ones. Because these women and their unruliness *matter*—and the best way to show their gravity and power and influence is to refuse to shut up about why they do.

CHAPTER 1

TOO STRONG:
SERENA WILLIAMS

Imagine all the female tennis players in the world: their tan legs, their perky ponytails, their tennis whites. "Tennis has always been a game defined by Whiteness," *Essence* magazine declared in 1998. "European players whose names sound of fjords and ice caps, Clorox-clean tennis togs, the blinding colorless sun, the pale fans sipping water and vodka tonics."[1] They are rich, they are beautiful—they are, at least in the mind's eye, and at least until the mid-1990s, white.

But then the Williams sisters arrived on the international scene and changed all that.

In some sports, there's an indelible marker that divides the history of the game—a particularly excellent team, a match, a player who slices the entire understanding of the sport in two. There was the game before, and then there was a different understanding, a different benchmark, afterwards. That's what the Williamses did to tennis—they reset the game. It's not as if there hadn't been black tennis players before: Arthur Ashe, most famously, but also Althea Gibson, the first black player in professional tennis, and Zina Garrison, who won a gold medal in doubles tennis at the 1988 Olympics. But those players always, as *Essence* put it, "stood alone."[2] The Williams sisters had something else: each other, and their absolute dominance.

And then there was the confidence, the pure, delighted swagger, with which they approached the game. Like so many male greats before their time, they knew, unequivocally, that they were the greatest. And Serena in particular: she served "like a man," had muscles "like a man," threw "tantrums" "like a man." She dressed in ways that were either not womanly enough (at least not for the historically demure, delicate world of tennis fashion) or too womanly, which is to say, too sexy, too confident in their announcement of her muscular curves.

Williams was, and remains, too strong: in her body, but also in her personality, her resilience, and her fortitude in the two decades she's spent holistically reorganizing the standards of a sport from which people with her skin color, class, and background have been historically excluded.

While Serena's narrative begins with—and is never truly absent from—that of her sister, over the last ten years, it has taken on a separate power of its own. Today, she is celebrated for her athletic strength, for the confidence that stems from her dominance, for the sheer amplitude of her personality. But every step of Williams's career has been shadowed with the sort of resentment that emerges whenever someone unsettles the status quo in an effective and unapologetic way. Put differently, when she stirred the pot, a whole lot of bullshit rose to the surface—and her refusal to try to perfume its smell has made her unruliness all the more potent.

To understand what makes Williams's body and strength so unruly requires an understanding of how black bodies, and black female bodies in particular, have been depicted, understood, and policed throughout history—and just how much friction resulted when the Williams sisters entered one of the most exclusive sports in the world. That friction has exposed the rotting wood at the center of an aging, if beautifully glossed, institution, forcing an uncomfortable examination of both the legacy of tennis and what a female athlete can and should do in public.

✦ ✦ ✦

From the beginning, the narrative around the Williams family was one of *difference*. In a 1994 profile, the myth of the family—woven, primarily, by the Williams's father, Richard—was already coming into focus.[3] Richard had decided that his girls—the fourth and fifth daughters in a family of five girls—would become tennis players. No matter that they lived in one of the "roughest areas of Los Angeles," as dozens of publications would put it, in slightly different variations—Richard and Oracene, the girls' mother, found tennis courts, dubbed them the "East Compton Hills Country Club," and began training every day.[4]

Richard and Oracene homeschooled the girls, learning drills and techniques from books and VHS videos. Even after drive-by shootings threatened their safety on the courts, they maintained their strict daily schedule. "To prevent against such dangers in the future," one profile explained, "Richard Williams struck a deal with the three dominant gangs in the area—a member from each stood guard during hitting sessions."[5]

The veracity of that anecdote matters less than what Williams was doing by repeating it to the press. His daughters were different, it suggests, and not just because of the color of their skin. Unlike other players—who arrived at the sport because their class and place in society afforded them the possibility—the Williamses *fought* their way in. Any victory from that point forward would not be out of luck, or proximity to privilege, or pedigree. It would be through sheer strength, work, and will.

In 1990, the family moved to West Palm Beach, Florida, so Venus and Serena could attend the tennis academy of Rick Macci, the man whose tapes they'd so diligently watched. They began to rise to the top of their age rankings, but Richard refused to allow them to compete in the junior tennis tournament scene—a move that boggled the minds of many. His logic, however, was sound: while other young tennis players were burning out their still-growing bodies on the tour, he was cultivating powerhouses.

When Serena was ten, Richard pulled the sisters from the tennis academy and resumed training them exclusively within the family. He took on a posture of offense, telling interviewers that he'd never played tennis himself because it was a sissy sport, that he didn't like "tennis people" in general. Taken together, it was another message: no one else will be responsible for our success.[6]

"I taught my children they were the best in everything they did," Richard explained. "And they believed it."[7] And they kept believing it over the course of the next decade, as Venus became one of the best players in the world and Serena gradually rose to join her. That first decade was shaped by the same conversations that would become themes for the rest of their careers, with continued emphasis on their race, their power, and their difference.

Richard had never been shy to invoke the way his daughters' blackness made other players uncomfortable: even before the sisters went pro, "kids would be afraid to walk off the court, because their parents would be there waiting for them, saying, 'Why did you lose to that black girl?'"[8] As Richards later recalled in his autobiography, he'd arrange for kids in Compton to stand outside the courts while the girls were playing and yell every racial slur they could think of—a way to harden them against the white recoil that was bound to accompany their rise.[9]

He wasn't wrong. That recoil manifested in forms implicit and explicit, from other players, parents, fans, and the press. Commentators marveled at their hair—in beaded cornrows—as if they'd never seen such a thing in their lives; *The Wall Street Journal* called attention to "their exuberant athleticism, blithe self-confidence and colorfully beaded braids," which "would stand out in any sporting milieu."[10]

A feature in *Women's Sports & Fitness* was less coded: "The truth is that no white player would have received such a raft of criticism for being different from—or the same as—everybody else. The truth is that there has been racism in tennis, and it has been directed at the Williamses, although it has rarely been explicit. Rather, it has been conveyed by innuendo and insinuation, and in a subtle disproportion in the way people respond to them, alternating between vitriol and over-congratulation."[11] As their attorney, Keven Davis, explained: "People talk about how smart and articulate Venus is, as if it's surprising."[12]

But the sisters had already developed their own mechanism for excluding those who would exclude them: they giggled. Around reporters, around other players, around fans, they "seem to take pleasure in showing people within the exclusive sport just what it feels like to be excluded." It had the effect of putting other people on edge: "I know people think they're laughing at them," Oracene said in 1998.[13]

Whatever the intent, it was the opposite of what most of America—and the sporting world in particular—had come to expect as the norm for dealing with issues of race and racism, which is to say, not deal with it at all. The 1990s were distinguished by the burgeoning ideologies of postracism and postfeminism, which suggested that the goals of the civil rights and feminist movements had been achieved, so why should we worry about all this political correctness? Within this cultural logic, it was unnecessarily inflammatory to bring up issues of race—it was impolite, in poor taste.

But that lie—whose purpose was to allow white people to continue to think they weren't racist, even when their actions and words indicated otherwise—was one in which the Williams sisters, like their father, refused to participate. They rejected the idea that they should assimilate to the white codes of the tennis world. Instead, they posed the question of their difference over and over again—in every clack of their densely beaded hair, in every powerful serve.

Serena, especially, was conceived as possessing a fearsome strength: the first profile of the pair in *The New York Times* said she'd been described "as everything from a fireball to a pit bull to a classically muscled natural athlete with a fierce netside manner."[14] In 1998, the St. Paul *Pioneer Press* reported that Serena "pounded winners so hard that people in the stands were ducking."[15] Their game was, as Serena would recall in 2013, "a power game," one "that could always grow, one we could always improve . . . We could develop bigger serves, we could develop more speed."[16]

Their power and charisma invigorated the world of tennis, but the Williamses rejected the presumed posture of gratitude and humility. Talking about the draw of his daughters, Richard told *The New York Times* that "I think the people who have helped the [Tennis] Tour to get where it is now, you should want to share some of that with them instead of keeping it all to yourself."[17] In *Sports Illustrated*, Serena declared that "I've never been intimidated by anyone, and unless I'm across the net from someone who's 10 feet tall and green, I won't be. On the other hand, because of my size and skills, I can intimidate anyone."[18]

The attitude of the Williamses versus the World made them formidable adversaries, but it also made them vulnerable to attack, especially, as Serena's talent began to equal Venus's, in terms of match fixing: falling ill and withdrawing from tournaments instead of facing each other. Even though the sisters showed no reticence to play each other ("Venus has no reason to fear me," Serena said in 1998; "I've never feared anybody"), the rumors came to a head in 2001, when Venus withdrew from the Indian Wells tournament in California four minutes before her semifinal match against Serena.[19]

As the sisters have confirmed in numerous interviews since, the last-minute withdrawal wasn't meant as a manipulation: Venus was indeed injured; they communicated as much the day

7

before, but no one had announced it until immediately before the match. But the crowd cottoned to the idea of a conspiracy, and booed Serena throughout her match, Venus and Richard as they made their way to their seats, and Serena as she took the podium to accept the trophy for roundly defeating Kim Clijsters. Richard turned to the crowd of fifteen thousand and defiantly shook his fist—a gesture interpreted by some as a black power salute. Amidst the boos, he'd later tell the press that he heard racial epithets—an expression, as he'd tell the press, of what the crowd had been wanting to say for years. "The white people at Indian Wells, what they've been wanting to say all along to us finally came out: 'Nigger, stay away from here, we don't want you here.'"[20]

In the years since, there's been debate over whether the use of racial epithets can be substantiated—Venus, for her part, said, "I heard what he heard," but no one else reported hearing similar insults.[21] Still, the incident—which prompted a boycott of Indian Wells that lasted until 2014—became the defining moment of the Williams narrative. More than any single tournament win or loss, it emblematized the resentment, skepticism, and racially in-fused postures of both the world of tennis and the Williamses within it.

The ability to articulate the racism and exclusion the family had experienced for years seemed to embolden Serena. Over the course of the next two years, she'd rise to be the number-one-ranked women's tennis player in the world—a feat that included beating her sister in the 2002 Wimbledon finals without drop-ping a single set, and completing the first of what became known as a "Serena Slam"; that is, winning four Grand Slam titles in a row. Her dominance was complete.

Still, as *The Guardian* explained, "she is, to many observers, little more than one half of the 'problematic' Williams sisters who have 'taken over' women's tennis with their power and their attitude."[22] Foremost among Serena's "problematic" behaviors: her fashion.

The Williamses had long challenged the traditional dress code of the tennis world: as *Vogue* editor André Leon Talley remarked, "They burned tennis whites!"[23] In the process, they'd become fashion muses: in 1998, the pair appeared in *Vogue* magazine in Carolina Herrera; at Paris Fashion Week in 1999, an avant-garde designer presented dresses "inspired by the sisters."[24] In 2002, Serena competed at the U.S. Open wearing what others called a "sleek and sexy black leather-look catsuit." "This is my new design," she told reporters. "It makes me run faster and jump higher and is really sexy. I love it."[25]

The *Daily Mirror* claimed the "dominatrix-style" outfit was "a shocker for many spectators"; the *Ottawa Citizen* wrote that "pacemakers went aflutter at every tennis club in town"; a *Sunday Telegraph* columnist declared that the skintight outfit "only serves to accentuate a superstructure that is already bordering on the digitally enhanced and a rear end that I will attempt to sum up as discreetly as possible by simply referring to it as 'formidable.'"[26] All descriptions, in one way or another, for "this makes me feel uncomfortable."

To spectators accustomed to the pleated skirt and the sleeveless tennis shirt, Serena's body was "formidable" simply because it refused to cloak itself in the traditional garments of femininity. Instead of hiding the parts of her that distinguished her from her (white) competitors—including her muscular thighs and arms, her hair, her black skin—she accentuated them. And she owned it: as she "paraded" in her outfit, she roundly defeated her opponent, Corina Morariu, 6–2, 6–3. As she told *Fader* in 2016, wearing the catsuit marked the moment that she truly became comfortable with her sexuality: "I remember wearing that and thinking, 'Wow, I can't believe I'm wearing this.' I was a little nervous before, but afterwards I was totally OK."[27]

But it wasn't just the catsuit that put people on edge. On her left wrist, she wore a $29,000 Harry Winston diamond tennis bracelet—the precise signifier of the sort of tennis bourgeois culture that she had so effectively disrupted. Pairing the catsuit and the tennis bracelet was a political sartorial act. And it infuriated many, including *Washington Post* fashion critic Robin Givhan, who decried her appearance, a few days earlier, at a Harry Winston press op. "She wore an orange crochet hussy dress modeled after something Wilma Flintstone might choose," Givhan wrote, describing Serena's U.S. Open outfit as "the stylistic equivalent of trash talk."[28]

Williams's trashiness is the opposite of the tennis image: to be sexy, to admit you have a body, to wear things that are flashy or sparkly, all of it flies in the face of the traditional tennis ideal, which corresponds with that of upper-class America. To wit: bodies are most beautiful when elegantly draped; wealth should be displayed in objects like the tennis bracelet, but never paired with something as crassly connotative as *black leather*.

But therein lay the genius: the catsuit may have looked like black leather, but it was a trompe l'oeil, an optical illusion— the suit was actually made of spandex, intended to cling and move with Williams's body. It was only from the distance of the

spectator—in the stands, sitting at home—that it took on the va
lence of trashiness.

As teens, both Williams sisters took fashion design classes,
in part because their father had instilled in them the idea that
one day their tennis careers would be over, and they'd need another skill to fall back on. But that interest, manifested on and off
the tennis court, was routinely framed as a frivolous distraction.
Serena's outfits, including black sneakers that transformed into
boots, a studded sports bra, and a jean jacket, dominated sports
pages. She appeared in a white bikini for the *Sports Illustrated*
photo shoot; she wore a minidress, again described as "dominatrix style," for an appearance on *The Tonight Show*, where she
talked about her newly launched fashion company; she wore a
full-length pink gown to the ESPYs, prompting Steve Hummer of
The Atlanta Journal-Constitution to comment, "The ESPY
Awards do not exactly mass-produce memorable moments, but
who will ever forget the outfit worn by Female Athlete of the
Year Serena Williams? You haven't seen that little support since
the Michael Dukakis campaign."[29]

Put simply, she wasn't just allowing the world to make her
into a sex object but actively asserting herself as one. "The swimsuit photo shoot has been a goal of mine for some time," she told
The Express. "I wanted to do some different pictures . . . I'm setting different standards in fashion, I always try to look trendy
and do different things. People are now seeing me in a new light,
seeing me for who I really am."[30] She attended the MTV Video
Music Awards; she made appearances at club launches; she dated
Hollywood film producer Brett Ratner and was photographed
"showing off her figure" in a "wild hairstyle" and "striking

brown-and-white bikini" with him on the "exclusive island of St. Barts."[31]

But the idea of Serena as sexy was divisive: *The Mirror*, for example, wondered, "Is her unique figure the sexy, athletic look that every woman wants and every man lusts after? Or is it an over-worked masculine turn-off?"[32] Such questions, and the dichotomy they presume, point to trenchant assumptions about women's athletic bodies, and black athletic bodies in particular. Even though women have been participating "in sport" for more than a century, such diversion has always been fraught: a distraction, but not a profession. Women were often encouraged to take up sports without strong male counterparts (field hockey, volleyball) or that demanded little physical exertion (golf). If women's high school sports programs existed, they were always secondary.

Title IX, passed in 1972, ostensibly righted that imbalance, forcing an equal number of girls' sporting opportunities for every boys' one, thereby paving the way for generations of women's basketball and soccer players. Yet this supposed equality—which coincided with the women's movement and sexual freedoms facilitated by birth control—amplified anxiety around women in sports, especially the figure of the tomboy, who eschewed the traditional trappings of femininity. If one played "like a boy," she'd never get a husband—or, even more dangerous, perhaps start to ask for the same privileges as men in other areas outside of sport, and never even *need* a husband.

Hence, the policing of the female athlete, who faces the daunting task of maintaining a body strong enough to excel at her sport of choice but contained enough so as not to incite fear about transcending her given place in the world. Jane Fonda helped popularize the lean, athletic body over the course of the eighties and nineties, and the rise of Pilates and yoga over the past twenty years has ushered in a new standard for the "ideal" feminine body: skinny but toned. A flat stomach, defined calves, nicely toned triceps. Muscular, but not *too* muscular; strong, but still undeniably feminine, lest it lose its attractiveness—the thing that women are taught to value most in the world, even above athletic dominance.

This ideal was, in many ways, encapsulated in the body of the tennis player: female tennis players weren't generally tall, and thus a threat to men's virility, like basketball players; they weren't better than their male counterparts, like the U.S. Women's Soccer Team. Tennis players were strong, but their uniforms made them look like ladies able to transition from the court straight to afternoon tea—even Martina Navratilova, one of the first athletes to come out as queer, had a markedly feminine style throughout the 1980s. Like so many women of the time, she often wore short-sleeve T-shirts that concealed the muscles she'd developed as a result of her powerful serve. Femininity cloaked power and strength, made it more palatable, less threatening.

Serena's body explodes those parameters—which is part of why it's been called "masculine," its capacity for beauty or sexual attraction called into question by men and women alike. In some ways, Williams has courted the comparisons: from the beginning, she wanted to play men, be considered as powerful as a man, be judged against men. In 1998, she walked around the Australian Open toting a page torn from the press guide featuring a German player named Karsten Braasch, ranked 226th in the world, whom she'd talked into playing a match, vowing that she was going to "take him out."

Later that year, Serena distributed a flyer, featuring a picture of her mid-stroke and the caption ANYONE. ANYTIME. ANYWHERE. In 1999, she asked the men's tour for a wild card: "Women's tennis is boring," she supposedly said. "I can beat the men."[33] And while she was likened to Michael Jordan—"The smile, the confidence, the way she carried herself—she plays like she knows she belongs"—her desire to play against men was treated as folly. "She is very masculine and very strong," Boris Becker said. "But if you compare her game to the likes of Pete Sampras or Andre Agassi in all honesty you are talking about two different sports."[34]

All of this took place while Williams was proving her mettle in the WTA tour, still struggling to equal her sister. As she began to rise in the ranks, her talk of playing men began to disappear— but the impact of her words reverberated in how she started being treated as too masculine in the public eye. In comparing Williams and opponent Justine Henin-Hardenne, *The Mirror* described them as "the girl with the gossamer touch against the woman with the heavy hands and the builders' shoulders."[35] She was criticized, like so many other women, for "grunting" while playing, as if evidence of physical exertion was somehow unseemly—even cheating, as Navratilova herself suggested.[36]

Serena may have been too masculine, but her signifiers of femininity were too much: her body has been described as "all bosom, bottom, and muscle."[37] Her butt has been explained as a feature of "the African American race. They just have huge gluteal strength."[38] Her breasts were dubbed large enough to be "registered to vote in a different US state from the rest of her."[39] Historically, women with bodies like Serena's—or fellow unruly woman Nicki Minaj's—have been exoticized, literally put on display, like the Hottentot Venus of South Africa. To turn black women into objectified others was to underline their difference: they may be beautiful, but they are of another kind, separate from the dominant understanding of attractiveness. Their bodies are treated as Halloween costumes or jokes, a concept manifested most blatantly when Andy Roddick and Caroline Wozniacki padded themselves up to play "as Serena."

The rhetoric around Serena's body also suggests that her skill and power stem not from hard work but from difference: the idea that black bodies rely on "natural athleticism," not strategy. Bodies blessed with power, in other words, but no intellect—that were a threat in no small part because they crushed their white opponents. As Brittney C. Cooper of Crunk Feminist Collective points out, "these narratives about Black bodies as 'naturally athletic,' 'more powerful,' 'more wild,' 'less thoughtful,' and 'less strategic' and black female bodies as '(un)naturally strong, invulnerable, and unattractive'—are central to Western narratives of white racial superiority."[40]

Put differently, the rhetoric of William's "different" body isn't just sexist—it's profoundly racist. But like all horrible reactions in pop culture, it's also a testament to how thoroughly she's usurped the worlds of tennis, women's sports, and celebrity at large. When faced with language that suggests she is a "female hulk with a bum to match," as an infamous editorial in *The Mirror* declared, with "the feminine curves and womanly shape of a brick outhouse"—or, as sportswriter Jason Whitlock put it, "proud to serve as a role model for women with oversized back packs"—her body, and her behavior, say *fuck that.*[41]

Or, at the very least, fuck the ideal against which her body has been measured and found lacking—an ideal rooted in how white women of a certain class and leisure level have decided to form their bodies. Serena's body isn't built to emulate the look of the model in an Ann Taylor shift dress. It's built—through an exacting and grueling regimen—to decimate her opponents. And the suggestion that that body, too, is beautiful and sexy—in spite of, or even because of, its threat to the norms of white femininity—will continue to be threatening until the standards of beauty are decentered from those of the white upper class.

Williams, along with a phalanx of other powerfully built women, have started that work: *People* magazine declared Williams's body as the "Most Amazing" of 2011; for *New York* magazine, she held herself aloft in the splits for a photo shoot, demonstrating the power and shape of her legs; in August 2016, she was the cover girl for *Self,* a place usually reserved for the Pilates bodies of the world. She told *People* that she gets the most compliments about her butt, which she likes to flaunt by wearing Brazilian-cut bottoms. "Some people think it's too small," she said. "But I'm like 'Whatever.'" When asked for her weight, she said, "I don't step on scales."[42]

"I love my body, and I would never change anything about it," she told *Self.* "I'm not asking you to like my body. I'm just asking you to let me be me. Because I'm going to influence a girl who does look like me, and I want her to feel good about herself."[43] Or, as she put it to *People*, "I represent ladies who want to be healthy and not starve themselves."[44]

Williams's general response to criticism of her body was to flaunt it, wearing clothes that made her difference *more* apparent. But that doesn't mean she didn't spend years internalizing the rhetoric of difference. In *Vogue*, she admitted that she "hated her arms" at the beginning of her career and refused to lift weights for fear that they'd get even bigger. "I wanted them to look soft," she explained.[45] Even today, she opts for TheraBands instead of weights because she doesn't want to overdevelop her arm muscles.

And while Williams has nabbed lucrative endorsement deals with Nike and Gatorade, her body—its size, its strength, its blackness—decreases her "value" as a celebrity body. As Stephen Rodrick put it in a 2013 *Rolling Stone* profile, "[Maria] Sharapova is tall, white and blonde, and because of that, makes more money in endorsements than Serena, who is black, beautiful, and built like one of those monster trucks that crushes Volkswagens at sports arenas."[46]

In 2016, Williams overtook Sharapova to become the world's highest-paid female athlete. But Rodrick's description, at once calling out and reinscribing the rhetoric around Williams's strength, is characteristic of so much of the writing and commentary around Williams. Compliments come off as backhanded; attempts to explain or celebrate her playing style are freighted with racism and sexism. Much of it comes from those who've been either players or analysts for years, and Williams destabilizes a tradition for which they'd become the primary custodians.

Which helps explain, but not excuse, the way that Williams

was routinely critiqued when she struggled to rebound from surgery, or suggestions, in 2007, that she had feigned injury in order to stall a match against Daniela Hantuchová. "I thought she was overreacting a little much, which she tends to do, having this injury," Michael Stich, a former tennis champion and match commentator told his BBC audience.[47]

"Overreacting a little much" is the sort of language used to censor unruly women. It's also the sort that's been directed, since the mid-1990s, at the Williamses' "sportsmanship"—a term with ever-shifting boundaries and deeply rooted class connotations. Historically, it's wielded to show who "belongs" in a sport and who does not. And the Williamses have definitively never belonged: as a 1998 profile put it, "If you were expecting easy answers, predictable behavior, or simple pleasantries, you can forget it. The Williamses do not do the expected or the pleasant, or the simple. They do the exact opposite. They raise contrariness to a performance art."[48]

That contrariness stemmed from their father's coaching tactics, from their hair and outfits and musculature, and the very way they played the game. Both sisters were known as "headhunters" for hitting the ball *at* their opponents. At the 1998 French Open, Arantxa Sánchez Vicario accused Serena, then sixteen, of trying to hit balls at her head and demonstrating poor sportsmanship. "She came to the net talking very aggressively," Sánchez Vicario said. "I don't think she can act that way. I don't think it's nice at all."[49] In 2003, Williams was fined for using obscene language during a match; in 2005, a tabloid condemned her "irritating habit of celebrating her victories by waving to the crowd."[50]

As Serena's perceived aggressiveness grew, Venus was figured not as a partner in crime, but as a foil. In 2003, the *Daily Mail* complained that Serena "appears utterly absorbed with her life in the fast lane. She recently admitted an addiction to internet shopping, and last month in Rome, I watched as she spent thousands on shoes, clothes and jewelry in one afternoon." By contrast, Venus was "positively bookish," devoting herself to learning foreign languages.[51]

In 2004, Serena's post-surgery decline was attributed to that lack of discipline: she made too many cameos in television shows, attended too many club openings, spent too much time designing her new line of formalwear. "Despite her absence from the tour," *USA Today* explained, "Serena was hardly unseen"—which is another way of saying that she was *too* visible, *too* much of a celebrity, all of which, in contrast to other players on the tour, was both unprofessional and tacky.[52]

As Serena struggled to regain her footing in the tennis world, others reveled in her difficulties: in 2005, the London *Sunday Times* declared that "the highly theatrical Williams family saw one of its leading ladies leave the stage last night" with Serena's elimination from Wimbledon, pointing to an "apparent lack of fitness" that manifested in "frustration and anger at her own inferiority, smashing her racket on the floor and frowning desperately to herself."[53] Tennis legend Chris Evert went so far as to pen an open letter to Serena in the May 2006 issue of *Tennis* magazine, declaring, "I don't see how acting and designing clothes can compare with the pride of being the best tennis player in the world."

Williams was condemned for her pride when she was the best in the world; judged for her lack thereof when she wasn't.

She was a bad winner and a poor loser; she made too much noise on and off the court. She was judged for her "petulance" and "divisiveness towards fellow top players" and snobbiness toward "more minor tournaments."[54] "Bad sportsman," in this case, was code for choosing to play the sport her way—a critique rarely levied on her white, male counterparts.

The most vivid example came in 2009, when, angry with a foot fault, Williams yelled at a line judge, threatening to "stuff this racket down your throat." The profanity-ridden exchange was called "graceless," a "tantrum" and "a disgrace"—sentiments that amplified when, in an appearance at the MTV Music Awards the next day, she treated it as a joke. A letter to *The New York Times* crystallized much of the public reaction: "The disrespect that Serena Williams showed the world of tennis—the professionals who spend their time and energy playing and administering this sport and the fans who play and support the game—demands a severe and swift penalty."[55]

Williams was fined $10,000 for the incident, but as another letter to the editor pointed out, her treatment was a clear example of a "double standard of decorum," as Roger Federer had recently been fined just $1,500 for cursing at an umpire. "Is the standard gender or racial?"[56] As Williams would later say, looking back at the reaction, "I just really thought that was strange. You have people who made a career out of yelling at line judges. And a woman does it, and it's like a big problem."[57] Williams is right: the USTA has long tolerated outbursts from white men, including Jimmy Connors and John McEnroe. As critical race scholar Brittney C. Cooper puts it: "White anger is entertaining; Black anger must be contained."[58]

When Williams tried to cloak that anger—as she did in 2011, when she remarked that Wimbledon "like[s] to put us on Court 2, me and Venus, for whatever reason"—her passive aggression was labeled "annoying."[59] "If she has something to say," *The Guardian* remarked, "she should say it, not lead the media on to fight her fights for her."[60]

Yet if Williams had spoken her mind, indicting her second-class citizenry—or, as *The Guardian* suggested, "storm into the committee, Serena, and demand to know why, as a long-time great player at Wimbledon, you have to put up with playing on a smaller outside court when others don't"—that, too, would've been taken as an affront.[61] To speak frankly about her treatment within the world of tennis would be received as playing the race card, as being too angry, as demonstrating disrespect for the sport that still seems to largely live in the nineties world of post-racism.

❖ ❖ ❖

The declaration, in *Rolling Stone*, that "Serena does what she wants, when she wants," is meant as a compliment, but it also singes.[62] It's the sort of thing you'd say about a child, a feckless teen, a trust-fund adult. It's also untrue: Williams's behavior is always already constrained by the expectations of a black female athlete. It's the moments when she transgresses those boundaries that she becomes an ungovernable, unsportsmanlike woman. Like in 2011, when another elevated disagreement with a line judge was dubbed an "outburst," "another tantrum," and proof of the end of refined tennis: "With Williams receiving no real punishment," one fan proclaimed, "trash-talk tennis has arrived. As long as no curse words are used, a player can say anything to an

umpire at any time. Is this new tennis game what we want children to learn?"[63]

Williams, in other words, has burned the old, respectable game
to the ground; in its place, she's built a game of trash to which
good parents would never expose their children. Another *New
York Times* reader from Kansas City, Missouri, declared the incident proof that "Williams is a spoiled individual who resorts to
threatening people who stand between her and what she wants";
another asserted that she should never be allowed on the tennis court again, especially since she had the bad taste to make
such a display on 9/11.[64] The problem with Serena was that she
was denigrating both America and one of its last remaining
"respectable" (read: white) sports, bringing it down to the level of
basketball, where players regularly confront their refs, or football,
where players rebuke, ignore, or otherwise refuse to play nice
with the press.

The anxiety centers on Williams, but it's really a manifestation of a larger fear that she'll turn tennis, one of the last bastions
of proper whiteness, into a black sport. To be nervous that Williams's behavior might rub off on one's children is to be nervous
that black people might talk back—that there might be a *reason*,
for example, that they are aggressive with the reporters who've
described their bodies with such distance and distaste.

Many tennis fans—like fans of any sport, or movie franchise,
or musician—would rather not think about the racist, sexist, and
classist underpinnings of their objects of affection, or the way
their fandom can work to reproduce and reify those same hierarchies of power. Williams's very existence makes that impossible:

she is the eternal question mark, the presence highlighting what so many would rather ignore. She is change manifest, which is to say she's never not a threat: the most unruly, and essential, of women.

✦ ✦ ✦

In 2012, Williams embarked upon her renaissance. Over the course of the next four years, she would reclaim the number one ranking in the world—the oldest woman in the modern era to do so—win a second ESPY for Female Athlete of the Year (2013), hold the number one ranking for the entirety of 2014, complete another Serena Slam (2015), and be named *Sports Illustrated*'s Sportsperson of the Year—only the third solo woman to do so since the magazine's inception. That she did so as a sort of second act of her career made it all the more powerful: a testament to her triumph over adversity, but also the simple fortitude required to endure years of being told she was on the decline.

Her experience, coupled with age, manifested in an aura of wisdom, of softening: a *Vogue* cover story in 2015 declared that "she has done something that has surprised many in the tennis world. She has mellowed."[65] That mellowing was evidenced by her "best" friendship with rival Caroline Wozniacki, and the "confident way she cruised to victory" (read: without an outburst) when playing Maria Sharapova during the Australian Open.

The greatest sign of her mellowing? She returned to Indian Wells. "After she made the announcement in February," the profile declared, "you could practically hear the tennis world sigh with relief." Relief that Williams, who appeared on the cover of the magazine in a simple, high-necked shift dress, the lettering of the cover obscuring her arms, was the angry, flagrant black woman no more. As former tennis champion Mary Joe Fernández explained, "She's changed, but so has tennis. We're never going to see anything like the Williams sisters again in American tennis, so having her back at such an important tournament is like seeing a circle close."[66]

Significantly, the word "mellowing" is *Vogue*'s—not Williams's. *Vogue*, whose preferred cover aesthetic might be described as "Blake Lively," has regularly softened the sharp edges of cover women (Lena Dunham, Kim Kardashian, Amy Schumer, Hillary Clinton) through both images and the profiles that accompany them. Which is why the profile suggests that Williams playing at Indian Wells is akin to "seeing a circle close" because, as Williams puts it, "I always talk about forgiveness, but I needed to show it. It was time to move on." "Forgiveness," however, doesn't suggest that there aren't still systemic issues plaguing the sport—or that the racist, sexist edges of the sport aren't still sharp.

Indeed, the disciplining rhetoric around Williams, and the periodic spikes of anxiety about the state of tennis and female athletes in general, remain. When, in December 2015, *Sports Illustrated* declared her Sportsperson of the Year, the *Los Angeles Times* channeled anger percolating across the nation when it wondered if a horse was more deserving.[67]

Granted, that horse had won the first Triple Crown in thirty-seven years, but the conversation encapsulated the manner in which Williams's achievements have been undercut and questioned over the course of her career. Instead of celebrating *Sports Illustrated*'s choice, readers questioned it. And whether that questioning stemmed from Williams's race, gender, or "sports manship" matters less than the fact that the preferred winner was *an animal*: an athlete ostensibly devoid of politics, unable to speak or challenge the norms of the sport in which it excelled.

For all Williams's recent visibility in the sports and fashion world, the most important, insightful writing about her came from a poet. In 2014, Claudia Rankine had invoked Williams in her National Book Award–nominated collection *Citizen*: "Every look, every comment, every bad call blossoms out of history, through her, onto you."[68] Then, in 2015, as Williams was about to play in the U.S. Open, Rankine was tasked with profiling her for *The New York Times Magazine*. In Rankine's description, Williams is not docile, is not mellowed, is not deterred. "For black people, there is an unspoken script that demands the humble absorption of racist assaults, no matter the scale, because whites need to believe that it's no big deal," she writes. "But Serena refuses to keep to that script. Somehow, along the way, she made a decision to be excellent while still being Serena."[69]

Even fifty years ago, it might not have been possible for Serena to be excellent while still being Serena. The wages might have been physical violence, or exclusion from the tour, or regular rounds of what she experienced at Indian Wells. But what remains, amidst it all, is the excellence: as Rankine declares, "The notable difference between black excellence and white excellence is white excellence is achieved without having to battle racism. Imagine."

Imagine, too, a woman whose dominance on the court leads to discussions of her skill, not her body. Imagine a scenario in which strength, manifest in physical and mental form, is figured as a pure testament to skill, not a means of distracting from it. Imagine a world in which female athletes do not provoke anxiety; in which black ones are not automatically perceived as a threat; in which unruliness doesn't need to be blunted in order to appear on the cover of *Vogue*.

Tennis hasn't changed; sports haven't changed; the way that we talk about strong women hasn't changed—at least not on their own. And yet: through sheer force of her presence, her enduring unruliness, her undeniable excellence, Serena has begun to change them all.

And so: Imagine Serena not as an aggressive, aggrieved participant in a sport that struggled to make room for her, but as one who forced her way in and made space for all who followed. Imagine her as she will be remembered: a woman in a catsuit, a woman in beaded braids, a woman yelling and cursing and grinning and laughing and twirling and dominating, in a way that may never be replicated, in a sport that recoiled from her at every serve. A woman who responds to the cries that "she's' too strong," then "she's too sexy," then again "she's too strong" with "Well, can you choose one? But either way, I don't care which one they choose. I'm me and I've never changed who I am."[70]

CHAPTER 2

TOO FAT:
MELISSA McCARTHY

Melissa McCarthy is a gimmick comedian who has devoted her short career to being obese and obnoxious with equal success," declared Rex Reed in a now infamous review of McCarthy's 2013 feature film *Identity Thief*. According to Reed, McCarthy was "cacophonous," "tractor-sized," and "a female hippo"; her sex scene was "grotesque."[1] It wasn't the first time this sort of rhetoric had been directed at McCarthy: three years earlier, Maura Kelly, a blogger at *Marie Claire*, had responded to the premise of *Mike & Molly*—in which a man (Billy Gardell) and a woman (McCarthy) meet at Overeaters Anonymous and fall in love—with disgust: "I think I'd be grossed out if I had to watch two characters with rolls and rolls of fat kissing each other," Kelly wrote. "Because I'd be grossed out if I had to watch them doing anything."[2]

Reed's and Kelly's pieces were explicit renderings of a widely held American attitude—one that fears and pathologizes fatness, even as it promotes the rhetoric of self-acceptance and self-confidence. Fat is ugly, and dangerous, and an epidemic sweeping the country, this logic suggests—but you should love yourself!

McCarthy's mercurial rise to stardom is rooted in her image's ability to reconcile that precise contradiction. She's othered yet embraced, but only to a point, and only because her behavior and body comply with specific parameters. Her comedic personas revel in the unruliness of the fat body; her most popular characters are some intersection of low class, sexually dominant, profane, and generally negligent of their place in the societal hierarchy. "If there is a McCarthy type," a 2016 *Guardian* profile declared, "it is the woman who does things you pretty much never see a woman do on screen."[3] But that unruliness is neutralized by her reassuringly "normal" persona, and the insistence that her most unruly performances are just that: a fugue state, an escape, a vent that can be opened and closed.

The thesis that unites press coverage of McCarthy is simple: she may be fat, but it's a nice, tasteful, contained sort of fat. The sort of fatness that doesn't complain about size-based discrimination, or speak out about the class and racial components of fatness, or wear clothes that aren't figure-flattering. And while McCarthy has, in many ways, leaned in to that coverage, she also challenges it, working to relocate the conversation away from her body, drawing attention to the ways in which the business practices of plus-size fashion stigmatize and ghettoize more than half the population. Her unruliness might be tempered, but that doesn't mean it's not quietly, consistently radical.

❖ ❖ ❖

In Western society, fatness is interpreted as failure: a failure of control, of societal expectations, of will. It's a health issue that's transformed into an ideological affliction, manifest through a continuous stream of diets, a culture of exercise fanaticism, and compounding shame when these myriad approaches don't lead to a thin, acceptable body type. Studies have shown that fat people have a harder time getting admitted into top colleges, landing jobs, and receiving promotions; to be fat in America is, in many ways, to be a second-class citizen. Modern capitalist society hinges on its citizens' constant drive to consume, but the successful American is someone who's able, whether through genetics or self-regimentation, to *contain* the effects of that consumption.

For decades, fatness was rare enough that it could be framed as wholly other. In films and in society, fat people were largely conceived as diabolical or comic relief. But as the percentage of the population that could be considered fat increases, the posture of shame and self-denial has been refigured to include the rhetoric of self-acceptance and confidence: "Beautiful at Any Size!" "Plus Is Equal!" "The Real You Is Sexy!" "Love the Skin You're In!"

Most of those slogans were generated by businesses, who've recently come to recognize the lucrative and largely untapped market of fat consumers. But those messages slam up against the resilient understanding of fatness as a societal ill—a symptom of weakness, low class, and general inferiority. That understanding is present on websites like "People of Walmart," on which the visible fat body is a punch line, or on *The Biggest Loser*, where fatness is figured as potential: a wildness to be gradually tamed, preferably through the sort of endless self-flagellation that suggests that inside every fat person there's a skinny, capable one begging to be set free. A good fat body, then, is one that's attempting—confidently! with love!—to erase itself. The body that refuses the pressure to do so, or even *celebrates* that refusal, becomes unruly.

Like all spectacles, the confident fat woman is magnetic; the *funny* fat woman doubly so. For a brief period in the 1930s, witticist Mae West, whose Schumer-like body incited a "curve craze," was one of the hottest stars in Hollywood; in the early 1990s, the 320-pound Roseanne Barr dominated television; today, McCarthy's performances of unruliness have made her one of the most bankable actresses in the business. The allure of these women oscillates between one of attraction and distance: one moment, the audience marvels at, even identifies with, their self-confidence, their command of the room, their refusal to be shamed by society's standards. But when the fat woman crosses some line—sexually, physically—and others herself in some way, she effectively encourages the viewer to step back. Instead of identifying with the character, the viewer defines herself *against* her.

Put differently, it's safe to *watch* a fat, unruly woman—so long as she's contained on-screen. Which helps explain why the careers of West and Barr were gradually destroyed by "real life" unruly behaviors: West loved to gamble and hang out with black men; Barr had a messy, flagrant relationship with Tom Arnold and savaged the national anthem in front of millions. Such actions made it impossible to conceive of their unruliness as something they simply performed on-screen. Instead, West and Barr were just intrinsically, holistically transgressive—and thus cast

aside as a means of shoring up the status quo. The shift in popularity was never as explicit as "I need to stop liking this woman
in order to maintain society's conception of proper femininity";
instead, their actions were gradually and sharply disciplined (in
the press, in conversation) as "just too much."

McCarthy has skillfully avoided that fate, cultivating a star image that balances unruly transgression with middle-class respectability. That image starts, as so many do, with a specific narrative
of childhood: her father grew up on the South Side of Chicago, part
of a large Irish family, and, as McCarthy tells it, wanted to raise his
children somewhere safer and more secure. So he moved them to a
working farm in Plainfield, Illinois, population 264, and McCarthy and her older sister grew up wholesome and creative. She was
a cheerleader before realizing that the team sucked, at which point
she "went to seed," as she describes it, and became a Goth, a punk,
an outsider: "I started going in to Chicago," she told *The Times* of
London. "Out came the long black raincoat and the blue-black hair
and Siouxsie Sioux and the Banshees and Robert Smith."[4]

That phase, McCarthy and others are keen to note, was essentially her "first role." "I looked like the most menacing psycho-
path," she explained, "and then we would be out at this club, and
everybody was supposed to be more depressed than the next person. I would look depressed until I couldn't take it anymore, and
I'd see somebody I knew and I'd be like: 'Oh my God! I love your
shoes!'"[5] She hung out at clubs with names like Medusa; she
danced and climbed to the rafters; she dyed her hair blue and
wore white kabuki makeup and capes. But as she reassured *Rolling Stone*, "I was pretty lame, though, and much more of a goody-
two-shoes than I looked."[6] Most teenagers experiment with

31

identity in some capacity, but this particular story is wielded as a means of emphasizing the "real" McCarthy: the inverse of the Goth, but capable of pulling off the act.

After "recovering" from her Goth phase, McCarthy went to college for a year, harboring dreams of a career in fashion, and moved to New York with the intention to enroll at FIT. But a friend convinced her to do stand-up, and unlike the other comedians, she didn't tell mean jokes about herself or others—instead, she recounted weird, meandering stories that the other comics didn't like. For most of her twenties, she appeared in off-Broadway plays; she took classes at the Actors Studio; she stayed between a size four and a six. Still, she was told, "You're never going to work at that weight."[7]

When McCarthy moved to Los Angeles—where she started performing with the improv group the Groundlings and started auditioning widely—she gained twenty-five pounds. "I stopped walking and ate shitty food," she explained. "But it wasn't like I ever wanted to play the stunning-girl lead part who just says 17 dry lines. That didn't seem like fun to me. But you go through everything, like maybe if I was taller, prettier, thinner, would I be going out on more auditions. But then in the back of my head, I didn't want to do those parts."[8] Here, McCarthy summarizes just how pervasive the cult of thinness is in Hollywood: even if the roles that go to thin people aren't great—and you objectively do not want them—you still want the sort of body that gets them.

The Groundlings, McCarthy says, "changed my life. . . . It taught me to write and how to do a character," she told *The Hollywood Reporter*, "rather than just play crazy."[9] It's where she developed the character Marbles, a cross-eyed, lisping, turtleneck-and-bad-sweatshirt-wearing woman who's framed as her authentic comedic self—a woman who, like Marbles's cinematic cousins (Michelle Darnell in *The Boss*; Megan in *Bridesmaids*), is "notably different but still confident and comfortable in [her] skin."[10] These women are bizarre, confident, almost castrating in their refusal to bend to the demands of patriarchy. In a YouTube video posted in 2006, for example, Marbles wears a white turtleneck and black Spock sweatshirt and addresses the camera with the unfettered confidence of a dad offering advice on car maintenance. As *Bridesmaids* screenwriter Annie Mumolo recalls, when McCarthy turned into Marbles, "she'd just get up on the stage and grab the crowd by the balls."[11]

McCarthy struggled to find steady work in Los Angeles, but she did find husband Ben Falcone via the Groundlings, where, according to their telling, they spent endless hours getting as weird together as possible. That weirdness, however, was almost entirely absent from her first major acting gig. While her Groundlings classmates went off to *Saturday Night Live* and other sketch endeavors, McCarthy took the role of Sookie St. James in the coming-of-age melodrama *Gilmore Girls*. The character of Sookie ran her own kitchen, but her defining characteristics were quirk and klutziness—a far cry from the likes of Marbles.

Mumolo admits feeling confused when McCarthy took the role of the "nice little chef," but for McCarthy, it was steady yearly work, with a narrative that could be bent, as it was in its final season, to allow for McCarthy's first pregnancy. After *Gilmore Girls*, McCarthy was cast as the nerdy, docile childhood best friend to Christina Applegate in the series *Samantha Who?*, and in 2010, she took the lead role in *Mike & Molly*, whose shooting schedule made it possible for her to spend much more time at home.

These roles—characterized by their deep sweetness, their oh-shucks loveliness—are far from McCarthy's star-making film characters. Yet like McCarthy's 2014 turn as a beleaguered single mom in *St. Vincent*, they feel foundational: proof, like the anecdotes from her personal life, that Marbles, Megan, Michelle, and Tammy are *departures* from, not reflections of, McCarthy's "true" self.

✦ ✦ ✦

From the beginning, *Mike & Molly* was surrounded by controversy. Producer Chuck Lorre had cut his sitcom teeth on *Roseanne* and *Grace Under Fire*, but he was most associated with his capacity as showrunner on *Two and a Half Men* and *The Big Bang Theory*—sitcoms that were "traditional" in both aesthetics (three-camera filming setups; shot in front of a studio audience; laugh-track) and tone (shallowly denigrating humor about women, dating, and nerds). A fine, sensitive, thoughtful touch—that wasn't Lorre's way.

Which is why the announcement of a show in which two fat people fall in love immediately incited concern. Lorre worked to assuage it: "This isn't a show about weight," he explained. "It's a show about people trying to make their lives better and find someone that they can have a committed relationship with. If we're still talking about [weight] come episode six, we've got a serious problem, because it would get tired really quickly."[12] Fat jokes nevertheless provided the narrative spine of the show, especially in the first season: in the twenty-two-minute pilot alone, twenty-five jokes invoke fatness in some capacity.[13]

In truth, most audiences are highly tolerant of fat jokes: they

34

pervade television and cinema, and have for decades. But many are offended by the *idea* of fat jokes: the theory is repugnant, not the practice, which makes most people laugh. And fat jokes aside, *Mike & Molly* had a surprising "inherent sweetness," as *Variety* put it, at its core.[14] "What I love is that for the first time ever, this type of show doesn't make you feel sorry for those who are battling the bulge,"[15] one critic wrote. Even more surprising, the characters of Mike and Molly seemed to authentically *like* themselves—even if that like was tempered by constant jokes, often made at their own expense, about their size. "Any time you see a broad spectrum of people on TV, it's good," one Canadian review declared. "It's good to have something a little more realistic."[16]

Which was the tone McCarthy espoused in press for the show, as she began to hone the rhetoric with which she would talk about her body and representation in general. She told the *Chicago Tribune* she hated the idea of gimmick casting: when she first heard about the premise for *Mike & Molly*, she "wanted no part of it"; she feared it would be filled with "potshots and cheap writing. . . . Just the thought of it upset me."[17]

McCarthy only signed on when she read the script and decided that *Mike & Molly* wasn't, to her mind, about weight: "I love that this show doesn't have any snarky quality to it, but is still funny and lovely," she explained. "If we lose weight, if we gain weight—that's just not the axis this show revolves around."[18] She especially liked how relatable and how much of an old-fashioned romance the show was: her character was a teacher, "and I love that she dresses like a teacher and wears things that are meant to be comfortable."[19] Which is part of why the show became such a success, albeit a quiet one: it wasn't flashy, it wasn't brilliant, but its plotlines and characterization of "normalcy" went down easy.

Still, constantly talking about weight—McCarthy's, her costar's—quickly became tiresome. "Not because it hurts my feelings," she explained in an interview with *Variety*, "but because, isn't this getting boring?"[20] When the *Marie Claire* blogger voiced her disgust with the idea of watching fat people make out, McCarthy didn't respond for nearly a year. Even then, it was measured: "My first thought was 'Gosh, I hope she doesn't have a daughter,'" she told *Entertainment Weekly*. "And then after a second I thought, 'What a sad, troubled person. You're making such a shitty judgment on people.'"[21]

With this early press, McCarthy was quietly challenging the rhetorical roundabout expected of fat stars. While she admits that she's gained more confidence since landing bigger roles, she's bored by weight conversations and refuses to stoke the outrage cycle by lashing out at others' disgust with her body. At the same time, she's attempting to reframe the conversation away from *her* body and toward representation *writ large*: the importance of bodies, of any size, that don't attempt to convince viewers that there's only one manifestation of normal.

That public posture remained steady through 2011, which the *Hollywood Reporter* dubbed "The Year of McCarthy": she won an Emmy for *Mike & Molly*, which had become the highest-rated new sitcom of the season, she hosted *Saturday Night Live*, and she stole every scene in *Bridesmaids*, earning an Oscar nomination for Best Supporting Actress—a rarity for a comedic performance. The character Megan is best remembered for shitting in a sink, but she's also just holistically, uniquely unruly: thoroughly confident in herself and her sexual magnetism, and aggressively dismissive of dominant beauty strictures.

Megan is a clear performative cousin of Marbles, McCarthy's "authentic" comedic self. She was also very much a McCarthy creation—a point driven home in the repeated tellings of how McCarthy won the role, which had been written as more of a "nervous oddball." But McCarthy decided to go in a different direction: part Groundlings characters, part Guy Fieri. She put on a pair of Dockers, pulled her hair back, and improvised a scene with Kristen Wiig in which she went off about a sexual encounter with a dolphin.[22]

The audition was one of what McCarthy describes as her near "fugue states"—when she accesses the far corners of her unruly characters, so far that she doesn't remember what comes out of their mouths. When she "came to," she was filled with regret— "Well, you dumbass, you did it, you fucked that up," she remembers telling herself. "There's not one thing you could have done to seem any stranger. Sex with a dolphin? Hand-play with a dolphin! You just could not have been any weirder. . . . But that's what happens when you really aren't there," she explained. "You do really weird stuff."[23]

Yet everyone present at the audition—director Paul Feig, producer Judd Apatow, screenwriters Kristen Wiig and Annie Mumolo—loved it. "My jaw hit the ground," Feig said. "I remember watching the first time, and we almost couldn't laugh because we were like: 'Oh my God. What is she doing? This is amazing.'"[24] Her "fugue state" won her the role—and, as *Rolling Stone* tells it, "enabl[ed] McCarthy to become all that she is today, just about the only comedian around who can almost single-handedly carry a movie to a $35 million opening."[25] Put differently, her ability to access an inner unruly woman made her a massive star.

Similar "fugue states" pop up all over McCarthy's life and career: there's the famous cameo scene in *This Is 40*, when she threatens to tear off Paul Rudd's and Leslie Mann's "slow-blinking eyelids" and drink their blood—and which she didn't remember until she saw it on tape. Anytime she's seriously lewd or crass or obscene, like in an uncensored bonus clip from *The Boss* when she says that a dead woman is not only a whore who fucked all the grossest guys at the company, but is probably now in hell fucking all the IT guys—fugue state.

The same goes for any troublesome behaviors in her personal life, like an oft-repeated tale of McCarthy shoplifting as a child: "Anytime I was doing it, I was thinking 'What the hell am I doing?'" she recalled. "I was in a fugue state. A security guard caught me. My mom was so disappointed. 'You broke the law to get a picture frame?' I was like, 'I don't know, I don't know.'"[26] One critic likened them to "biblical tales of xenoglossy," highlighting that McCarthy is "probably more shocked than anyone by her behavior."[27] "Apparently there's pretty big reserves of rage I've got," she explained.[28] But that sort of rage is unacceptable in polite society—so she has to effectively *leave her body* (or, more precisely, her head) to access it. In order to be unruly, she has to effectively lose consciousness.

And if they're not fugue states, they're at the very least drag. In a more detailed (and much more queer) version of her high school Goth days, recounted for *The Advocate*, she remembers "being undressed and then redressed by two drag queens up on a pillar and in the end I looked like Bea Arthur," adding that the LGBT community "was just my world. I was a little odd, and I found them to be the most accepting group. . . . I wanted to be a drag queen so badly. I'll bet I still own more wigs than any drag queen—I love me a wig."[29] McCarthy keeps about twenty-five wigs in her possession, and relied heavily on them for her characters in *Identity Thief*, *The Boss*, and the vast majority of her performances on *Saturday Night Live*, but the wig itself matters less than the transformation it provides: when she embodies these crass, profane, transgressive women, she's essentially in unruly woman drag.

The political power of drag resides in its ability to draw attention to just how *performative* gender can be. By amplifying characteristics of femininity or masculinity, it highlights their absurdity, their arbitrariness, and just how easily they can be applied and abandoned. The drag of unruly womanhood, then, points to the constrictions of traditional femininity. McCarthy's characters are *liberated* by their transgressions: they're confident, self-assured, sexual, and secure in their jobs, especially in comparison to their female foils (Sandra Bullock in *The Heat*, Kristen Bell in *The Boss*, Kristen Wiig in *Bridesmaids*). It's no coincidence that several of her roles were originally written for men, or mapped onto traditionally "male" genres, like the buddy cop film, the spy movie, or the ghost-busting narrative— McCarthy's characters have the confidence and shamelessness of a pompous white male.

When she discusses her characters, McCarthy's main focus isn't their size but their capacity for assholery. "At some point in the past it was decided that women in comedy are never supposed to be shown in an unflattering light," she told *The Daily Telegraph*. "But in comedy you need all your tools to be funny. You need to be able to look ugly, and act ugly, and to be an ass, and then come groveling back. So when actresses are cleaned up to the point that they look perfect, and dress perfect, and never act inappropriately, and never say the wrong thing, you've taken away every tool they have. And then they're told: 'And now be funny.' What else can you do? You have no personality left."[30]

It's also a double standard: all the best male characters are unkempt or flawed in some capacity. "A woman does the same thing and people are actually offended," she said. "They're offended that I don't preen myself—even though it would be completely inappropriate for the character. . . . Don't you go to the movies to see real people with real flaws and watch them try to get better? Without the mess you've got nothing."[31] "The mess" can manifest in lack of preening, but it can also take the form of general unlikability, which is just another way of saying that a character doesn't comply with expectations of femininity. By insisting on a character's messiness, McCarthy is pushing depictions for "real people with real flaws," but she's also suggesting the most compelling characters, male or female, are those who live their lives out of bounds.

✦ ✦ ✦

With success, McCarthy gradually ratcheted up her rhetoric: she's called Hollywood sexism "an intense sickness" in which female actors who aren't "skipping along in high heels" are branded "unattractive bitch(es)," and suggested that her role in *Spy* was a comment on the ways in which women are "trained to some degree to, you know, mind your manners, don't say this, don't do that. I think as women you're taught not to trust your gut, not to be rude."[32] She thinks identifying as antifeminist is flat-out ridiculous: "Oh, that sounds so dumb," she told *Redbook* before pulling back in her trademark way. "And I don't mean that in a hateful way. It just sounds so ill-informed."[33]

Still, that's powerful rhetoric—made even more so when articulated in a venue like *Redbook*, which has helped reify notions of "proper" femininity for more than a century. But no matter how strong McCarthy's language, or how unruly her characters, they're accompanied—both rhetorically and visually—by the mild, sweet domesticity of McCarthy's "real" self. It's the self that shows up on the cover of those same women's magazines in tasteful color-blocked outfits, a lovely smile, and messages like "She looks more like your neighbor than a Barbie" and "She's living proof that self-acceptance and perseverance can make any dream come true." Because the real McCarthy, according to Feig, is "what you want out of every comic hero: She's you. She's not intimidating, yet she's aspirational, because she's a beautiful woman, but she's a real woman."[34]

The real McCarthy seldom swears; she shares her simple recipe for vegetable soup; she declares "I make a mean coconut macaroon" and assures readers, "I'm nothing like I am in the movies."[35] She exclaims "Holy smokes!" when she wins an Emmy and uses her speech to proclaim, "I go to work and show up early, like a dork." For date night, she goes to five o'clock dinner with Falcone so she can come home and tuck in her daughters. She loves HGTV. She lives in an unassuming part of the San Fernando Valley, in part because she's "too friendly" for Hollywood.[36] She wears a thirty-dollar ASOS dress on the red carpet and feels horrible when she loses her character's wig while shooting a Jet Ski scene for *Tammy*. She and her husband hold hands while they watch the day's footage on set. She could never handle hecklers because "I don't really want to fight with people," and she loves *Ellen*; she once told DeGeneres, "You put a little love and kindness in the world, and it does good things when you do that."[37] She grew up Christian, and prays every night with her daughters. "I believe it matters how you treat people," she told *Good Housekeeping*. "I believe in heaven . . . I have a lovely relationship with God."[38]

Critics describe the real McCarthy as "gentle, feminine and exceedingly polite," "everyone's favorite every woman," an "ingenuous Midwesterner," and "deceptively delicate," a person who lives by the principles of being "courteous and outgoing."[39] She's "all smiles and warmth" and "much closer in spirit to Sookie St. James, the endearing cook."[40] She's also "a much gentler person than you would ever know," "far more demure in person," and "the sweetest person you'll ever meet." She was chosen to host Ivory Soap's "Soap Dish" discussion group on Facebook, where she discussed "everyday topics including motherhood, marriage and meatloaf," because, as Ivory's brand manager put it, "Melissa's humor, simple charm and down-to-earth attitude fit with every bit of Ivory's persona. More than refreshingly honest and sincere, she is every woman and modern mom."[41] Which is to say: like Ivory Soap, she's white and fundamentally inoffensive.

The ethos of "honesty and sincerity" extends to the way McCarthy talks about her own body. When she put on weight after the birth of her second daughter, she told *People* that instead of focusing on a certain size, "I want to be healthy. I don't have a goal weight. I'll know when I feel good."[42] She doesn't work out constantly; instead, she does activities, like "Piloxing," a blend of Pilates and boxing, that she finds fun. "I want to be a good example to my girls," she explains, which includes telling them to focus on what's important: "Being older, I'm not so hard on myself. The important things in my life—my family, my kids, my job—are so wonderful. I feel really lucky."[43]

McCarthy admits she's not immune to the ideologies of thinness: "Do I sometimes hope I wake up in the morning and people are like, 'What's wrong with her? She looks emaciated.' Of course I would love that. I'm such a clothes whore I would love the opportunity to be a hanger."[44] But, she demurs, "I'm more confident than I've ever been in my life." Yet she also periodically indicts those same ideologies: "Everyone I know, no matter what size, is trying some system," she told *Good Housekeeping*. "Even when someone gets to looking like she should be so proud of herself, instead she's like 'I could be another three pounds less; I could be a little taller and have bigger lips.' Where does it end?"[45]

She remains conscious of the extreme care she must take in talking about those issues. In a 2013 *New York Times* profile, she said, "There's a strange epidemic of body image and body dysmorphia," in which articles like Rex Reed's "just add to all those younger girls, that are not in a place in their life where they can say 'That doesn't reflect me.'" Then, the restaurant in which the interview was taking place started testing its fire alarm, disrupting the conversation. "I imagine that's my publicist," McCarthy averred. "The gods didn't want us discussing this."[46]

According to the profile, McCarthy laughed when she said it. But her words point toward a greater reality: audiences don't want any woman, even one as clearly wronged as McCarthy was by Rex Reed, to speak out forcefully. Her publicist's advice was most likely to let the storm pass, and keep using the same inward-focused language, instead of pointing to the ways in which the focus on her weight, even the *positive* focus, bespeaks a society-wide obsession with women's bodies and how they do or do not adhere to certain norms.

Look closely, however, and you can see the tension between these two postures throughout McCarthy's career—in the way she diffused outrage over her appearance, in a full-length coat, on the cover of *Elle*, by pointing out that she picked the coat, or anger directed at the Photoshop job for the poster for *The Heat* that significantly slimmed her neck by joking that her husband was responsible.

Anger, after all, makes other people angry. And while that sort of righteous rage can elevate a public figure into a cultural icon, it rarely prompts fans to purchase cute dresses—which is exactly what McCarthy is hoping for in launching her clothing line. McCarthy's name has been linked with fashion ever since her first year of prominent stardom, when she admitted she couldn't find a designer willing to make a red-carpet dress in her size, sparking a firestorm of "Why Melissa McCarthy Couldn't Find Anyone to Dress Her for the Oscars" think pieces. (Answer: fashion is size-ist!)

Many of McCarthy's complaints were couched in humor ("The things out there are either made for a 16-year-old hooker or an 89-year-old grandmother of the bride. And they're made from the material used for haircutting capes"), but she's incisive when it comes to fashion's bad business sense: "Seventy percent of women in the United States are size 14 or above," she told

Refinery29, "and that's technically 'plus-size,' so you're taking your biggest category of people and telling them, 'You're not really worthy.' I find that very strange."[47] Her own line thus aims to provide what the business at large would not: choices. As she admitted in an interview with *Vogue*, "some days I want to be prim and proper, and others I want to be in a band. I lost the ability to do that with clothes."[48]

McCarthy's clothing line serves sizes 4 through 28. Within that range, she refuses to distinguish between "standard" and "plus-size": "My whole goal is to stop categorizing women," she explains. "I can't control who puts what where in the store—that's out of my abilities—but it's all for sale, all together, on my website. I have a five-year plan for my line, and it included this: I wanted all my clothes, in all sizes, to be down on the regular floor of stores. I know what it's like not being able to go shopping with my friends, because 'women like me' have been hidden away on a different floor next to the tire section."[49]

These interviews, and the clothes line itself, are ostensibly about selling clothes. That's why McCarthy appeared on the cover of *People* to promote them, why she penned a five-point essay on how to "Love the Way You Look!" inside, why she spent hours on the Home Shopping Network selling them.[50] In many ways, it's the classic McCarthy approach: she identifies a real problem, indicative of larger, and serious, societal ills, and softens it. Which doesn't mean that the idea isn't still radical: McCarthy may be speaking to the women who subscribe to *People* and watch the Home Shopping Network, but she's still saying what most know but are reticent to say—that fat people receive vastly different treatment than non-fat people. And in a country where power largely resides in your status as a consumer, declaring fat people a viable market is effectively asserting their equal citizenship. The clothes line, like McCarthy's very presence in Hollywood—on the cover of magazines, on billboards, and on the red carpet—makes fat people, and fat women in particular, visible.

Which is why McCarthy's recent weight loss—what some have called her "post-success body"—has proven difficult to process. McCarthy prepared readers for the idea of a weight fluctuation: whenever she's asked about her size, she's quick to point out that she's moved all over the scale. But her weight loss also highlights the discourses about her body that McCarthy has held in tension since *Mike & Molly*. When McCarthy begins to lose weight, she disrupts that logic: she's "fixing" the problem, but doesn't that underline a *lack* of pride in her size?

Of course, it's possible to both change your body *and* continue to take pride in it—but that's an understanding too nuanced for most press coverage, whose headlines revel in her transformation: "Melissa McCarthy's Body Evolution"; "Melissa McCarthy Shows Off Slim Figure in Pink Jumpsuit"; "Melissa McCarthy Looks So Slim, Even Under Multiple Layers"; "Melissa McCarthy Looks Slimmer Than Ever"; "Melissa McCarthy Continues to Flaunt Impressive Weight Loss." Such headlines invite the reader to marvel at the spectacle of McCarthy's shrinking body, often pairing "before" and "after" shots that ostensibly "celebrate" her weight loss journey yet reinscribe the idea that if her "new," smaller body is beautiful, the "old," fat one was repellent.

McCarthy's body, like Oprah's or Adele's, has become overdetermined with meaning: a decrease or increase in size is tantamount to a press release about the state of her psychological health, her status in the entertainment business, and how other women should feel about *their* bodies. Dozens of celebrities contribute to this understanding, fetishizing their diets, exercise routines, and body "tricks" to the point that the fixation cannibalizes their personality, as their ability to regiment their bodies becomes their value as women.

McCarthy, by contrast, has refused that cycle—the "How I Did It" cover story, the exercise tape, the tell-all interviews. She doesn't specify how much she lost; when asked, as she was, repeatedly, during press for *The Boss*, she deflates the question altogether: "No trick, nothing to tell," she told *Extra*. "Just super boring life." And that's been McCarthy's consistent stance when publicizing her body: "I'll be up, I'll be down, probably for the rest of my life," she told *Refinery29*. "The thing is, if that is the most interesting thing about me, I need to go have a lavender farm in Minnesota and give this up. There has to be something more."[51] Asserting that women are more interesting than their size or what they put on their body shouldn't be a radical or unruly idea. But that doesn't mean, in today's society, that it isn't.

❖ ❖ ❖

Over the past five years, McCarthy has proven herself one of the most successful women in Hollywood—and one of the few whose success has not hinged on a major superhero franchise. Just look at the numbers: $173 million global gross for *Identity Thief*, $229 million for *Heat*, $100 million for *Tammy*, $235 million for *Spy*, $78 million for *The Boss*, and $229 million for *Ghostbusters*. "This is not just a remarkable run," historian Mark Harris writes. "It is a literally singular one."[52] "You can count her among the most consistent box-office draws out there," box-office analyst Paul Dergarabedian told *The Hollywood Reporter*. "She ranks among very few actors who can boast actual star power and the ability to draw big audiences based on their name alone."[53]

Her draw is likened to Eddie Murphy's in the 1980s, Jim Carrey's in the 1990s, and Adam Sandler's in the 2000s; her paycheck now hovers between $12 and $14 million, making her the third-highest-paid female star in Hollywood. In 2012, a Fox executive said, "Every script I see these days has a character described as 'a Melissa McCarthy type.' I've seen literally 100 scripts like that in the last six months."[54] Yet industry press has been quick to write off, or at least hedge, those accomplishments, framing *The Boss*'s $23.9 million opening on a budget of $29 million as "a cautionary tale," even though it went on to gross $78 million worldwide, a not-insignificant feat for a film that's not a sequel or a superhero film. Still, the fact remains: thin or fat, young or old, a female star simply has to do more, gross more, be more in order to be valued in the same way as her male counterparts.

For all of McCarthy's significant strides and uncontested talent, her success—and Hollywood's reticence to acknowledge it—is a sign of just how regimented the rules for a fat womanhood remain. Not everyone speaks as loudly, or forcefully, as Rex Reed. But that doesn't mean that his attitudes about fatness, especially in the female body, don't continue to structure the logic of the industry.

As Harris argues, "Hollywood is now fine with actresses being powerful, as long as it can maintain some control over how 'power' is defined. The kind of powerful woman the industry likes is Reese

Witherspoon, who uses her power to buy a lot of deserving books and give work to a lot of deserving scriptwriters, and every once in a while takes a role that will get her an Oscar nomination but is fine doing supporting roles or HBO."[55] Power, in other words, that actually threatens the logic of Hollywood. Because McCarthy's success, like Roseanne's before her and Schumer's beside her, suggests that audiences *do* like unruly women—unruly in size, unruly in behavior, unruly in the way they control their projects.

That unruliness must still be tempered—configured as a momentary embrace and release of the rage she's collected at her treatment as both a woman and a fat person. And while that compromises the potency of her star image, it does little to diffuse the anarchic power of her performances, which remain so vital, combustive, and, when finely tuned, impossible to resist. McCarthy onscreen is the unruly woman at her most magnetic—and the very best argument that good behavior, in body or bearing, is for suckers.

CHAPTER 3

TOO GROSS:
ABBI JACOBSON
AND ILANA GLAZER

All the gross stuff the bros of *The League* and *Workaholics* do, Abbi and Ilana of *Broad City* do worse: they stuff sachets of marijuana up their vaginas; they Skype during sex; they find condoms hiding inside them; they catalog their poops and live in rat-infested apartments and announce their farts in yoga. If a dude did any of these things, it'd be called "epic" or "legendary" or maybe just a "casual hang" with the guys. When a woman does it, it's unruliness in the highest degree.

Or so the theory goes. In truth, the women of *Broad City*—costars Abbi Jacobson and Ilana Glazer—*aren't* too gross for most people, especially not for the type of people who watch Comedy Central. Reviews, which are overwhelmingly positive, admit to its raunch, but revel in the show's depiction of New York, the intimate female friendship of the protagonists, the gonzo surrealist structure of their adventures. The grossness in the show isn't for grossness's sake; rather, it's a form of radical honesty and transparency: they simply talk about all the things that happen to women and few dare to say aloud, let alone on television.

All of Abbi and Ilana's unruliness—wading through the most abject corners of their bodies, their sex lives, and New York City—is made possible by their liberty: they go where they want, take up space how they want, behave how they want, get stoned how they want. Usually those freedoms are reserved for the rich, or at the very least men; Abbi and Ilana's escapades are proof that white, middle-class, educated women, operating in a multicultural, bourgeois, urban space, can pretty much do whatever they want. They might get some funny looks, but they're ultimately free of consequences—or the sorts of pressures (jobs, families, unattractive bodies) that would curtail their control of their bodies and the space they fill with them.

They're free, in other words, to be semi-worthless wastrels. It might sound like a dubious achievement, but it's a critical one. Men have long been represented in the fullest spectrum of sinner to saint; in their refusal to submit to dominant cultural norms, unruly women like Abbi and Ilana help flesh out the spectrum of female representation that had previously been limited to the likes of evil prostitutes and Cruella de Vil. The deeper unruliness of *Broad City* has less to do with shit and bongs and dicks, then, and everything to do with the leisure time in which they're able to amuse themselves with any of the above. Abbi and Ilana hang out, waste time, and refuse labor in the same manner as their male counterparts. And that, far more than the general abjection that fills their days, is what makes them a problem in need of solving.

✦ ✦ ✦

Over the course of *Broad City*'s first three seasons, its protagonists have matured in the way that many people mature between ages twenty-four and twenty-six: the pressure to be something or be with someone increases, but only marginally. The pursuit of sex, or weed, or a wormhole of adventure remains the primary mode of existence, with pockets of work in between. Seeking the best way to hang out at all times, devoid of true responsibility, the entire city as your playground—it's the utmost in freedom and privilege.

This type of freedom was, until fairly recently, only available to rich white men. Working-class men rarely had time for that sort of unencumbered leisure, but with the rise of the middle class—and the white-collar job—came the Wednesday afternoon golf game, the booze-soaked lunch. Working-class women labored both in and outside the home, while middle-class women, their lives supposedly liberated by the likes of the washing machine and the dishwasher, were still largely relegated to the suburbs, isolated in their homes, their time filled with caring for their children, their appearance, and their husbands.

When middle-class women moved into the workplace, it was celebrated as women's "liberation"; in practice, it meant that women simply doubled their labor. Women had greater control of their own finances and, by extension, their lives—but, as late as 1990, they were still getting married at an average age of 23.9 and having their first child at the age of 24.[1] To "have it all" generally meant laboring nearly constantly: the first shift at work, the so-called second shift at home. Over the course of the 1990s, the age of "responsibility"—when people first married, or the age of their first child—began to rise. In 2009, 46 percent of adults below the age of thirty-four had never been married—a twelve-point jump from just a decade before.[2] And the longer marriage and children are delayed (or refused altogether), the longer women have to explore or switch careers, or to experience weekends and non-work times not as time to serve others' needs, but their own, or none at all. The more time they have, to put it bluntly, to fuck around.

The ability to fuck around has long been the provenance of the very rich—think of the characters in a Jane Austen novel, filling their days with walks and teas and flitting about Europe. Starting with the so-called slackerism of the 1990s, it became the privilege of the children of the middle class: highly educated kids in their twenties, clustered in urban areas, who came to understand labor as something that should always feel meaningful or fulfilling. You could perform non-meaningful, non-fulfilling labor while you waited for that other occupation to realize itself, but never as an end to itself. Factory jobs, serving "the man" in middle management, service work in non-artisan restaurants—those were *jobs*, not careers, and to be avoided at all costs, even if it meant relying on parents to fund that dream, or working for free as an intern at a place that did feel meaningful and fulfilling.

The privilege to fuck around intertwines with the privilege to only accept labor that makes you feel good. That attitude is usually ascribed to the hazy swath of the American population known as "millennials," but it's a particularly raced and classed and educated sort of millennial—one whose ideas about work are often shaped by their parents, who desire more fulfilling work for

54

themselves, and the media, which limits its conceptualization of desirable labor to that in creative fields.

Enter *Broad City* and its creators. Jacobson and Glazer are textbook members of the millennial population described above: Jacobson grew up in a well-to-do suburb of Philadelphia, the daughter of an artist and a graphic designer, and attended Maryland Institute College of Art, where she studied video production. Glazer grew up on Long Island in a fairly standard Jewish middle-class household and attended NYU. Jacobson found her way to New York after college and, following some lonely months in Queens, heard about the Upright Citizens Brigade, or UCB, the leading improv troupe in New York. Both she and Glazer, who was finishing up at NYU, tried out to be part of the main troupe, but neither made the cut, finding themselves together on the UCB approximation of a farm team.

They were paying for practice space and an improv coach, and making essentially nothing, money-wise. And they had nothing tangible to show for it—or, more specifically, to show their parents—as the fruit of their labor. So in 2009, the pair decided to produce a web series with themselves at its center and their New York, filled with similarly striving, hooking-up, weed-smoking, educated twentysomethings, as their set. The name *Broad City* both reappropriated the term "broad" (a historical pejorative for promiscuous women) and yoked it to the city, implying that the New York of the series isn't just filled with broads, but a city defined by them. Glazer describes a broad as "a full person," which is an appropriate reflection of the ethos of the series: unruliness as the completion of personhood, not a perversion of it.[3]

The first episode—a two-minute sketch that pitches the desire to donate only a certain amount to a homeless man against liberal guilt at not doing so—premiered in February 2010. Subsequent episodes honed in on the ethos and DIY aesthetic that still structures the show: the inanity of bar conversation, the fetishization of the in-house washer and dryer, the truly bizarre people who live and breathe and walk the streets of New York.

The webisodes focus on tiny slices of (non-work) life while voicing a strong antipathy toward so-called adult life. In one early episode, Abbi and Ilana find themselves in a cheap yoga class in what seems to be Park Slope—an area of Brooklyn known for its abundance of children, strollers, and preschool talk. At first, Abbi and Ilana feel like they've found an accepting place where they belong. But once the yoga class ends, the other participants begin to talk manically about child care options, telling the pair that they'll never understand life until they have children. Parenthood and marriage aren't just lame, the episode suggests— they're also repressive and exclusionary.

Once the web series accumulated a modest following, Jacobson and Glazer started paying their directors, and the series began to look less like a thesis project and more like a polished product. They kept working their day jobs (waitressing, working at a bakery), wrote at night, and bent their work schedules around their shooting ones. Eventually, they both ended up at a company that provided deep discounts on health and beauty services (and on which Ilana's employer in the television series is based). There, they sat next to each other, Gchatted constantly, and collected show ideas in a spreadsheet. It was the apotheosis of the millennial-job-as-placeholder-while-seeking-a-career, down to using the job's resources to facilitate your more fulfilling (and, according to this logic, rightful) employment outside of it.

For the end of season two of the web series, Jacobson and Glazer decided to shoot for a high-profile guest star. As the story goes, they contacted Amy Poehler, a fellow UCB alum, to see if she'd appear; she responded, "Sure! I love *Broad City*!" at which point Jacobson and Glazer lost their collective shit. Poehler appeared in the episode chest-bumping, high-fiving, and falling amidst a sea of oranges; seven months later, she signed on to executive produce a pilot of the television show.

Poehler was a perfect match for *Broad City*. Back in 2008, she'd created a web series called *Smart Girls at the Party*—now an online community called "Amy Poehler's Smart Girls"—that aims to "emphasize intelligence and imagination over 'fitting in,'" and "wants you to be your weird and wonderful selves!" *Broad City* combined that cultivation of the wacky with the warmth of Poehler's other project, *Parks and Recreation*. Abbi and Ilana might have been far less straightlaced than Poehler's conception of Leslie Knope, but they share a ball-busting stubbornness and a devotion to their female friends. When it comes to characters like Abbi and Ilana, Poehler told *The New Yorker*, "there aren't enough like them on TV: confident, sexually active, self-effacing women, girlfriends who love each other the most."[4]

The pilot was originally destined for FX, but as Poehler later recalled, the network "really blew it."[5] So she took the series to Comedy Central, where Kent Alterman, head of original programming, decided that Poehler's assertion that *Broad City* would be a good fit for the channel was "good enough for me."[6] But Alterman was also responding to an industry-wide demand for a specific sort of show: when *Broad City* debuted in 2014, *Girls* had already proven that audiences were ready to watch young (white) women behaving badly.

Girls's ratings have always been deceptively low, yet its swift domination of the zeitgeist prompted television execs, from basic cable to extended cable, to set out in search of their own show starring and directed toward millennial women. The broadly palatable network version of that show was *2 Broke Girls*; the basic cable rendering was *Broad City*. But if *2 Broke Girls* took all of the meanness of *Girls* and none of the heart, *Broad City* did the inverse: less ugliness, more zaniness, a sort of "Unruly Girls Just Wanna Have Fun! (and Get High)."

Instead of a series of sketches like *Key & Peele, Inside Amy Schumer*, or *Kroll Show*, each *Broad City* would have a loose, simple, elliptical "goal": retrieve a package, make money by Airbnbing their apartments, go to a Lil Wayne concert. Elements that were hinted at in the web series—their distance from each other, their ridiculous jobs, Ilana's lust for Abbi—became major plot points. Abbi's art school past becomes more pronounced as several episodes address some component of that dream deferred: the sadness of finding out that the "gallery" exhibiting her painting is just a vegetarian sandwich shop, or the general indignation of working as a cleaner, literally getting her hands in rich people's shit and pubes, at a swanky gym.

Ilana works in a different sort of abyss—the light-filled, hip Brooklyn offices of an Internet "deals" site, always desperate to think up new ways (discounts on Vajazzling!) to make people buy coupons for things they didn't know they wanted. It's a riff on Jacobson and Glazer's own employment at a similar site, yet with the absurdity ratcheted to eleven: Ilana doesn't "work" so much as occupy a space at a desk and generally disrupt the work-space. She knows she's supposed to have a job—in order to buy produce at the grocery co-op, to acquire weed—but she refuses to discipline herself into performing as an efficient, responsible person. She wears dog hoodies to the office; she terrorizes her co-workers; she terrifies her boss. She navigates the world with the swagger of a mediocre white man. Which doesn't make her actions any less despicable, or less lazy. It simply points to the liberating powers of confidence: to succeed or, in Ilana's and many white men's cases, to coast on other people's hard work.

Abbi's and Ilana's confidence is fueled, in part, by weed—the consumption of which blunts the pressures of perfection. Smoking weed is unruly not because it's illegal, but because it makes women care less about everything in general and societal expectations in particular. Men have been getting stoned for decades, but when a woman admits to getting high and *liking it*—as Jennifer Aniston did in 2000—it's viewed as "tarnishing" her image. "There are things good girls are supposed to do," *Paper* magazine's Gabby Bess explains, "and marijuana, apparently, isn't one of them."[7]

Weed culture is male-dominated and often blatantly sexist: in California, men are estimated to do 80 to 90 percent of the purchasing; advertisements regularly feature the sort of alluringly posed, big-breasted, blonde women of the beer ad; many women still smoke "in secret" and in private, eschewing joints, bongs, and the public visibility of weed consumption. The stoner, slacker lifestyle, according to cultural critic Ari Spool, is "an accepted part of modern maleness."[8] Women, by contrast, have to go to college, get jobs, have kids in the limited biological time available to them: "there is not time for women to be slovenly and relax."

Broad City eschews those expectations: Ilana hides weed all over her house and her body; she rolls joints like a pro and for everyone who wants them. When she's nervous about getting an HPV shot, her quasi-boyfriend Lincoln calms her by surprising her with a massive Gingerblunt Man. For her, being high isn't an act of rebellion, but a way of experiencing the world. As Glazer explains, "People latch on to the party thing. But it's more about their spirit."[9] *Slate*'s Willa Paskin describes that spirit as "IDGAF," or "I don't give a fuck," and points to just how rare it is to see a woman inhabit it: not because women aren't intrinsically capable of such lack of concern for what others think of them, but because they've been taught for so long that it's the primary barometer of one's life.[10]

That IDGAF attitude is part of why work doesn't structure Abbi's and Ilana's lives, let alone disrupt them: it simply pauses their everyday rhythms of getting high, having sex, and hanging out, all of it in bold excess. They don't just Skype each other; they Skype each other *on the toilet*; they have never-ending brunch *while* discussing anal sex; they don't just take weed with them everywhere; they stash it in their vaginas. It's that sort of compounding unruliness that earned the show its immediate label as "raunchy," "sort of a crude, transgressive and poorly typed treatment," and "outright gross."[11] Yet that grossness is remarkable because the filth is emanating from women's bodies. If a "proper lady" never curses, ignores the existence of bodily functions, and possesses a sex drive solely activated by male desire, then Abbi and Ilana are impropriety manifest: they play profanity like a personal piano, they talk openly about piss and shit and periods, and their sex drives are autonomous and fulfilled on their own terms.

But they're dirty only insomuch as they acknowledge the existence of what all women know to be true. A vibrator becomes gross when it's not hidden; poop or a tampon becomes abject when its existence is acknowledged. Or take the scene when they decide to get their facial hair waxed: the camera zooms in close on the dripping, disgusting wax, the repeated cries of pain, the puffy pinkness that deforms the face for hours afterwards. They're presenting the grotesquerie of performing femininity.

The goal of such scenes, according to Jacobson and Glazer, is humor—but also visibility. "We're doing it so everyone can be like, 'I do that.' Everyone does that," Jacobson told *The Hollywood Reporter*. "I remember the joke in middle school or high school that girls don't fart or girls don't shit," Glazer added, "and it's like fuck you. Because that's not a funny little joke; that's a big statement that women are somehow property of men, and they should stay in line, missy."[12] And while they acknowledge that individual scenarios—pooping in a shoe during a blackout, for example—are indeed gross, it rarely feels shameful, in part because their attitude toward their unruly selves is always one of compassion. Take the night when Ilana ignored her shellfish allergy in order to eat a fancy birthday dinner out with Abbi—and her face, as a result, swelled to the point of hideous distortion: it's not a point of embarrassment, but a testament to Ilana's devotion.

Which is part of what makes *Broad City* feel so tonally different from depictions of bodily humor that have come before. Men have been trained to think of women's excess as abject, an understanding that manifests in film and television (the "Battleshits" scene in *Harold & Kumar Go to White Castle*; the menstrual blood joke in *Superbad*; any movie in which a woman gives birth) and in obscenity standards on social media, in which Instagram dictates that an image depicting period blood soaking through the back of a pair of pants is "inappropriate content." According to this logic, men's bodily functions are funny—but women's bodies are fundamentally obscene.

Women often internalize this contempt for and shame of their bodily fluids, but not Jacobson and Glazer. They don't find the scenarios gross, or excessive—"A lot of it feels more casual when we're writing it," Glazer told *New York* magazine. "I think some of it has to do with being young women and having agency over our behavior and our words."[13] That agency, like the privilege to fuck around, is a more positive, shared characteristic of the middle-class white millennial. Glazer explains that "with my girlfriends of 20 years, we always talk about the disgusting stuff first: sex, poop, the fundamentals. Then, if we have time, the other things." "Maybe not a lot of women on TV act the way we do," Jacobson adds. "But a lot of women we know act that way."[14]

That disconnect might explain why so many outlets have struggled to encapsulate the show, describing it, variously, as "two mismatched friends who embark on zany adventures," "BFFs navigating their 20s in New York City and making a mess of things," "two young, single, cash-challenged gals," "wacky, deliciously bizarre comedy," "Like the *Friends* cast, they're goofy and irrepressibly good-humored."[15] If those all sound like studio-generated tag lines for a rom-com, it's because reviewers possess a paucity of reference points when it comes to female-centric texts. In many ways, *Broad City* demands a new language, to start a new lineage: it's a "totally unhinged game changer," according to *Out* magazine. "Now shows (like *Crazy Ex-Girlfriend* and *Idiotsitter*) are being compared to *it*."[16]

There is some merit to the rom-com comparison—it's just that *Broad City*'s central romance is a platonic one between two women. As the series went from web to television, the contrast between Abbi's "straight man" and Ilana's manic id became bolder. Whereas in most shows, a character like Abbi would take on the role of Ilana's centering force, the foil that reminds her how to behave like a good girl, in *Broad City*, Ilana's dick-swinging bravado is the magnetic force: instead of shutting it down, it activates Abbi's own swagger, pulling her past her typical timidity into a confidence usually reserved for men.

Both Abbi and Ilana are deeply weird, but within the vividly rendered world of *Broad City*, their actions make some sort of sense, always in relation to each other. Of *course* Abbi would pose as Ilana for a six-hour shift at the co-op, or Ilana would devote an entire day to caring for Abbi after oral surgery—they're each other's first and foremost. Which is why there are no "bottle episodes" that focus uniquely on one character or the other: not because they're not individuals, but because they're always in each other's orbit.

From the beginning, Poehler pushed Jacobson and Glazer to maintain their narrative focus on the friendship: "We wanted to make sure that everybody knew that at the end of the day, this show was a love story between Abbi and Ilana. They're the couple, they're the two that you have to care about."[17] Which doesn't sound revolutionary until you put it in context: the majority of female-oriented texts from the last twenty years, from *Sex and the City* to *Girls*, retain traditional, heteronormative romance at their narrative core. One early executive who was pitched the idea of *Broad*

City couldn't even conceptualize a show about two twentysome-things without romance: as the pair's manager explained, "I had one agent, a woman, tell me, 'I don't get why we'd watch this. Are they going to get married?'"[18]

But who needs romance when you have friendship with just as much texture and affection? Abbi and Ilana are each other's boosters and facilitators; always best friends, in a way that never feels schmaltzy, just enviable. They have none of the humor-generated friction of the buddy-cop movie; they don't scrape against each other like the characters of *Seinfeld*. Unlike other female protagonists, they never compete; they're not passive-aggressive; their friendship is never toxic. In their world, men are as secondary as female friends are in the traditional rom-com. With the exception of Ilana's "sex friend" Lincoln, men are props, foils, caricatures: ways to entertain themselves or learn about each other. When Abbi and Ilana call each other after hooking up with a guy, it's not to brag so much as to revel in each other's plea-sure. "These girls are horny, but not under the male gaze," Glazer told *Out*. "They're horny, period. Just starting from the vagina, not starting from some man looking at them."[19]

Operating without the male gaze frees women from self-consciousness, and *Broad City* highlights just how liberating that can be. They walk the streets and dress and enter restaurants and dance, truly, like no one's watching. They're never cruel or mean to those they encounter, but they also don't naturally oc-cupy a posture of submission or niceness, the way even women of New York are expected to greet the world. It's not Abbi's comfort zone, but Ilana's gravity and self-assurance brings her there. As Paskin points out, "Ilana is uniquely unburdened by what people think of her. If that sometimes makes her a jerk, it also makes her a unicorn—a rare being that, once spotted, you don't take your eyes off her."[20] A woman navigating the world with the confidence of a man is a beautiful, magnetic, and periodically unnerving sight to behold.

For television scholar Phillip Maciak, Ilana's dancing—which isn't an event so much as a state of being—is both an act of resistance and an expression of fluidity. "She's finding a groove," Maciak writes, "but she's also dodging bullets, ducking under boundaries." Boundaries of gender (when she gets turned on, she says she's "hard"; she wears tuxes and men's underwear) and sexuality (she prides herself on her desire for Abbi—and insists on an open relationship). And while sometimes that quest for fluidity is misplaced—as Abbi says, sometimes she tries so hard to not be racist that it's actually racist—it's also, in Maciak's words, "a sincere, if preposterous, statement of purpose. . . . It's a comfort that leads her to be offensive, to be an asshole, to be unruly. But it's also a comfort the show presents as admirable, that the show understands to be a type of unassailable virtue."[21]

Ilana and Abbi also both conceive of their own bodies—and each other's—as intrinsically beautiful. They constantly tell each other they look amazing; Ilana's outfits could best be described as bra- and midriff-centric; both agree that Abbi has "the ass of an angel." They're frequently nude around each other and others, which becomes all the more powerful given that they have, in Glazer's words, "womanly bodies." As she told *Flare*, "I think we both have these bodies that, because you just see such thin people represented all the time, when you have any tits, any ass, it's like va-va-voom."[22]

Unlike *Girls*, which employs unfetishized nudity as part of the argument of the show, the breasts and vaginas of *Broad City* get covered with blurred lines. "Lena is like a vessel for the message that normal bodies are so beautiful and sexy and powerful," Glazer told *New York* magazine. But "Lena's isn't a joke, you know? Ours is always a joke."[23] As she elaborates, "I am very sensitive about my boobs; I was literally nine when I got them, and for so many years, before I got to enjoy my body, it was for other people's evaluation. To enjoy your body on a comedy level is a whole other level of pleasure. Boob humor: it's like, this is not for you—it's for me." That's a stark contrast to the scene in *Neighbors* with Rose Byrne's heavily engorged and spurting breasts as punch line—a male-authored moment that upholds the notion that women's bodies are a horror show. The women of *Broad City* aren't horrified by their own bodies—but that doesn't mean they can't find them deeply hilarious.

In refusing to conceptualize women in relation to men, *Broad City* reaches its greatest theoretical unruliness. Whether through the embrace of a queer sexuality or single status or a relationship in which they remain financially or psychologically independent of a man, women have spent the last two decades gradually disarticulating their destinies from men's. That freedom has often been conceived as "fucking around"—wasting time, in this case, better spent navigating toward marriage and children and domesticity. The refusal to prioritize or achieve those things has been pathologized for years, and still sticks to the women of *Broad City*: part of the reason they're "zany" or "unhinged" or "boundary-pushing," to use the language of reviewers, is because they are, simply put, outside the gravitational sway of men.

✦ ✦ ✦

That separation from men, both as creators and in their characters, has proven especially discombobulating for the press, which has grouped *Broad City* with any slightly unruly female-oriented film or television show of the last five years: *Girls, New Girl, The Mindy Project.* "To be compared to any of those shows is so cool," Jacobson told *The Washington Post.* "But you know, no male shows are ever grouped into a category as being so similar just because there are guys on them."[24] The comparisons, according to Glazer, are "reductive": "It's minimized and dismissive and unproductive. Lena Dunham is a true, hardworking genius. But it's up to other people to differentiate the shows. Taking that comparison shortcut passes over a lot of details."[25]

Apart from centering on white women in their twenties in New York, *Broad City* and *Girls* are profoundly different—in tone, in aesthetic, in attitude toward the world. The world of *Girls* is inward-focused, both in psychology and in space; their New York is a small corner of Greenpoint, Brooklyn, with occasional, necessary, epiphany-facilitating trips out of the city. The look of *Girls* is filmic and crisp, befitting Dunham, whose previous work was all in filmmaking; the narrative is linear; the aesthetics are realist.

Broad City is equally obsessed with its protagonists, but their world—which becomes a character unto itself—is the marvel of New York, an ever-expanding utopia that opens up, at any given moment, to reveal secret worlds of weirdness and bliss. In *Broad City*, it's always summer, always sweaty, the haze of the city transposed onto the look of the footage, which retains the digital, haphazard, quixotic feel of the show's web series origins. If *Girls* is all deep, rich colors and moody introspection, *Broad City* is pulsing fluorescence, a chain of happenstance and a surrealist, self-defeating journey toward events the characters never reach or that never even happen.

Which isn't to elevate one show over the other so much as highlight the different registers in which they're operating, different depths they're plumbing, different understandings of the world they're negotiating. They're both using the figure of the unruly twentysomething woman to achieve those narrative goals. The tendency to group *Broad City* with *Girls* thus highlights just how ideologically ill-equipped and inexperienced the industry is with narratives produced by and for women: "It's like women in their 20s, you are all the same!" Glazer told a panel at Internet Week New York. "If it's not a white dude thing, it's compared to whatever group you're in."[26] It's a tendency that reflects the age-old understanding that (white) men can contain multitudes, while members of every other group are pitted against themselves, as if there can be only one show about black families, or queer dudes, or, in the case of *Broad City* and *Girls*, young women.

Jacobson and Glazer refuse to play nice—the way all celebrities, and women in particular, are expected to—when publicity fumbles its coverage. In addition to repeatedly and unflappably disabusing the comparisons to *Girls*, they've talked back when interview questions turn flat-out sexist. When, in a 2014 video interview for *Vanity Fair*, they were asked if they ever fight, Glazer's response was cutting: "Would you ask Key and Peele if they fight?"[27] Later, people told Glazer, "You were so right to tell that guy off." But as she explained to *Grantland*, "I'm like, no, baby, that was a *woman* doing that interview. Women can put you in a box just as much as men can."[28]

It's also, frankly, insulting: "What allowed us to rise out of web series saturation was our business mentality," Glazer told *Flare*. "We took it so seriously. I'm a businesswoman, not a cat fighter."[29] That status—as incredibly hardworking business-women who not only created and produced a web series, but now run their own television show—points to a central tension of the show: that a narrative based on *neglecting* labor actually requires a tremendous amount of it.

Granted, it's a different sort of labor—creative, self-satisfying—but in the six years since Jacobson and Glazer first began filming the web series, they've gradually distanced themselves from their *Broad City* doppelgangers. In a 2014 interview, Glazer said those characters were "like 15 percent of us blown up to the full 100 percent."[30] "My character goes out and parties at night," she continued. "I kind of never have done that but to show my eccentricities I gotta be going 24/7." And while they smoke weed (at dramatically lower levels) than their characters, they distance themselves from their behavior: when Glazer lost an earring during an interview with *Rolling Stone*, she chastised herself: "Goddamn it, Jesus Lord. This is so fucking *Broad City*. I hate the scatterbrained side of myself—I don't wanna be like my character. I hate being chaotic and harried in real life. I want to be mistakeless."[31]

It's not that they dislike their characters so much as they increasingly conceive of them as operating in a universe that's parallel, but not identical, to their own, aging and maturing at a delayed, but not necessarily stunted, pace. In "real" life, Abbi lives by herself in Brooklyn Heights; Ilana is dating a post-doc from NYU. They have a not-insignificant amount of money. They sometimes even take *cabs* instead of the subway. And by the end of season three, their characters have changed in different, but no less significant ways: Abbi and her long-loathed roommate, Bevers, have developed a quiet dependency and affection for each other; Ilana is crushed when Lincoln breaks up with her in order to seek monogamy, but doesn't know how to express her sadness at the loss. Abbi realizes she authentically likes a guy who's sweet, albeit slightly douchey; Ilana is finally, definitively fired.

In a different show, those developments would be framed as maturation—putting away childish things, and habits, and attitudes. But the triumph of *Broad City* is its ability to emphasize how characters can learn more about their behaviors and still not dismiss their essential selves. In other words, they're leaning *in* to their feelings—not because of societal expectations, but because they want to do what feels good. At the end of season three, they are still gloriously at home in their unruliness, but they're also diving deeper into what satisfaction and fulfillment might look like for each of them—an equation that might include boyfriends or babies or jobs but will, above all else, include each other.

❖ ❖ ❖

Watching the fuck-up freedom of *Broad City* can be intoxicating, but it can also feel tone-deaf: as Kyla Wazana Tompkins and Rebecca Wanzo explain in the *Los Angeles Review of Books*, their "economic precarity" can be played for laughs precisely because it is, ultimately, escapable. For millions, it isn't. "Some people spend much of their lives cleaning up after others," Wanzo explains. "Many of them are working poor, working class, immigrants, and people of color. So the show's joke relies on the idea that people who clean are not, should not be, people like Abbi." Many of the jokes thus turn on "how incongruent it is for white girls to live demeaning lives."[32] The poor and people of color are yoked to the abject; white people use its exploration as a path toward self-liberation.

It's a valid critique—and one that *Broad City* has increasingly interrogated, suggesting, especially in later seasons, the extent of Abbi and Ilana's privilege. The characters' disgust at the treatment of women in Saudi Arabia is juxtaposed with their disgust at the absence of free mimosas, highlighting the superficiality of their concern with inequality that doesn't directly affect them; Ilana's roommate, Jaime, gives Ilana a decimating lecture on how the hoop earrings she wears to masturbate—which spell out "Latina"—are a mode of neocolonialism. These moments sound strident, but they manage to be both incisive and humorous—evidence, as *New Yorker* critic Emily Nussbaum points out, that "great comedians don't fold and sulk when people raise questions—they just make better bits and bolder, more ambitious jokes."[33]

The joke, increasingly, is on their characters, especially in the moments when they fail to realize just how unique and privileged they truly are, or the faults in what Nussbaum terms their "well-intentioned but barely informed fourth-wave, queerish, anti-rape/pro-porn intersectional feminism."[34] Because embracing their particular brand of unruliness—the freedom to fuck around, the ability to act "like men," or act like "the boss bitches we are *in our minds*"—without considering the ways other people are still excluded from doing so, is the height of white girl feminism. The progression of *Broad City* ultimately suggests that freedom should not be equated with enlightenment—and while being a woman who doesn't define yourself in relation to men is incredibly powerful, the danger is when you fail to see yourself, or the freedoms you enjoy, in relationship to those of anyone else.

In this way, Glazer and Jacobson have used the more recent seasons of the show to move from "Too Gross" unruliness into "Too Honest" territory. There are parts of their characters that are beautiful and liberating and glorious to behold, but others that shine an unbecoming mirror up to the often good intentions of certain swaths of their privileged generation. The willingness to contemplate the ramifications of these freedoms is by no means an exclusively female trait. Yet the refusal to fall into the easy posture of denial or defensiveness, like so many comedians under fire, requires a sort of bravery, of brazenness. Unruliness isn't just calling attention to arbitrary expectations of how a woman should behave. It's also a willingness to expect better for all other women—and better of oneself.

CHAPTER 4

TOO SLUTTY:
NICKI MINAJ

Like that of so many celebrities, Nicki Minaj's Instagram feed is at once incredibly boring and incredibly beautiful to behold. It's filled with promotion for her upcoming concerts and film appearances, images of the dozens of products affiliated with her name, inspirational quotes, and shots of her looking, well, amazing. Selfies, sometimes in triplicate—shots of her ass, shots of her outfit, shots in profile—a constant carousel of the grainy shoot-your-own variety expertly mingling alongside high-gloss paparazzi shots.

These images routinely amass tens, if not hundreds of thousands of likes, but attract little outside attention. But when, in June 2014, Minaj posted a preview of the album cover for her new single, "Anaconda," she sparked a firestorm. In the image, Minaj is squatting, wearing a G-string, bra, and high-tops, and peering over her shoulder; a "Parental Advisory: Explicit Cover" sticker hangs in the right lower corner. "Most iconic day in music history," one of thousands of commenters asserted. "She is a musician, she doesn't need to be showing off her ass and boobs to sell her music," chided another.

The photo spread swiftly across the Internet, posted with headlines like "Nicki Minaj's NSFW 'Anaconda' Cover Will Make Your Jaw Drop" and transformed into an ever-replicating meme. Speculation mounted that the image had been Photoshopped or that Minaj's ass was fake, but the real "controversy" was over the example Minaj was setting for young girls, encapsulated in an open letter from AllHipHop.com CEO Chuck Creekmur:

> I'm trying to raise a young girl that will eventually grow into someone greater than the both of us. I know that this requires great parenting, great education, great luck and an assortment of great influences. I'm sure you know the influence you wield, but now, if you told the "Barbs" [Nicki's name for her fans] to scratch my eyes out, some would attack without thinking about it. I'm sure some will also replicate the "Anaconda" image without thinking about it too. . . . Is this the path you want to lead impressionable kids down?[1]

Minaj responded by posting a series of similarly revealing photos on Instagram—only all the exposed butt cheeks were those of "classy" (read: *not* black) women, posing for publications like *Sports Illustrated*. With her captions, Minaj highlighted the ways in which those bodies were deemed "Angelic" and "Acceptable," while hers was automatically considered the opposite.

Later, she told *Complex* magazine that the picture was not

"premeditated"—her photographer had been on set, snapping photos; later, when Minaj saw the shot, she loved it. "What made me excited about it was that people hadn't seen me do a picture like that in years," she said. "The reason I stopped taking pictures like that was because I needed to prove myself. I needed for people to take me seriously. I needed for people to respect my craft. I've proven that I'm an MC. I'm a writer; I'm the real deal, so if I want to take sexy pictures, I can. I'm at the level in my career and in my life now where I can do whatever the hell I want to do."[2]

The tendency to label Minaj "too slutty" or sexually explicit is a symptom of a much larger anxiety: how to process a woman, and a black woman in particular, who has taken control of her body, her formidable talents, and the way they are marketed, monetized, and received. Minaj is unapologetic about who she is and how she chooses to live—exercising a form of self-determination that has been almost entirely unavailable to black women in America. Which is why, in a society still very much dominated by white men, that sort of sovereignty doesn't just threaten the existing cultural hierarchy, it compromises its very foundation.

For centuries, white men have largely controlled the way black women's bodies have been represented in both culture and civil society, whether in painting, sketches, sculpture, lyrics, photography, or film. In a world structured by Christian morals, including the disavowal of sexuality and lust, artists often displaced those qualities onto the black body. Black bodies were figured as more "earthy," more animal, more primal, more sexual—and, despite the black woman's historical subjugation, *more free, more* open. In this way, the black female body was made available for consumption and titillation, yet still distanced from the (pure, virginal) white body. With positions of power and production unavailable to black women themselves, this mode of representation was so common, so consistent, so unchallenged, that it came to be accepted as truth.

Within this paradigm, the only way for a black woman to excel—especially in a public, performing sense—was to embody the very understanding that's been mapped on her, regardless of its veracity. As feminist scholar bell hooks explains, "many black women singers, irrespective of the quality of their voices, have cultivated an image which suggests they are sexually available and licensed. Undesirable in the conventional sense, which defines beauty and sexuality as desirable only to the extent that it is idealized and unattainable, the black female body gains attention only when it is synonymous with accessibility, availability, and when it is sexually deviant."[3] Hooks points to the example of Billie Holiday, but it's a lineage that also includes Dorothy Dandridge, Tina Turner, Diana Ross, and, more recently, Janet Jackson, Beyoncé, and Rihanna. To study these women is to consider larger questions of power, self-objectification, and false consciousness: If women of all races have been objectified for centuries, what happens when one decides to do it herself? Is it liberating—and if she thinks it's liberating, has she simply accepted the ideology of the oppressor? And how do the questions of empowerment function differently when applied to white women and women of color?

This approach to thinking about women's bodies and their representation falls under the broad umbrella of "intersectional feminism," which suggests that the only way to talk about the lives of women under patriarchy is to also consider the ways in which those lives are constructed at the nexus of race, sexuality, class, religion, ability, and nationality. It's a feminism that, in the words of cultural critic Teresa Jusino, "acknowledges that different communities of women within our greater Sisterhood have concerns that are specific to them, and deserve focus if Women as a group are ever going to move forward."[4]

Scholars and astute critics have taken an intersectional approach to analyzing Minaj, working to place her within a sublineage of how black women have been represented in hip-hop. If hip-hop is, as cultural critic Touré wrote in the *The New York Times*, "primarily a celebration of black masculinity," women's bodies have often been used in service of that celebration.[5] The typical representation of a black woman's body in a rap music video is one of little or no agency: "We see black women whose rear ends are either the theme of the song or the star of the music video," cultural anthropologist Nikki Lane argues, "but rarely do these women get to express anything outside of sexuality that is already shaped by the desire of the male artist."[6] Their personalities, like their purpose, are one-dimensional, limited to their ability to provide sexual satisfaction to the subject of the video and/or the audience viewing it.

This mode of representation stemmed from the male dominance of hip-hop—which went unchallenged until the first female MCs broke through in the early 1990s. Scholar Savannah Shange divides this generation of women into a rough dichotomy: the "Righteous Queen" (Lauryn Hill, MC Lyte, Salt-N-Pepa, Queen Latifah), whose music offered positive messages of empowerment and self-love, and the "Gangsta Boo" (Lil' Kim, Foxy

Brown, Eve), all of whom were linked with a male rapper "mentor" figure, and whose lyrics focused on crime and sex. A "Righteous Queen" like Queen Latifah was capable of transcending the traditional boundaries of black women in hip-hop, winning roles in mainstream Hollywood films, even as it meant eschewing major parts of her personality (and remaining pointedly mum on matters of her sexuality).[7]

By contrast, the careers of "Gangsta Boos" have been curtailed by prison or dead-ended by the decline of the male rappers with whom they rose to prominence. As critic Julianne Escobedo Shepherd explains, "Lil Kim and Foxy Brown put their sexuality on a platter, which was complicated, but at times revolutionary, like a reclamation—but the sexual power from the money/power/respect–era became diluted and sad as the years went by." Yet exploiting their sexuality "pigeonholed Kim and Foxy into caricatures of what they thought men wanted"—and those caricatures gradually cannibalized their underlying talent.[8]

But Minaj—like Missy Elliott, another iconoclastic artist to whom she is often compared—complicates the dichotomy of Righteous Queen or Gangsta Boo. She cites Lauryn Hill as her most significant influence, yet her early raps, and the artwork that accompanied them, place her within the lyrical lineage of the Gangsta Boo. On the advice of her manager, she changed her given last name from Miraj to Minaj, a play on "ménage a trois"; her first mixtape opened with a sex line call to 1-900-MS-MINAJ.

Minaj occupied the stereotype only long enough for it to gain her notice—specifically, that of Lil Wayne, who signed her to his Young Money label—and then disposed of it. "When I grew up I saw females doing certain things, and I thought I had to do that

exactly," Minaj told *Vibe* magazine in 2010, just as she was rising
to national prominence. "The female rappers of my day spoke
about sex a lot . . . And I thought that to have the success they got,
I would have to represent the same thing. When in fact I didn't
have to represent the same thing."[9]

Instead, she adopted a cornucopia of identities, some more
fully fleshed than others, to accompany the various aural personalities that distinguished her rapping style. Most prominently,
there's Roman Zolanski, a gay British boy with a cockney accent
and a deep reservoir of rage, and Harajuku Barbie, with a girly
voice and hyper-feminine aesthetic, but there are nearly a dozen
more: Nicki the Ninja, Point Dexter, Female Weezy, Nicki the
Boss, Nicki Lewinsky.

These personas, Minaj explains, allow her to occupy attitudes often viewed as "unacceptable" for women: they're angry,
lewd, coy, uncouth, violent, and frequently at odds, as in the
video for "Monster," when two of the personas verbally spar as
one binds and whips the other. They also serve as a commentary
on the fractured, performative nature of femininity: as Minaj explains, "Every woman is multifaceted. Every woman has a switch,
whether she's going to be maternal, whether she's going to be a
man-eater, whether she has to kick ass, whether she has to be one
of the boys, whether she has to show the guys that she's just as
smart or smarter, she's just as talented or creative. Women sup-
press a lot of their sides."[10] It's a form of "code switching"—a
term to describe how one speaks and behaves differently in order
to match an intended audience. Code switching is, at heart, a sur-
vival mechanism: a way of showing, at any particular moment,
that you fit in, you're not a threat, you *belong.*

Minaj's alter egos were also a means of figuring her own identity when the role of "female rapper" had become too overdetermined with meaning. "I don't know where I fit in the spectrum of rap yet," she told *Fader* in 2010.

> I think now I'm kind of proving myself, but before, people thought I was more of a sex symbol or a wannabe sex symbol—and I never wanted to be a sex symbol. Now they're seeing. That's why I make the goofiest faces. I don't want people to think I'm up there trying to be cute. I'm trying to entertain, and entertaining is more than exuding sex appeal. I don't think that's fun. I don't find it fun watching someone trying to be sexy. It's sad. I'm trying to just show my true personality, and I think that means more than anything else. I think when personality is at the forefront, it's not about male or female, it's just about, who is this weird character?[11]

Cultural historian Uri McMillan calls Minaj's "ever-expanding oeuvre" of wigs, outfits, voices, and personas "Nicki-aesthetics"— a means through which the *performance and spectacle* of character becomes the focus, even more than the characters themselves. "Through these aggressive aesthetic acts," McMillan explains, "Minaj not only crashes hip-hop's proverbial boys club, but also refuses its constitutive element—a street-savvy authenticity, or 're-alness'—in favor of girly artifice." Put differently, as observers, we're too busy marveling at the artistry to even consider the questions of legitimacy that often swirl around hip-hop artists and women in particular. McMillan sees "Nicki-aesthetics" as a black, female, and feminist form of camp, in which "the female spectator laughs at and plays with her own image," observing it as a construction, distancing herself from it, and deriving pleasure by "making fun of, and out of that image."[12] Which is another way of saying that Minaj is constantly messing around with her audiences: she understands her image *as image*, and delights in playing with it, making it as confusing and contradictory (and beguiling) as possible. Unruliness, then, through illegibility.

Part of this illegibility is a refusal of all labels, genres, or boxes—and residing in the spaces in between. Like that of "bisexual"—a label that, in the early days of her career, she didn't court so much as *not* reject. Granted, as Marquita R. Smith explains, many of her mixtape-era lyrics also invoke a queerness, or *performance* of queerness, in the service of male desire: the lyric "Can I squeeze your boobs, let me see your boobs," part of a guest verse on Gucci Mane's "Girls Kissing Girls," figures "homosexual desire as titillation for male fantasy"; a similar configuration goes down in the video for Usher's "Lil Freak," in which she searches for a suitable woman for a ménage a trois.[13]

In the June 2010 issue of *Black Men* magazine, Minaj addressed the issue without clarifying her stance: "I don't date women and I don't have sex with women," she told the lad mag. "But I don't date men either." At least not publicly: as Minaj would later reveal, she had been in a long-term relationship with her hype-man, Safaree Samuels, but kept it private, in part because of the industry logic in which female artists are poised as always available to men, but also because she simply did not want a label dictating her identity. "People who like me—they'll listen to my music, and they'll know who I am," she later told *Out*. "I just don't like that people want you to say what you are, who you are. I just am. I do what the fuck I want to do."[14]

As Smith points out, Minaj is not an "ideal (or willing) spokeswoman for queer women of color."[15] And yet her image points to the perceptions of gayness that run through hip-hop, "unmasking assumptions that parade as truths"—like the idea that a woman who presents as femme, or a man who's butch, should automatically be figured as straight.[16] What others might perceive as a maddening insistence on obliqueness doesn't just blur lines; it calls the very need for them into question.

It also steers the conversation away from her love life and back toward her art. Female celebrities are faced with limited choices when it comes to publicizing their private lives: romance, and the corresponding gossip and narrative that accompany it, can be a shortcut to fame, but it also feminizes and often delegitimizes their work. Remaining unattached makes the artist seem more sexually available, and thus more attractive to fans, but it can also open up other narratives: she's too focused on her career; she's asexual; she's queer. Yet Minaj circumvents those prescribed paths, in part because they're profoundly boring. "Everyone knows I can go out and pick a dude and date him," she told *Out*. "But I want to do what people think I can't do, which is have the number 1 album in the country and be the first female rapper to sell albums like dudes in this day and age."[17]

Minaj also refuses the identity of "feminist": as she told *Rolling Stone*, "I don't like to put a label on myself, because then people will tear that apart."[18] She's not wrong: the media has often wielded female celebrities' public embrace of feminism as a tool to pick at their failures, instead of accentuating their successes. As a result, focusing on control of one's career—showing, as Minaj says, that "a young black girl from Queens can maneuver through corporate America" and advocating for "women who take control of their careers"—is more powerful, both on the level of representation and in terms of what she can actually do to change the status quo, than embracing a term and watching as—mostly white—writers complain about how her actions fail to fulfill their definition of the word.[19]

Refusing to embrace the term "feminist" pissed some people off. But her refusal to maintain the sanctity of hip-hop has angered far more. Minaj's career has often been segmented into two parts: the "mixtape era," spanning from early forays into mixtapes to guest appearances on more than thirty songs, and the "album era," starting with the release of *Pink Friday* (2010) and extending to the present. "Mixtape Nicki" is more "traditionally" hip-hop (visceral, fast-spitting), while the voice of "album Nicki" is clearer, cleaner, more pop, more accessible. Her first massive single, "Your Love," is a radio-friendly ballad; "Super Bass," the fifth single from the album, took off after a video of Taylor Swift and Selena Gomez rapping along to it went viral. Her second album, *Pink Friday: Roman Reloaded*, is even divided into two halves: one pop, one hip-hop.

As a result, hip-hop purists have routinely accused Minaj of selling out. In 2012, Peter Rosenberg, the host of Hot 97's Summer Jam concert, referred to "Starships," the poppy single off of *Pink Friday: Roman Reloaded*, as "bullshit" that wasn't "real hip-hop." Minaj responded by pulling out of the concert, prompting a genre-wide discussion of the function, if any, of policing the lines of hip-hop. As Minaj later told Rosenberg, "I wanted to experiment. My whole career has been a playing field for me to try new

things. I never put a limit on myself. And I don't like it when—
especially black—women put a limit on what they can do."[20]

The self-appointed guardians of the purity of hip-hop criticiz-
ing Minaj were, naturally, all men. As music critic Ann Powers
explains, the play between genres, like the play between the egos of
Barbie Nicki and Roman Zolanski, is a message itself: "Though
many critics have accused Minaj of making these more 'girly' tracks
for strictly commercial reasons, they do make a statement about
femininity: that it's a form of drag as potentially ridiculous as the
strap-on machismo of Roman."[21] In rejecting labels, Minaj makes
even bolder, more complex and incendiary statements—about what
it means to be a woman, an artist, or a person in power. "With her,
the point is plenitude," critic Jody Rosen explains. "More boasts,
more hooks, more craziness, more shape-shifting, more cognitive
dissonance, more pleasure."[22]

Minaj's most incendiary act has been to exercise complete
control over that plenitude—as well as agency over her body, her
sound, her social media, her business deals, and her image at
large. It's a strategy years in the making: when the change of her
last name comes up in interviews, it's like a specter of the one
time she let someone else control her career, continually framed
as the misstep that ensured she'd make her own path from that
point forward. During her mixtape days, rumors circulated that
someone else wrote her lyrics—in part because of the sexist assumption that no woman would have the skill to write lyrics as
good as hers, but also because other female rappers who were the
protégés of men, such as Lil' Kim, often had those men write lyrics for them. But Minaj is unequivocal when it comes to her authorship: "I am so territorial, that [from the start] I just felt like

whatever I was gonna do I was gonna write myself," she told *Fader.* "It's my personal preference to always be in control of everything I do in life."[23]

While other celebrities host profile writers in their homes or over lunch or on an adventure in the desert, when they visit Minaj, she's always working—going back and forth with the color correctors of a video short, posting to social media, overseeing every detail of a mix, testing perfume scents. If other celebrities perform leisure in their profiles, Minaj is always laboring—or, as in the case of a now-famous *GQ* profile from 2014, falling asleep out of exhaustion from that labor.[24] "When it comes time to retouch and do color correction, those are little things that can turn into big things if they're not done properly," she told *Rolling Stone.* "So I oversee it, too. I would save so much time if I didn't care about things like that. But I do."[25]

Same for her outfits, her fashion, her look: "My hard-core fans know that everything I do has been approved by me personally," she explained. "That's very important to me—and to them. Even though my team is mostly made up of guys, none of them would ever think about telling me what to wear or what to do with my hair. I ask for my team's opinion, but they know that ultimately I'm gonna do what I'm gonna do."[26]

Minaj conceives of her image not as a frivolity, but as a business, and oversees it accordingly. Which significantly undercuts any attempt to argue that the return to sexual images—like the one on the cover of "Anaconda," and the images throughout the video for the song—somehow decreases, or otherwise compromises, her unruly potency. Instead, it's simply the next chapter in the extended narrative of experimentation, control, play. Between

Pink Friday: Roman Reloaded and her third album, *The Pinkprint*, Minaj began to put away her alter egos and the "Nicki-aesthetics" that accompanied them. Increasingly, she appeared in "natural" form—on the cover of magazines (the April 2013 issue of *Elle*, for example, promised "Nicki Minaj Unzipped: No Wig, No Costume. The American Idol Diva Like You've Never Seen Her Before"), at the Met Ball, in her capacity as a judge on *American Idol*.

Rumors swirled that she had fired her entire "glam squad" in an attempt to be taken more seriously—a point unconfirmed by Minaj and, it seems, a misreading of Minaj's decision-making. As Carrie Battan points out in her 2014 *Fader* profile, "just before the cartoonish, attention-demanding outfits that had become her signature began to limit her, she stripped them away."[27] The alter egos, like her previous sexed-up persona, was simply an instrument: if the latter helped put her on the radar of Lil Wayne, then the former helped put her on the radar of America at large. "I always thought that by the time I put out a third album, I would want to come back to natural hair and natural makeup," she told *GQ*. "I thought, I will shock the world again and just be more toned down. I thought that would be more shocking than to keep doing exactly what they had already seen."[28]

Cue "Anaconda"—so "shocking" it broke the Internet, sparked a firestorm of opinions, and incited the wrath of moralists across the country. The video for "Anaconda" features sequences of Minaj twerking with a clutch of similarly buxom women, another in which a pink-wigged Minaj maniacally chops, devours, and then disposes of a banana, and a closing interlude where she dances around and nearly astride Drake, but never lets him touch her. The YouTube comments oscillated between "Is this porn?" and "This bitch has no talent at all, so she decided to shake her ass just to be famous, am I right?" A white female writer for *Mic* claimed that the video "isn't challenging anything, it's only playing by the game that the entertainment world has foiled on women for decades," relying on "the tired trope of hypersexualizing women's bodies."[29] And then there was the letter from Creekmur, with its paternalistic demand for Minaj to contemplate "How is Onika Tanya Maraj doing? How does she truly feel about Nicki Minaj right now?"[30]

When Minaj was asked about the backlash—and the letter from Creekmur in particular—her response was cutting: "Shut your stupid ass up. Bye, dad. I laughed at it. But I also didn't even know that that was happening."[31] Bigger than the backlash, after all, were the sales, the exposure for several of her brands, which were featured in the video—and her own intentions: "With a video like 'Anaconda,' I'm a grown ass fucking woman!" she said. "I stand for girls wanting to be sexy and dance, but also having a strong sense of themselves. If you got a big ol' butt? Shake it! Who cares? That doesn't mean you shouldn't be graduating from college. When I'm twerking and having fun, I still want to instill self-worth in young girls."[32]

Minaj knows exactly what she's doing—and that includes forcing critics to treat the way she represents herself as a mindful act. If she's rejected easy categorization to this point, why would she embrace it at the peak of her powers? There's something much more complicated, albeit difficult to parse, with this current iteration of her image: it's almost as if she's daring us to underestimate her, to think that she's not conscious of what she's doing. And if you looked and thought hard about it, it was easy to go beyond the simple "bad representation" argument, as evidenced by a slew of nuanced, intersectional takes on the video. As *Feministing* columnist Mychal Denzel Smith put it, "whenever black women own their own sense of sexuality and it appears to not be controlled by the hetero-male gaze, the whole world gets in a tizzy."[33]

The video is like the most beautiful, irresistible inkblot test: the way you react to it says more about your own assumptions—about women, about asses, about black women, about the level of intelligence women who watch this video possess—and less about Minaj herself. To label her "too sexual" is to underestimate just how complicated women, and the pleasure and power they can take in their own bodies, can be, even if—*especially* if—that power and pleasure have historically been wrested from them.

Minaj put it best when describing her character, Draya, in *Barbershop: The Next Cut*: "I didn't want her to be, you know, an Instagram thot," she told *Nylon*. "I wanted her to have some sort of purpose and meaning."[34] Which is why, when the script called for her character to twerk, she declined: "Not every sexy woman out here is twerking all damn day." Here, like with her videos, and her interviews, and her lyrics and her transformations, lies a simple yet highly provocative suggestion: that women are far more complicated than others have come to assume.

Many female celebrities, especially unruly ones, have demanded, and required, reconsideration. But Minaj is also demanding a reconsideration of the entire paradigm of celebrity—and the way the exchange of ideas, and the assumptions that accompany them, travel from the producers of culture to those who consume it. If other celebrities are in the business of playing nice with the press in order to soften their image, Minaj is unafraid to play bold, callous, and abrupt—characteristics often rewarded, or at least tolerated, when it comes to men—and undermine the mechanisms that would paint those actions as unruly in the process.

You can see it in a widely publicized appearance on *The Breakfast Club*, a popular morning radio talk show, when she let loose on the hosts' lack of preparation: "I don't understand why I'm coming to radio and y'all don't even have my songs ready." When one of the hosts admitted she hadn't yet watched Minaj's video for the song "Freedom," Minaj questioned her legitimacy: "How are y'all on the radio, especially if you know an artist is about to come up to your show and you know, she just put out a video. What would make you not watch it? When I go to the UK, my fans are like, 'Oh you always have the best interviews out there,' because it's a knowledgeable interview. They know what they're talking about. They've done the research."[35]

Then the coup de grâce: "I'm gonna start holding y'all responsible and up to a certain standard," she said. "If every other artist wants to come up here and be fake, I'm not doing it no more." It's a threat that, due to the massive reach of her social media, she could make reality: she can afford to ignore, or at least inflame, the traditional press, but they cannot afford to do the same to her.

The language used to describe this encounter—Minaj "Gets Turnt Up," "Goes Off," "Lets Loose," "Goes HAM [hard as a motherfucker]"—was the rhetoric of unruly womanhood. Instead of containing her thoughts, she ignores the standards of behavior for a female celebrity. Similar language was used when she criticized MTV for not nominating "Anaconda" for Video of the Year, which prompted Miley Cyrus to describe her as "not very polite" and "not too kind." (Which, in turn, prompted Minaj, accepting her award for Best Hip-Hop Video, to point at Cyrus, who was hosting the show, and declare, "This bitch had a lot to say about me the other day in the press . . . Miley, what's good?")

But Minaj wasn't *acting out* or behaving outlandishly so much as revealing the crude framework behind the manufacture of celebrity, and her natural frustration when someone else fails to match her work ethic in the critique of her art, or when the system itself shows its underlying racism. She regularly tells interviewers when a question is dumb, or calls them out, as she did in a 2015 *Rolling Stone* exchange, when, after describing an incident when she didn't want to call an ambulance for fear of TMZ coverage, the interviewer suggested she might have had a bad acid trip.

"I didn't have a bad trip," she responded. "I'm a businesswoman, and I have too many partners out there for me to be out here joking about shit like that."[36]

The most powerful rejection of the publicity apparatus, however, came in the form of an October 2015 *New York Times Magazine* cover story.[37] The profile, written by veteran celebrity journalist Vanessa Grigoriadis, starts off like so many others in the genre: there's a history of Minaj's accomplishments, a discussion of her lineage in hip-hop. But there's also a slight tone of disparagement throughout, evidenced by observations like "'Bitch,' in music, used to be insult, a sneer, and it still can be. But female empowerment is a trend, and the word has been reclaimed—by Minaj, in many a track; by Rihanna, in 'Bitch Better Have My Money'; and triumphantly by Madonna, in her recent track 'Bitch, I'm Madonna.' This is good for business and either good for women or not good for women at all." The end of that statement can be read as an acknowledgment of the multiple interpretations of feminism—or a haughty cut at those who've even participated in the conversation.

Minaj's voice is wholly absent from the first half of the profile. Instead, her presence, meaning, and importance are filtered through Grigoriadis's skepticism and, judging from her reductive history of women in hip-hop, a lack of familiarity with the racial and artistic context from which Minaj emerged. As nearly two dozen cover stories make clear, Minaj has a keen sense of what makes for a good profile, what sells magazines, what gets people interested in her. But she also understands when the questions asked of her to arrive at that point serve a different, divisive purpose. Like when Grigoriadis brought up the feud between Minaj's new boyfriend, the rapper Meek Mill, and Drake—along with another disagreement between her mentor, Lil Wayne, and a label executive—asking Minaj, "Is there part of you that thrives on drama, or is it just pain and unpleasantness?"

Minaj's response was cutting. "That's disrespectful," she said. "Why would a grown-ass woman thrive on drama? What do the four men you just named have to do with me thriving off drama? Why would you even say that? That's so peculiar. Four grown-ass men are having issues between themselves, and you're asking me do I thrive off drama?" It's the sort of response that cuts to the inner mechanics of the celebrity profile—the give and take between the profiler, pushing buttons; the interviewee, avoiding them. It was also the sort of thing that usually gets excised from an interview entirely.

But *The New York Times Magazine* and Grigoriadis kept them, and Minaj's subsequent remarks, in. "That's the typical thing that women do," Minaj told Grigoriadis. "What did you putting me down right there do for you? Women blame women for things that have nothing to do with them. . . . To put down a woman for something that men do, as if they're children and I'm responsible, has nothing to do with you asking stupid questions, but you know that's not just a stupid question. That's a premeditated thing you just did." Minaj called Grigoriadis "rude" and "a troublemaker," said, "Do not speak to me like I'm stupid or beneath you in any way," and then cut the interview short: "I don't care to speak with you anymore."

The profile was celebrated in some corners, debated in others: perhaps Minaj's behavior, as Grigoriadis suggested elsewhere in the piece, was symptomatic of the softball profile of the "social-media" era, in which interviews are about "being adored, not interrogated."

But it was also about a celebrity seeing the publicity game for what it is—calling out Grigoriadis's questions not because they were aggressive, but because the assumptions behind them were reductive, sexist, and purposely incendiary. In many ways, Grigoriadis was trying to lasso Nicki back to the physics of dominant celebrity culture, and the gender hierarchies and feuds and melodrama that accompany them. But that's not Minaj—and not how her gravity works. When, in 2015, she appeared in the pages of *GQ*, it was to promote Meek Mill's career.[38] Not to make hers secondary, but to announce her ascendency to the role almost always reserved for men—now *she's* the doyenne of taste and the kingmaker. In this way, Minaj has effectively inverted the Gangsta Boo hierarchy: men revolve around Planet Nicki, not the other way around.

The *New York Times Magazine* profile could've been adjusted to a more traditional format: Minaj's most cutting answers removed; the focus on the accompanying images increased. But the magazine's editors might have also known that the unruliness of the interview—the mixture of confidence and brazenness, the refusal to conform to the guidelines of proper, feminine celebrity behavior—was far more compelling than whatever puff piece they could've carved out of the original transcript.

That's the thing about Minaj: she understands, like few celebrities before her, how to get people to tell her story, pay her attention, appreciate her artistry, propagate her message, acknowledge her mastery—and all of it on her terms. As countless interviews and interactions have demonstrated, she's not the passive participant in someone else's story of who she is. She bursts through the glossy veneer of the celebrity industrial complex, wrests control of the narrative, calls bullshit on the rhetoric and mechanisms that would frame her as unruly, acting out, overly aggressive. Because Minaj is not, in fact, too slutty—or too rude, or too weird, or too manipulative. She simply has something that's long been inaccessible for female celebrities, and black ones in particular: total control.

CHAPTER 5

TOO OLD:
MADONNA

"She looks like some Old Hooker." "Granny hands." "Skeletor arms." "Saggy Ass." "Oldanna is just sickening looking." "Cobweb-filled Vagina." That's the rhetoric that swirls around the most recent incarnation of Madonna, the Queen of Pop and the richest female singer in the world, whose 2015 world tour grossed more than $300 million. And while the reception to Madonna's thirty-year career has always been split between anger and adoration, the antipathy leveled at her as she approaches her sixtieth birthday is of a different tenor. While "Like a Virgin" and her *Sex* book may have been obscene, this version of Madonna was something different, something worse: she was repulsive, inappropriate—and worst of all, *sad*.

The problem with Madonna's body isn't that it's old—it's that she's allowed it to be sexual, powerful, and *visible* in a culture that expects women of a certain age to hide themselves. When other aging female singers opt for a Vegas residency and long ball gowns,

Madonna goes on a world tour. She refuses to cover all the things women over fifty aren't supposed to show in public—arms, boobs, butt. While postmenopausal women are generally represented as asexual crones, she cycles through gorgeous men in their twenties. She kisses Drake in public; she bares her breasts for *Interview*. She behaves, dresses, and flaunts her body like a millennial. She doesn't just "not act her age"; she refuses to conceive that age should limit her career.

The norms that dictate how women should behave as they age may, however, be the one taboo too ingrained in culture for even Madonna to smash. In the past, her iconoclastic power stemmed from a constant looking forward—a devouring of the future in order to explode the past. Today, she's increasingly obsessed with retreading her history—her past image, her past looks, her past body—in a manner that doesn't feel liberating or unruly so much as self-obsessive. Is Madonna battling ageism—or battling for her own particular body to remain forever young?

✦ ✦ ✦

Madonna has been judged so harshly because, to be blunt, she is a woman—and the compulsion to maintain the body, face, and mobility of a much younger woman is rooted in gendered norms about the place of women in modern society. In premodern (read: agrarian) society, actual age was far less important than one's capability. Your physical capacity (and gender) largely dictated your labor, your value, and your place in society, not the number of years you'd been on the earth. The development of modern society and the separation of certain classes of men and women from constant physical labor along with the development of the standardized calendar, and the cult of the individual—made one's precise *age* more important.

The continued development of the middle class, the accessibility of the birth certificate, the demarcation of official life dates (driver's license, drinking, smoking, consent, school) accelerated society toward its current fetishization of age. Before, one's life was broadly divided into one's status first as a child, then as a parent of a child, and finally as too old to have a child—the last of which, given the state of healthcare at the time, often lasted little more than ten years. Today, the average (Western) human's lifespan has not only grown, but become even more segmented, with distinct delineations among children, tweens, teens, college students, delayed adults, "Thirty and Flirty," "Fabulous at Forty," the middle-aged, retired grandparents—with established physical and societal standards for each.

These groupings and the norms that govern them are far more powerful for women, largely because our value has so long resided in our beauty—and in the face in particular, which, in modern society, women are expected to cultivate like a most valuable garden. As Susan Sontag writes in "The Double Standard of Aging," a woman's face is separated from the body, treated like "the canvas upon which she paints a revised, corrected portrait of herself." Her face becomes "an emblem, an icon, a flag. How she arranges her hair, the type of makeup she uses, the quality of her complexion— all these are signs, not of what she is 'really' like, but of how she asks to be treated by others, especially men. They establish her status as 'object.'" Makeup is central to this transformation: a teenager who wears makeup declares her status as a sexual object; the grown woman who doesn't wear makeup signals classiness; the aging woman who wears too much makeup becomes gaudy in her insistence on her continued objecthood.[1]

The crafting of the face is a billion-dollar industry because there's actually only one truly acceptable face to create: that of "the girl." The girl's face is always dewy, unblemished, and un-wrinkled, her eyes bright, her forehead uncreased. In recent years, similar strictures have applied to the woman's body: the most desirable form is that of a fourteen-year-old girl, down to the perky breasts, the lean arms, the slender, athletic legs. "Wom-anly" hips and ass might be theoretically fetishized, but they're desirable only when the rest of the body remains that of the girl.

As girls become women, they discipline their bodies and faces to remain girl-like: there is but one standard of beauty, and much of the labor of self is dedicated to preserving what has long departed. Men have very different expectations: some men might shave or wax to preserve a boyish look, but they are allowed to "exchange one form of attractiveness for another," as Sontag puts it, as they transition into adulthood. A boy can become a man and still have others find him handsome, and furthermore, a man can enter his later years and find that his aging qualities command even greater respect/admiration. Which explains why Cary Grant, George Clooney, and Sean Connery can be considered "the world's sexiest men," with their deeply lined faces, square jaws, and silver hair. Women, by contrast, continue to strive for the ever-more-elusive ideal of the girl—and spend endless hours com-bating the shame of their failure to achieve it.

✦ ✦ ✦

There's a highly circumscribed performance of femininity expected at each stage of a woman's life—a certain way her face and body should look. All of these ideals are some form of striving for youthfulness, but only to the extent that it's "appropriate," and with any part of the body that fails its duty hidden from sight.

Before plastic surgery and Photoshop, the only way to defy those expectations was to lie about your age, as Mae West, Constance Bennett, and Joan Crawford famously did for most of their careers. Lying about one's age was a natural strategy to stay visible and vital and public for longer: if females of "a certain age" were expected to gradually fade from society, lying meant that you could remain a valued woman (and a more bankable star) for longer. You could be considered beautiful; you could be represented in art; you could be sexual and sexually attractive, even if you were no longer able to bear children.

While Hollywood stars today have still been known to lie about their age—both Rebel Wilson and Jessica Chastain were recently "caught" doing so—there's a new, more clever way to lie. You keep the number, but transform the body, either digitally or surgically or through physical discipline, to present as a lower age. So many of the attributes that "give away" one's age—wrinkles, sagging, loss of muscle mass, gray hair—can be fixed this way. When a magazine cover declares that someone looks "amazing" for her age, it's an affirmation that she looks like someone *younger*.

Societal repulsion, like that directed at Madonna's body,

occurs not when a woman turns a certain age, but when some part of the body evades or otherwise rejects attempts to discipline it into a younger version of itself. See: the unflattering paparazzi photo on the beach, the misplaced Botox, the unwrinkling brow, or, in the case of Madonna, the hands that, in the words of the *Daily Mail*, "betray" her.

Lying about one's age, Photoshop, surgery, exercise, and diet all become ways of hiding the *abjection* of aging: the gradual decay of the body, the leakage and excess skin, the terrifying mementos of death. All aging bodies are abject, but women's bodies are especially so—there are more areas, the breasts and neck and butt in particular, to sag, disappoint, and signal their lack of viability. That's why a woman's actual age becomes her "dirty" secret, why the inability to fight the appearance of wrinkles is a humiliating defeat. Why, as Sontag points out, growing old "converts the life of women into an inexorable march toward a condition in which they are not just unattractive, but disgusting."[2] But the aging body only radiates abjection when the woman tries to deny it. A grandmother's soft, deeply wrinkled cheeks aren't abject, nor is her amorphous frame under a loose-fitting muumuu. Judi Dench's regal carriage, that's not abject—nor is Helen Mirren in a tasteful black one-piece. They're aging "gracefully" and "elegantly"—words that connote class, the opposite of trash and abjection. By contrast, Madonna's arms and ass in a leather corset are repulsive, and making out with Drake onstage at Coachella prompts the headline "Drake and Madonna Kiss . . . and It's Super Gross!"[3]

The aging body is grotesque—but so, too, are the attempts to keep that aging process a secret. That fundamental contradiction becomes most visible in the rhetoric around plastic surgery, which underlines the necessity of such procedures in order to remove the signs of aging, but becomes its own source of abjection, especially when done poorly. The overplumped lips, the Botox-frozen forehead, the overstretched eyelids—"bad" plastic surgery is just the ballad of the celebrity who tried too hard to stay employable.

Female celebrities are thus forced to walk "an incredibly narrow and precarious tightrope," as celebrity scholars Su Holmes and Deborah Jermyn explain, in which "the aesthetic and discursive space in which one can age 'well' is severely delimited, as well as contradictory, capricious, and subject to change."[4] Work out, but don't get arms like Madonna's; work hard to keep your body ageless, but make that labor invisible. Put simply: you're damned if you do; you're damned if you don't. Try too hard, and you're disgusting; don't try at all, and you're invisible.

This sort of contradiction is nothing new for Madonna, who's spent her career exposing the double standards applied to women, especially when it comes to sex. It's equally fitting that her celebrity image would be the one through which America first truly grapples with the aging and sexual body: at every point in her career, she's been a "repository," in the words of critic Steven Anderson, "for all our ideas about fame, money, sex, feminism, pop culture, even death."[5] What we've always talked about when we talk about Madonna, in other words, is some ideology in flux. In this case: aging.

The anxiety swirling around Madonna's body—and her ceaseless desire to preserve it—is amplified by her status as both Queen of Pop and the foremost avatar of postmodernism. Pop and postmodernism both revel in surfaces, transformation, and pastiche; while rock stars have authenticity and R&B singers have soul, pop singers have artifice. That's why Stevie Nicks, Bonnie Raitt, Joni Mitchell, and Aretha Franklin have been "allowed" to age, while Madonna has to continue reinventing and revitalizing herself, in part because pop music, and its fetishization of the new, demands it. As a result, there's no "real, authentic" Madonna for her to settle into as she ages; there's only forward motion.

That motion has defined Madonna's career, and has been made possible by Madonna's exhaustive work ethic, her curious mind, and her fearless appetite. From an early age, she surrounded herself with geniuses, seeking out boundaries—of proper femininity, of pop music, of what others thought she was capable of—and then purposefully breaking them. Part of that process was proffering her body as a playground for different ideas of obscenity, sexual play, and the performance of femininity. Her sexually explicit music videos, award show performances, *Truth or Dare*, the *Sex* book, nude photos, and dozens of photo shoots not only asserted her body as a fundamental component of her art, but also helped create the culture of body surveillance that accompanies female celebrity today. In this way, Madonna became one of the primary architects of the apparatus that is now rejecting her.

Up until very recently, Madonna was able to keep pace with its demands. To understand how she arrived at her current, assailed position, media scholar Lucy O'Brien structures Madonna's career progression into three mythological phases: the Maiden, the Mother, and the Crone. Madonna's early career, spanning her first performances in New York clubs to *The Immaculate Collection*, is the "Maiden" phase. She may have been married to Sean Penn for part of that time, but her image was rooted in the sexual freedom and provocations that traditionally accompany maiden-hood, that is, life before devotion to children, husband, and the domestic. That image began to change with the birth of Madon-na's first daughter, Lourdes, in 1996. As O'Brien explains, Ma-donna put away the dominatrix gear as she pursued the role of Eva Perón in *Evita* and became deeply invested in the mysticism of Kabbalah, which, along with introspection and exploration of her own mother's death, manifested on *Ray of Light*, a critical smash—and a departure from her "pop" self. "Approaching 40 years old," O'Brien explains, "she had ditched the arch, glittering blonde of 1992's *Erotica* album to re-emerge with subtle makeup and flowing pre-Raphaelite hair." Thus: the Mother.[6]

Through the release of *Music*, in 2000, Madonna embraced the reputation as a "serious" musician—and her videos, while as visually stunning as ever, focused less on her body and more on aesthetics, genre play, and artistry. Her next album, *American Life*, featured an indictment of the Bush administration; an ac-companying video filled with military imagery caused uproar in the still-sensitized post-9/11 society. Madonna decided not to pub-licly release the video, explaining that "it was filmed before the war started, and I do not believe it is appropriate to air it at this time." Still, sales were disappointing, and she retreated into her role as mother and wife (this time, to director Guy Ritchie, with whom she'd had a son, Rocco, in 2000), wrote children's books, and hung out in the English countryside, hunting, riding, and in-habiting what O'Brien calls a "Lady of the Manor" persona.[7]

This conservative, upper-crust, family-oriented persona might have persisted. But in 2005, on her forty-seventh birthday, Ma-donna was involved in a serious riding accident that left her bedridden for three months and purportedly prompted a renewed consideration of her career and image. *Confessions on a Dance Floor*, released the same year, was far more electronic/dance than pop; its hit single, "Hung Up," like the rest of the album, was "market tested" in dance clubs, and went to number one in forty-one different countries. The video showcased a fit, leotarded Madonna dancing by herself in a dance studio, juxtaposed with footage of dancers in various feats of acrobatism. Its popularity announced to the world: Madonna was cool with the club kids once more.[8]

But *Confessions*'s obsession with coolness also signaled Madonna's progression to the status of the Crone: the stage "most deeply hidden, the most difficult to understand . . . She is unavoidable Time, the One with whom we must make our peace if we are to really grow in the greatest spiritual depths." The Crone is mystical, at times alluring, at others defensive and controlling; to maintain her beauty, the Crone practices some sort of magic— and Madonna's particular magic was exercise, the details of which she publicized so as to ward off rumors of plastic surgery.[9] Every day, she did one hour of "Olympic level" Ashtanga yoga, one hour of strength training, one hour of cardio. She subsisted on a heavily regimented diet, which allowed for only one glass of wine on Sundays. She turned her body into a machine strong enough to fight time: the product of the same workaholic, perfectionist tendencies that had defined her earlier career.

But the machine could only do so much. It was during this period that the first murmurs of disgust began to coalesce around her body—from the press, which called out the "virtual roadmap of veins" on her hands, from her husband, who said that Madonna "looked like a grandmother" when compared with her backup dancers, and from the leak of pre-Photoshopped images from the shoot for the cover of *Celebration*, which prompted the *Daily Mail* headline "As Madonna Poses for Yet Another Raunchy Album Picture, Will She Still Be Doing This at 70?" It's also when she acquired the aforementioned nicknames of Vadge, Oldanna, Granny Madonna, Old Hooker, and Skeletor: terms that suggest just how fully she'd come to occupy the intersection of anxieties about aging female sexuality.[10]

Yet as Madonna continued to age into her fifties, she doubled down on looking, and acting, twenty years younger. She would regularly wear gloves to shut people up about her hands. For her concerts, she started doing even more physically demanding feats—she aimed to always do "something really impossible," as she told *Rolling Stone*, like jumping rope while singing.[11] She adopted two children. She brought on Justin Timberlake and the Neptunes to produce her new album. She divorced Guy Ritchie. She dated a man in his twenties. She opened a line of gyms, named after her *Hard Candy* album, in locations across the world, with the motto "Harder Is Better." She joined social media; she adopted teen slang; she debuted a single on Snapchat. She made flagrant gaffes online—including using the n-word to describe her son—and appropriated images of civil rights heroes to promote her latest album, *Rebel Heart*. She likened ageism to racism and homophobia. She spanked Katy Perry. And Diplo. And appeared in assless pants at the Met Ball, and bared her (heavily Photoshopped) breasts for a photo shoot in *Interview* that also featured facial bondage wear.

And then there was the video for "Bitch I'm Madonna," essentially a collection of "I'm cool" set pieces: Madonna wearing a grill; Madonna making out with a random young guy in the hallway; Madonna dancing with a giant TV showing Nicki Minaj's rapping face. The cameos—from Minaj, Katy Perry, and Kanye West—felt less like endorsements and more like sad courtesies. Even the song itself felt pitiful: an assertion of iconicness instead of a demonstration of it.

Madonna may have outwardly refused the shame of age, but the effort she applied to fighting getting older stunk of it. And that effort felt fatiguing—a little too much like Amy Poehler's "cool mom" character from *Mean Girls*, whose quest to make herself fit in with her teen daughters' friends reveals a deep emptiness within. Labor slowly became the central theme of her image, instead of the means of expressing a larger artistic purpose within. Put differently, her attempts to fight age may have been working— but they were also consuming all that was interesting about her.

And that, far more than the repulsion at an "old" body owning its sexuality, is what repels many from Madonna. As Lindy West explains, "It's not that she's forgotten how to be young, it's that she's forgotten how to be *new*."[12] She's taken to cannibalizing her past, and all the ideas about sex and race and provocation that accompanied it, including the manner in which she regimes and displays her body. What was once transgressive now feels regressive, including her ideas about the primacy of the body as a mode of power. As cultural critic Julia Baird observes, "When Madonna refuses to age, when she turns her body into a scientific experiment, she stops representing rebellion and starts representing obedience. An obedience that requires wealth, time, and an enormous, unending amount of effort."[13] An obedience that's not just regressive—but boring and exclusionary.

When, for example, she responds to criticism of baring her ass on the red carpet of the Met Gala with "This is what a 56-year-old ass looks like, motherfuckers!" she's not actually breaking ground for fifty-six-year-old asses—just *her* fifty-six-year-old ass, disciplined to belie its age. When confronted with this idea in a 2015 interview, Madonna redirected the conversation:

> Well, you know what? It could be the average one day. That's the thing. When I did my *Sex* book, it wasn't the average. When I performed "Like a Virgin" on the MTV Awards and my dress went up and my ass was showing, it was considered a total scandal. It was never the average, and now it's the average. When I did *Truth or Dare* and the cameras followed me around, it was not the average. So if I have to be the person who opens the door for women to believe and understand and embrace the idea that they can be sexual and look good and be as relevant in their fifties or their sixties as they were in their twenties, so be it.[14]

Madonna's logic is not wholly wrong: she has broken boundaries so dramatically, so incandescently, that they've never been reconstructed. But what she's suggesting with age isn't that *all women* in their fifties and sixties should be relevant. Rather, she believes that women *who look like her* can be relevant. It's a highly individualistic approach to a societal affliction, but it shouldn't be surprising: in addition to pop and postmodernism, Madonna also embodies the ideologies of postfeminism, with its attendant privileging of the desires, power, and pleasure of the individual woman over actual equality and rights for women in general.

It makes sense, then, that Madonna never complained about ageism until she experienced it. Even if, all the way back in 1992, she famously questioned, "Are people just supposed to die when they're 40?" she never championed older women artists, or defended them when they went through their own attacks for being "too sexual."[15] And while she conceives of her work today as kicking down the door for female musicians to come, she hasn't sought to collaborate with those, like Jennifer Lopez, or Gwen Stefani, on the cusp of "old age," instead opting to associate with Ariana Grande or Katy Perry, who might call her "Grandma" onstage but for whose youth she seems desperate. A song like "Bitch I'm Madonna" is a perfect encapsulation of this individualism: her power, at least at this point, is welled in others' recognition of that power.

❖ ❖ ❖

In a 2016 interview with *The Daily Beast*, Shirley Manson, lead singer of Garbage, spoke to the vitriol directed at Madonna. "It has a lot to do with society's expectations of women and also highlights the inequality between male and female artists to this day," she explained. "There are very few women willing to fight the idea that beauty is the highest currency. That's the problem: that women are scared to fight against that currency, fight against the idea of, 'Does a woman have any worth past youth and beauty?' I believe they do, and I will fight that fight until I die, but I think a lot of women feel they have to give up."[16]

But Manson's fight is not Madonna's. In fact, they're at odds: not only has Madonna's career traded on the currency of her body, and the vibrant, variable beauty that attended it, but through this, she increased the value of its economy at large, as well as other female celebrities' near-compulsory participation in it. It's not that there weren't constantly surveilled sex symbols before Madonna; it's that today, there are so few ways to become a celebrity without being one.

Granted, the ideology that yokes a woman's worth to her beauty—instead of her accomplishments, or her intelligence, or her integrity—has been ossified through centuries of patriarchy. But just because Madonna participated in its fortification doesn't mean that she can't be part of its disassembly. That would take something flagrant and incendiary, something, like her earlier work, that made people think through the presumptions they'd made about women's bodies, and sex, religion, and race, and any number of intersections in between. It would have to be something more powerful than the thesis-less manicness of the video for "Bitch I'm Madonna," more to the point than a kiss or a bared ass or a bondage image or any of her past repertoire.

It would need, in other words, to be from the future: an image, an attitude, an argument heretofore unseen, profound and robust enough to position not just Madonna's talent, as she moves into her sixties, as viable, but *any woman's* skill, at any age, any race, any size, as the font of her worthiness. It would have to rattle the presumptions of patriarchy, challenge the norms of femininity, occupy the heart of unruliness. It would have to be the sort of gesture, argument, and gut punch that's historically come from an incredibly rare, and all the more valuable, sort of female celebrity. A woman, in other words, like Madonna.

CHAPTER 6

TOO PREGNANT: KIM KARDASHIAN

There's a picture of Kim Kardashian in a color-blocked black-and-white dress from February 21, 2013—about five months into her first pregnancy. Her "bump," as pregnant bellies have come to be called in the mainstream media, is visible, as are her white pumps, red lipstick, black wrist cuff, and perfectly made-up face. It's a look that *E! News* called "absolutely stunning." But there was another photo from that same appearance—taken from the side as Kardashian turns her head back, presumably at the beckoning of one of the paparazzi who, at that point, were tracking her every pregnant move.

This image is cropped closer, ending before the hem of her dress; her legs aren't visible, nor is the overall silhouette of the look—just black-and-white fabric hugging the growing curves that helped establish Kardashian's famous, and incredibly lucrative, celebrity brand. That image was paired with a picture of a killer whale, whose black-and-white color scheme echoed the color-blocking of

Kardashian's dress, and the caption "Who Wore It Best?" The photo circulated swiftly across the Internet, but it didn't stop there: *Star* magazine put it on its cover, along with the headlines "65-lb Weight Gain!" "Binges on Pasta, Cake and Ice Cream!" and "Kim's Pregnant Nightmare!"

The photo wasn't the first image of the pregnant Kardashian, but it became the indelible one, encapsulating all that was "wrong" with her pregnancy: her weight gain (not cute) and her strategy for clothing it (not appropriate). From that point forward, the already Kardashian-frenzied paparazzi went into overdrive. The ultimate prize wasn't just a picture of Kim, but one of Kim eating, Kim looking fat, Kim looking miserable, Kim looking uncomfortable, Kim looking, in other words, not like Kim: a betrayal of the image of celebrity maternity that, over the last ten years, has become the norm.

Yet in transgressing the boundaries of the "cute celebrity pregnancy," Kardashian effectively called attention to the constrictive, regressive norms of how women, celebrity or not, are now expected to "perform" pregnancy in public. When she writes on her blog that "for me pregnancy is the worst experience of my life," she's not just "keeping it real," as she proclaims at the beginning of the paragraph; she's working to mainstream the truly unruly idea that pregnancy—and, by extension, even motherhood—is not the pinnacle, or even defining purpose, of every woman's life.[1]

Kardashian *wanted* the cute little basketball bump. She wanted a "normal" pregnancy. But when her body refused to give her one, she became the unlikely means by which the cracks in the ideology of "good" maternity became visible.

♦ ♦ ♦

If you were born after 1991, you've never known a time when pregnancy wasn't performed in public: 1991 was the watershed year in which Demi Moore appeared naked, seven months pregnant with her second daughter, Scout, on the cover of *Vanity Fair*. The cover became instantly iconic, mocked and replicated and spoofed in the manner of meme culture decades before online memes existed. In some quarters, it was considered obscene: many supermarkets displayed it with the sort of paper wrap reserved for *Playboy*; others, like Safeway and Giant, refused to sell it entirely. "It's tacky," one twenty-three-year-old woman told the *Los Angeles Times*. She couldn't imagine "why anyone would want to display her swollen stomach like that—and why people would want to look at it."[2]

The titillation was purposeful: *Vanity Fair* editor Tina Brown, who would go on to serve as editor in chief of *The New Yorker*, made the decision to put the image on the cover, knowing how it would drive sales. The issue ended up selling more than a million copies—250,000 more than normal circulation. "The Demi Moore cover is a radical statement of New Hollywood values," Brown declared. "It breaks the mold of every stereotype of celebrity glamour. For too long, women have felt that pregnancy is something they have to conceal and disguise. It takes the courage of a woman as modern and innovative as Demi Moore to cast aside the conventions of traditional beauty and declare that there is nothing more glorious than the sight of a woman carrying a child."[3]

Moore, who was promoting her new movie, *The Butcher's*

Wife, obviously agreed. "I have no regrets," she said. "Attitudes are changing. I feel beautiful when I'm pregnant . . . I was just on vacation in Mexico, in my bikini with my big belly hanging out and my low-cut top."[4] Even before the shoot, Moore's attitude had been catching on: swimsuit designer John Koerner reported that his maternity bikini, released three years before, was now his number one seller. "Women's whole attitude toward pregnancy is changing fast," he explained. "It's what we call a paradigm shift— none of the old rules apply."[5]

It's taken twenty-five years to see just how right Koerner's statement would be. Today, pregnancy and motherhood are one of the primary ways in which a female celebrity maintains attention. The baby bump has become, as Molly Jong-Fast declared in *The New York Times*, the new Birkin bag: it's "cute" and "adorable" and "feminine," something to dress up, to rub in photos, to have photographed as your partner leans down and kisses it. Celebrities model these behaviors on the red carpet, in selfies, and in paparazzi photos, and as a result, women across America have adopted them en masse.[6]

It's difficult to emphasize just how radical this attitude would seem to women experiencing pregnancy even thirty years ago. To be pregnant in public was in poor taste—unsophisticated, trashy, unbecoming, obscene. That sense of the pregnant body as abject goes back millennia, as the pregnant body is a woman's body at its most fecund, but also in its most grotesque figuration: the body swells, expands, and oozes, the boundary between inside and outside permeable. New motherhood is often depicted as something darling: sweetly sleeping babies on all crisp white sheets and gurgling babies in the bath. But childbirth is a messy, primal process: consider the afterbirth, the leakage of breast milk, the caked gunk scraped from the newborn's body, the blood and screaming, and the fact that for so long, so many otherwise healthy women died in the process of giving birth.

The pregnant body was also profoundly contradictory: as scholar Jane Ussher explains, pregnancy is, at its most essential, the most vivid proof of women's sexuality—which is precisely why representations of mothers took on the opposite characteristics. The most significant mother of Christianity, for example, is the Virgin Mary: asexual, idealized, immaculate. Mary is rarely represented while actually pregnant, only afterwards, when the child is safely born, both mother and child clean and content. This beatific mother is contained, pure—the antidote to the abjectly pregnant mother.[7]

Historically, the easiest way to contain that abjection was to keep the pregnancy out of sight. Women of a certain class often receded entirely from public view until after the baby was born and the visible signs of pregnancy had diminished. When the birth occurred, it happened in the domestic space and was managed by midwives. Like all things hidden for fear of abjection (women's sexuality, menstrual periods, feces), it became societally unacceptable to even speak openly of pregnancy: according to historian Carol Brooks Gardner, in nineteenth-century America "talk of pregnancy was forbidden even between mother and daughter, if either hoped to claim breeding and gentility." Colloquialisms were developed to refer tactfully to the obscenity of a woman's condition: she was "with child" or "in a family way," never "pregnant."[8]

Up until the 1950s, the word "pregnancy" was not even allowed on-screen. In 1953, the Motion Picture Association of America refused to approve the script for *The Moon Is Blue* because

115

it included the word "pregnant"; the MPAA's list of "13 Don'ts and 31 Be Carefuls," which determined what could and could not make its way on-screen from the 1920s to the 1960s, included a ban on any depiction of childbirth, even "in silhouette." In silent film–era Hollywood, most stars avoided motherhood in one way or another so as to sustain their marketability; those who did become pregnant removed themselves from public view, even as the studios offered access to all other parts of the stars' homes and family life. As late as the 1950s, stars like Elizabeth Taylor and Debbie Reynolds were seldom photographed while pregnant—just during the blissful, bonding aftermath.

The attempt to erase pregnant bodies from the public sphere took place alongside women's increased freedom to control when they became pregnant. In 1965, the Supreme Court upheld the right to privacy when it came to birth control; in 1973, it protected the right to access abortion services in *Roe v. Wade*; a year later, the court denied a Cleveland school the right to ban a pregnant teacher from continuing to work when the administration "worried that her pregnant body would alternately disgust, concern, fascinate, and embarrass her students." As legal scholar Renée Ann Cramer points out, these decisions "set the stage for openness to the bump, and pregnancy, that we have today."[9] The idea that women shouldn't work while pregnant, after all, is predicated on the fact that women would have some other source of income while absent from the workforce. In many ways, the decision of the court underlined that this was no longer, or could no longer be expected to be, the case.

Even after the Supreme Court ruling, pregnant women were largely exempted from having to perform the same sort of femininity and body surveillance that accompanied their non-pregnant existences—in part because they were not yet considered a lucrative market. Put differently, industries weren't yet selling the idea of the "cute" pregnancy—or the products to maintain it.

There was no maternity yoga; no maternity Spanx. Maternity clothes were largely hideous and/or homemade, making "pregnancy style" an oxymoron: even Princess Diana, whose early 1980s pregnancies were arguably the most visible in history, still dressed in what might best be described as polka-dotted baby doll dresses. But the popularization of spandex and Lycra in the 1980s and '90s changed all that: a fabric that could stretch was one that could be crafted into something (relatively) cute for the growing pregnant body.

Before Moore, the paparazzi generally respected the boundaries of the pregnant female celebrity (even Madonna, who'd so willingly embraced public documentation of her body throughout her career, remained largely unphotographed during her first pregnancy). All that changed within the decade—when the combination of digital photography and *Us Weekly* not only created a market for pregnancy photos, but helped turn "bump watch," and the cultivation of the "cute pregnancy," into one of the female celebrity's primary modes of publicity. Suddenly, the taboo of the pregnant body turned into a spectacle that could be stylized, exploited, scrutinized, and interpreted as emblematic of a woman's overarching success or failure.

Janice Min dates the shift to around 2003, when she had just taken over the reins of *Us Weekly* from Bonnie Fuller, who'd turned the long-flailing magazine around. "Not only were an unprecedented number of top actresses suddenly pregnant ([Courteney]

Cox, [Brooke] Shields, [Gwyneth] Paltrow, [Debra] Messing, [Denise] Richards, to name a few)," Min explains, "but they were—for the first time in history—well, *flaunting* it." Min lists all the products that had become associated with pregnancy—the Bugaboo stroller, designer cribs, the Bikram yoga post-pregnancy workout routine—before declaring "the once frumpy bump industry was suddenly big business."[10] And with the availability of the means to create a "cute" pregnancy came the compulsion for all women, celebrity or not, to do so.

Min points to the ways other companies were making money off the "bump industry," but it was *huge* business for her own magazine—in part because it fit its ethos of "Just Like Us." *Us Weekly* had become a genuine competitor to *People* through its reliance on paparazzi photos—of stars doing mundane things like grocery shopping and pumping gas—that cost very little. In the process, it effectively created a market for photos of celebrities in all aspects of their lives outside of the home. Even more valuable, though, were shots of female celebrities performing these tasks *while pregnant.* The pregnant celebrity body is the perfect consolidation of "Just Like Us" and "Nothing Like Us," the mundane and the spectacular: it doesn't matter what the celebrity and her body are doing, because her body's growing. And like the aging process or weight gain, that process, and how a celebrity chooses to embrace or conceal it, is one of the most perversely engrossing images to observe.

All of this—*Us Weekly,* Demi Moore, fashionable baby clothes, surveillance of celebrities that translates into their own hyper-vigilant surveillance of self—funnels toward Kim Kardashian, the most important and influential celebrity of the twenty-first century. Paris Hilton understood that power (initially, through her sex tape; afterwards, through *The Simple Life*) at the beginning of the 2000s, but Kardashian—who established herself as part of Hilton's circle by volunteering to organize her closet for her—was observing her closely. Then she beat Hilton at her own game: with the help of her "momager," Kris, and her extensive, blended family, Kardashian transformed the banalities of "everyday" life, and the surveillance thereof, into a narrative far more gripping than most reality television.

Part of that watchability stems from the *Pride and Prejudice*-style plotting, in which a controlling mother attempts, in some ways more overt than others, to pair off her gaggle of daughters or otherwise ensure their success. There's also an addictive quality to how rich people live so beautifully, with so little legitimate friction: their days are spent getting ready, talking on the phone, half paying attention to one another, deciding on clothes, eating salads out of plastic containers, and taking care of family drama, the vast majority of which gets solved by the end of each episode. But *Keeping Up with the Kardashians* is also a glimpse into what it's like to live under surveillance. Kris and the sisters appear almost exclusively in full hair and makeup; their conversations, phone calls, and questions gradually become the sort that don't even need editing to feel like the setup and resolution of a classic sitcom.

As the show and the Kardashian family grew in popularity, so, too, did their surveillance outside the bounds of the television show—whether at the hands of the paparazzi, who tracked their mundane activity (which functioned as a sort of "supplementary" narrative to the show itself), or, increasingly, by themselves, via social media. Boyfriends, children, fiancés, marriages, shopping trips, weight gains and losses, brands consumed, diet tricks

119

endorsed, clothing lines launched—all of it was catalogued. And when you spend so much time acting for an audience, your entire life becomes a performance. The Kardashians became the apotheosis of what it means to be a celebrity today: instead of deflecting surveillance of the body and the personal, they embraced and exploited it.

✦ ✦ ✦

In 2013, *Keeping Up with the Kardashians* was entering its eighth season. The family had never been more popular: Kourtney had given birth to two children, the gestations of whom were incorporated into the show; Khloé was in her fourth year of marriage to basketball player Lamar Odom; Rob had launched a successful sock line; Kendall and Kylie Jenner had their own clothing line for Pacific Sunwear; Kendall was embarking on the beginning of her career as a model. And Kim—who had married and separated from basketball player Kris Humphries and started dating Kanye West, all within the span of two years—had never been more surveilled or valuable.

When Kanye announced Kim's pregnancy on December 30, 2012, it felt sudden—largely because Kim's divorce from Humphries had yet to be finalized. Yet in addition to whatever personal feelings Kim might have had at the prospect of becoming a mother, she also understood the pregnancy in terms of marketability. When your body and personal life are the source of not just your fame, but your income, that's not callous so much as the new corporeal due diligence.

But Kardashian's pregnancy refused to make itself marketable—at least not in the way she envisioned it. If, before, women had to hide from public view, today, the bump is imagined as "a new freedom"—not an "embarrassing or abject physical state," as Imogen Tyler explains, "but an opportunity to have a different fashionable and sexy body shape."[11] But the actual liberating power of what Tyler calls "pregnant beauty" is dubious, in part because there's really only one acceptable way for it to manifest. Min describes that model, demonstrated en masse by celebrities, as "one day you'd look as though you swallowed a basketball. The next day it would be gone."[12] There's no swelling, no barfing, no hemorrhoids, nothing abject about this pregnancy experience: you feel great, and you talk about feeling great, and everyone knows you feel great. Kim herself admits to buying into this understanding: as she says, on camera, late in her third trimester, "I always envisioned [that] only my belly would get big."

Yet Kardashian's pregnancy failed to fulfill that vision of pregnant beauty on both a physical and an emotional level. In the first episode of season eight of *Keeping Up with the Kardashians*, when Kris accompanies Kim to a sonogram appointment, she exclaims, "I'm more excited than she is," a point driven home when Kim doesn't even want to *see* a picture of the sonogram. Kim avers that "once I start showing I'll get excited." Once the bump appears, or, in other words, once she's able to style it and make it available for public consumption—that's when she'll start enjoying pregnancy.

Kardashian's anxiety over the "in-between" time—from when a woman knows she's pregnant to when her body strongly signifies as such—is widely held. Few things in American society, after all, are considered as terrifying as getting fat, and with good reason: for most people, fatness means a harder time getting a job, garnering respect, or navigating the physical world; for celebrities, it means all of those things, plus incessant public ridicule. And as the cult of the baby bump developed, so, too, did the idealized post-baby body—one that, just months after giving birth, looks exactly as it did before pregnancy.

Which is part of the reason that Kim, who was thirty-two when she became pregnant, was anxious: "Our parents had us in their twenties and their bodies bounced back," she tells one of her sisters. "My mom had Kendall and Kylie in her forties and she still can't lose the weight." She was not only nervous that her body would, in its early pregnant state, signify as fat, but that whatever weight she gained would haunt her in the future. It makes sense that women's inclination toward disordered eating spikes so sharply during and after pregnancy: that's how strongly weight gain of any kind, even related to pregnancy, is stigmatized.[13]

But as Kardashian's pregnancy became unequivocal, the rest of her body refused to conform to the cute ideal she'd internalized. Her feet, like the rest of her body, began to swell—early indicators of what would later be diagnosed as preeclampsia. She yearned for the body that hid beneath her pregnant one: when brother-in-law Scott Disick walked in on her in pregnancy Spanx, he exclaimed, "Your voluptuous pregnant body shouldn't be in bike shorts around people," to which Kardashian responded, "It's less attractive than my skinny toned body . . . Can we just reminisce for a second?" Over the course of that one scene, Disick tells her: "You're gonna get back there"; "Your boobs are getting a little big for you to do that"; "How big *is* that baby"; "You look like the Nutty Professor." It's the sort of contradictory messaging a pregnant woman receives: you're hot, but on the border of obscene; you're perfect, but you're huge; don't feel bad about yourself, but your thin body is better.

Early in her pregnancy, Kardashian also began experiencing sharp pains—so severe that her doctor initially believed it was appendicitis. Her body was making it impossible for her to revel in pregnancy—a thought that thoroughly distressed Kris. "It was the most wonderful time of my life," she tearfully tells Kim, "and I want you to have the same experience"; "the fact that she can't enjoy being pregnant breaks my heart," she says in her one-on-one "confessional" interview. In episode three, as Kim writhes in pain, it's again juxtaposed with Kris's commentary: "I want her to relish in this pregnancy; I feel like it's the most amazing experience, and she's just not having that."

Like so many other women, Kris has internalized a single understanding of how pregnancy should be, look, and feel, which is part of why Kim's persistent dislike is so powerfully unruly. "I hate this so much," she moans, in a clip shown multiple times throughout the episode. "I'll never do this again." Later in the episode, she admits that "the anxiety that I have is so ridiculous"— in part out of fear for the baby, and fear of the pain, but also because of an overarching fear that the experience of pregnancy was not what she had been led to believe. "This is definitely not the picture she painted for herself," Khloé explains.

There was another part of the pregnancy picture that Kim hadn't anticipated: ridicule at the hands of the press. The comparison to a killer whale soon joined pictures of her feet, swelling painfully out of her high heels. At the beginning of episode five, Rob greets Kim with "What's up, fat feet?" clearly alluding to her coverage in the press. It's one of dozens of moments, interspersed throughout the season, that highlight the ways in which coverage of their celebrity *outside* of the show disrupts the illusion of the hermetically sealed Kardashian world. It's also one of the unspoken allures of the show: viewers are essentially watching celebrities react, respond, and oftentimes alter their behavior based on how they're covered in the press.

It's a window, in other words, into the highly reactive, yet usually invisible, production of celebrity. What's fascinating about Kardashian's pregnancy, then, is how she refused to allow her changing body to be policed by it—especially when it came to fashion. Maternity wear has become a $2.4 billion business, with thousands of options for every pregnant body, yet there's still an unspoken demarcation of "appropriate" maternity fashion.[14] It can be feminine and flirty, but shouldn't be slutty or sexual; you can show your bare belly at the pool, but not in any other circumstance. And when you begin to show, you should wear clothes designed specifically for maternity wear.

Kardashian ignored each of those rules. She'd always worn clingy dresses, so she kept wearing them. She'd always shown skin, so she kept showing it—outfits with see-through mesh strips, short dresses that showed off her legs, low-plunging necklines that revealed her substantial cleavage, high-waisted pencil skirts that broadened, rather than hid, her girth. She kept wearing heels, and full makeup, and "body-con" dresses, performing femininity and sexuality the same way she had her entire celebrity career. Those decisions were met with disgust: "Would someone please tell Kim she's pregnant!" the cover of the *New York Post* screamed, along with a picture of Kardashian in a high-waisted, flared dress.[15] *Us*

Weekly called her style "controversial"; *People* explained that the "tough and edgy" style of one outfit was "usually reserved for non-pregnancy moments."[16] "We give you a woman at the tail end of her pregnancy who refuses to ditch the Rich Bitch bodycon dresses, hose, and sky-high heels," VH1 declared. "What is she trying to prove? And to whom is she trying to prove it? We'd love her more if she rolled out in yoga pants, toe socks, and pigtails. She's eighteen months pregnant."[17]

What was Kardashian trying to prove? That there are myriad ways to clothe a pregnant body. That the way you feel sexy in your own body doesn't have to change when you get pregnant. That even at "eighteen months pregnant," she'd actually be shamed, in some capacity, for "rolling out" in yoga pants and pigtails. If she tried to keep the baby healthy, she was too fat. If she put on a dress that made her feel attractive, she was too sexy.

Take, for example, the skintight floral dress she wore to the Met Ball—which purportedly prompted Anna Wintour to cut her out of *Vogue*'s coverage of the event. Wintour's move made sense, in a messed-up way: *Vogue* is a fashion magazine, but it's also a policer of class, and Kardashian's pregnancy troubled the magazine's trenchant distinctions between high and low. Not just in her body's inability to hew to the ideal of the basketball bump, but also in Kardashian's conception of how to dress it. Just look at the language used, across the press, to describe her style: "Kim isn't shy about showing off her cleavage," "never one to keep things simple," "overly-opulent," and "disastrous"; "illusion netting, feathers, leather leggings—any one of these items would be over the top," *OK!* magazine declared, "but of course Kim feels no fashion fear."[18]

She spilled out of her dresses; she purportedly broke zippers:

125

her flesh was too ample, too much. She tried *too hard*. Coded language, all of it, for a disrespect of the boundaries that separate class from trash—a distinction that has afflicted Kardashian from the beginning of her career, first because of her association with a sex tape (tawdry) and then for her affiliation with reality television (lowbrow). That's why Wintour famously would only allow her on the cover of *Vogue* with Kanye. It doesn't matter that Kardashian grew up rich, or that she currently pulls in more than $100 million a year: she'll always be perceived as new money, and her fame will always be centered on her body and, as such, easily dismissed and delegitimized.

It was easy to code Kardashian's pregnancy in the same manner as her career—especially when it played out in near-synchronization with that of the Duchess of Cambridge, popularly known as Kate Middleton. As novelist and cultural critic Hilary Mantel explains, "Kate seems to have been selected for her role of princess because she was irreproachable: as painfully thin as anyone could wish, without quirks, without oddities, without the risk of the emergence of character."[19] She was, plainly put, incredibly, wonderfully, perfectly palatable. Fashion scholar Maureen Brewster points out that Middleton's style "relied heavily upon knee-length dresses cut in A-line with Empire waistlines" that "also displayed her as very clearly slim despite her growing bump, further establishing her pregnancy as a fit and fashionable performance."[20]

No matter that her slimness was due to her hyperemesis gravidarum, also known as acute morning sickness, for which she was hospitalized early in her pregnancy—Middleton's classy, contained bump incited approving commentary from *People*'s "Style

Watch" Facebook page: "Very classy & pretty"; "Simple and elegant!"; "Pregnancy suits her very well! She looks beautiful." The opposite, in other words, of Kardashian. If Middleton's body was impossible to interpret as fat, Kim's always threatened to be read as such; if Middleton's style was feminine and classy, Kardashian's was whorish and trashy. The contrast was made explicit in photo spreads throughout the pair's pregnancies: "often, the slimmer star was portrayed as the most able to police her desires to eat and grow large," Cramer explains, as "the press valorizes the women most able to exhibit self-control while pregnant."[21]

It didn't matter that Kardashian was carefully monitoring her diet: the tabloids claimed not only that she "couldn't stop eating," but that she was doing it *on purpose* so as to then strike a deal with a weight-loss company after the birth of her daughter. One magazine said she'd gained "65 pounds" through "binges"; another put her at more than two hundred pounds through "waffle cones and fries." *Keeping Up with the Kardashians* features a handful of scenes in which Kim "indulges": in one, she eats mozzarella sticks; in another, she eats fries with her brother. But the vast majority of the time she's filmed eating the same boxed green salads and chef-prepared meals as the rest of her family. "All I eat is carrots, and celery and ranch, and like, protein bars, gluten-free stuff, sugar-free stuff," she told Maria Menounos in an interview on *Extra*. "I am waiting for the moments when someone's like, go to McDonald's and Taco Bell [but] that's not happening for me."

If she were to go to those places, the paparazzi would be waiting for her. After the "whale photo" went viral, unflattering images—any shot of Kim eating, looking fat, or in situations that could be construed as overindulging or disgusted at her own body—were at a premium. When she arrives at a frozen yogurt shop to meet with her stepbrother Brandon and his wife, Leah, in a midseason episode, the paparazzi swarms the windows, forcing Kim to hide behind Brandon as she attempts to get a taste of yogurt. "I'll get like a sample and they'll be like, 'she's five hundred pounds, she's trying like a million yogurts!'" she explained. When, later in the scene, Kim calls the actions of the paparazzi "bullying," she is referring to their physical presence in her life, but it applies equally to their purpose: making it as difficult as possible for her to appear in public in a way that won't be *construed* as a pregnant body out of control.

Most of the paparazzi policing was published in "unsanctioned" gossip outlets—the tabloids and gossip blogs that don't rely on cooperation from the celebrities they cover. But there was an opportunity for a counternarrative, and *Us Weekly* took it, publishing photos of Kardashian on vacation in Greece with her family, with the caption "You Call This Fat?" next to her clearly pregnant stomach. Kim looks relaxed and unpretentious, her hair in a loose braid; her makeup replaced by a bronzed glow. Instead of "stuffing" herself into inappropriate maternity wear, she's wearing a bikini that frees her body. It was easy to frame the photos as an embrace, on Kim's part, of her pregnant form: "She's loving the seventh month," a source told *Us*. "And she thinks pregnancy is so cute."[22]

It wasn't until months after the issue hit newsstands and the footage of the family in Greece aired on E! that the discordance of that claim became clear. In her seventh month, Kardashian found pregnancy distinctly miserable. "I feel like I've turned into a different person," she said, just before putting on the bikini captured on the cover of *Us*. "I just feel like a huge roly-poly . . . It's like an alien inside of you." In the next episode, the rest of the family discusses Kim's inability to enjoy herself at the breakfast table: "She's so not happy," Kris says. "I mean pregnancy isn't for everyone," Khloé responds. "It doesn't seem like she's enjoying hers."

Kim's family at once bemoans her inability to enjoy the pregnancy *and* reinforces the very anxieties that've made it difficult: the obscenity of her body, and her fear of it. When Kim comes down to breakfast, for example, she's the most disheveled she's been all season—no makeup, her hair tied up in a truly messy, not performatively messy, bun. "I just don't care right now," she says. Kris starts commenting on the size of her breasts: "I don't know how she goes day to day with those boobs," she says, to no one in particular. "Shit, you've got some big fucking boobs. I've never seen anything like them; it's two watermelons." "There's not even milk in them yet," Kim replies. "Which is the scary part."

The three episodes in Greece offer a portrait of a pregnant body so thoroughly surveilled that it begins to discipline itself: while her siblings are goofing around and jumping off the yacht, Kim stays out of sight, typing on her phone and lying in bed. She wears long dresses in the hot sun; she acts as family photographer. She tries not to scratch her stretch marks, for fear that the scratching will make them permanent. She holds up her feet at dinner and pushes into the flesh to demonstrate just how swollen they've become. She says, "I've been really scrutinized my whole pregnancy, about what I wear, my weight, which is ridiculous, and it's so frustrating that the paparazzi are here," and "I just want to fulfill a craving without a picture of me stuffing my face." In other words, Kardashian wants to defy the expectations of pregnant beauty, but she's been so steeped in its rhetoric that she can't help but feel shame, and anger, at her inability to do so.

Kim's family urges her to engage further in the public spectacle of her pregnancy—even when, as Kim admits, "to say that all the scrutiny doesn't get to me, I would be lying." When they return stateside, Kim tells her sisters she doesn't even want a baby shower, because of all the "negative attention" she's already garnered. But Khloé and Kourtney keep planning one behind her back, and Kris insists Kim watch footage from when she was pregnant with Rob to see just how meaningful a shower was to her. Kim's family ultimately wins the argument, in part because a baby shower—and the inclusion of one's friends and family in the anticipation of a child—is now compulsory: to *refuse* a baby shower is much more unruly than to have a lavish one filmed by a host of cameras.

And while Kim eventually comes around to the idea of the shower—and the shower itself comes off as loving, inclusive, and emotional—it only solidifies her anxiety over how the rest of her pregnancy will be documented. "I just want to make sure I'm doing it all right," she says while discussing her birth plan. "I just wanna be perfect." That perfection includes being in "full glam" for the birth—her face made up, her hair done, her nails done in a shade that will look good, as Kim explains, when her daughter Instagrams the photo in twenty years.

She also starts planning what she'll do the instant she reinhabits her old body: "The first thing I want to do is some nude shoot," she tells her sisters. "I just want to walk down the street fully naked," but only "when I'm skinny again." Everyone thinks Kim's being ridiculous, but her behavior is simply the next level of the ideology that's been policing her all along: if her body can't "be perfect," she wants everything else—the look on her face when she gives birth, the composition of the Instagram her daughter will someday post, the body that she'll return to—to be as close to ideal as possible.

With an official diagnosis of preeclampsia, Kardashian ended up giving birth nearly six weeks early. After the delivery, she suffered from a condition called placenta accreta, which meant the doctor had to reach his hand inside her and physically scrape the placenta from the uterus. Her delivery, like the rest of her pregnancy, was not "perfect." But that's only if you believe there's such a thing as perfect: ultimately, both Kardashian and her baby, North Kardashian West, survived the labor in good health. North was treated overnight for jaundice, but everything was *just fine*.

The takeaway from Kardashian's very public pregnancy, however, was that "just fine" just isn't enough when it comes to the contemporary pregnant body. Even if the concept of "perfect" is wobbly and contradictory, it remains the pregnant woman's goal. A perfect pregnancy style, a perfect weight gain, a perfect attitude toward pregnancy. When a woman is unable to achieve that perfection, or refuses its pursuit altogether, she's shamed: if not by her immediate circle of friends and family, whose shaming is often cloaked in the language of "advice," then by the representations of "ideal pregnancy" that, over the course of the last thirty years, have become regular fixtures of our media diet.

Kardashian's unruly pregnancy punctured that ideology. By speaking about her discomfort, by airing its minutiae on television, even by continuing to wear clothing that compelled the press to shame her, again and again, it sent a message: if one of the most beautiful and valuable women in the world can't have a perfect pregnancy, then maybe we can rethink what "perfect," and its connotations of docility, femininity, containment, and good taste, might mean. Granted, Kardashian was rebelling not by choice, but out of necessity: her body forced her to. If she had the choice, she would've loved to reinforce the norm—a posture borne out by her second pregnancy, in which she was more circumspect in how she dressed and dealt with far less press scrutiny, in large part because her body wasn't dealing with preeclampsia and, as such, didn't provide the same spectacle.

But an accidental activist is an activist nonetheless. In August 2015, Kardashian Instagrammed a selfie of her naked pregnant body, ostensibly as a means of silencing speculation that she'd hired a surrogate to carry her second child. "First they said I'm too skinny so I have to be faking it," she wrote. "Now they say I'm too big so I have to be faking it . . . Some days I'm photographed before I eat & look smaller, some days I've just eaten & I look bigger. It's all part of the process. I think you all know me well enough to know I would document the process if I got a surrogate. Everyone's body is different; every pregnancy is very different! I've learned to love my body at every stage! I'm going to get even bigger & that's beautiful too!" The more representations of the ways in which "everybody's body is different" and "every pregnancy is different," the less pregnancies like Kardashian's—or Jessica Simpson's, or that of any woman who doesn't have a Kate Middleton–style pregnancy—will feel unruly, or deserving of censorship, or ashamed.

The pregnant woman has more "freedom" in the public sphere than ever before—and yet women are experiencing the largest war against their reproductive freedoms in more than fifty years. It's contradictory, of course, but that's the guiding structure of any ideology: no matter how emancipatory it might seem for the preg-nant body to be visible, that visibility means subjugation to re-gimes of respectability and regulation under patriarchy. As Cramer points out, it was no coincidence that as audiences watched Kar-dashian's preparations for labor, Wendy Davis was filibustering against anti-choice laws in the Texas state legislature. When the body becomes public property, as the pregnant body has indubita-bly become, it not only liberates the populace at large to comment and cast judgment on it, but the (male-dominated) legislature to institute legal controls over it.[23]

Kardashian may have felt bullied, saddened, and otherwise hurt by the reception of her pregnancy; she was certainly disap-pointed in her own failure to live up to the ideal. But when things didn't go as planned, she planned differently: watching the sea-son, you get the sense of a woman figuring out how to navigate, on her own terms, a world that's told her not only that she's "too pregnant," but that she's also been too fat, too superficial, too fake, too curvy, too sexual. The anxiety over Kardashian's body is, of course, actually over her power: that a woman whose pri-mary skill is the way she lives life could so effectively market that life. That even if she's married to the best rapper in the world, she's still the most influential person in the room.

It's easy to mistake Kardashian for a falsely empowered wo-man, so thoroughly enmeshed in the ideology of self-surveillance and the performance of docility and submission it implies. Yet she has spent the last decade of her life, and her first pregnancy in par-ticular, being labeled as too much of something. She may not own the label of feminist, averring that she's not a "free the nipple" type girl—but that doesn't mean that her work to make the labor of femininity visible or reduce the stigma around the "non-beautiful" pregnancy isn't, at heart, a feminist project.

It will take years for the cultural influence of Kardashian's particular brand of unruliness to become clear. But just as Demi Moore's appearance on the cover of *Vanity Fair* has become a pivot in attitudes toward pregnancy in public, Kim's pregnant body, likened to a whale, excised from *Vogue*, pursued specifically at its worst angles, might mark another era: in which the Supreme Court declared unconstitutional those same anti-choice laws that Wendy Davis filibustered against, in which the most famous woman on the planet declares that every body, every pregnancy is different— and in which the business of being a woman in public, even with an audience of millions, still remains that woman's business alone.

CHAPTER 7

TOO SHRILL:
HILLARY CLINTON

Not to be sexist, but it is what it is," Dennis, a sixty-three-year-old teacher from Stillwater, Oklahoma, told *Esquire*. "I do not trust that she, a woman, would be able to do what a man could with the same capabilities." Dennis was one of dozens of men, of various ages and vocations, surveyed by *Esquire* as to their opinion of Hillary Clinton for their February 2016 issue. And while these men differed in their opinion of Clinton, their comments share a common ideological core. Sometimes, as in the quote above, they disavow sexism before explicitly engaging it. In other comments, their dislike is more subtle: "I don't think she has mastered the art of becoming a warm, likable person to the American public," says Jeremy, a fifty-eight-year-old CEO from Albuquerque, New Mexico. "To me, she comes across as cold and stiff." Or this quote, from Russell, a fifty-seven-year-old farmer from Sumter, South Carolina: "There's just something about her personality—it's a little abrasive and a little arrogant," he explained. "You know, after so many years of Hillary, it's like, 'Oh, go away.'"[1]

Over the course of her public life, Clinton's been called unlikable and uncharismatic, bitchy and ball-busting—all expressions, in some way, that imply unruliness. For many, she is a nexus of disgust, a vector through which all anxieties about the changing world flow. With good reason: Hillary Rodham Clinton has spent her adult life being first. She was the first female partner at her law firm, the first professional woman to take the role of First Lady. And until a stunning upset by Donald Trump, she was slated to become the first female president.

While the other unruly women in this book have learned to tread a narrow lane of acceptability, Clinton's lane has been attenuated to a tightrope. She should be assertive but not bossy, feminine but not prissy, experienced but not condescending, fashionable but not superficial, forceful but not shrill. Put simply: she should be masculine, but not too masculine; feminine, but not too feminine. She should be everything, which means she should be nothing.

That Clinton has weathered more than two decades of these critiques is a testament to her resilience and fortitude. And her endurance has paid off: for the 2016 election, Clinton was able to find a foothold, and something like sympathy, among the voting public—in large part due to twenty-five years of accumulated sexism. The combination of an openly misogynist opponent and Clinton's undeniable qualifications prompted both journalists and voters to question the standards by which politicians are judged—standards that are unquestionably masculine. What had previously felt like a smattering of objections and disappointments about her treatment by opponents, the press, and voters coalesced into something substantive and persuasive, with bite of its own. It felt like a reckoning—even if, as we now know, it was false hope, like celebratory fireworks that distracted from the fact that the house was getting torched.

"Shrillness" is just a word to describe what happens when a woman, with her higher-toned voice, attempts to speak loudly. A pejorative, in other words, developed specifically to shame half of the population when they attempt to command attention in the same manner as men. And that's the core of Clinton's unruliness: she has demanded the same stature, power, and attention as a man. Ultimately, Clinton's campaign didn't just illuminate the corrosive rhetoric that accrues around women in power. It amplified and invigorated it. What seemed like the beginning of a gradual transformation of what power looks, sounds, and behaves like now feels like startling rejection: not just of Clinton, but of the very notion of unruly women in general.

✦ ✦ ✦

Clinton has been considered unruly in some capacity for more than forty years. Her 1969 commencement speech at Wellesley was so incendiary that, according to dozens of retellings, it prompted a seven-minute standing ovation. The speech, which was later featured in *Life* magazine, was about the future—her hopes for it, her curiosity about it—but it was also a critique of the university life that had sheltered her and her fellow students.[2] After graduation, she went to Alaska and worked in a cannery until she was fired for complaining about working conditions. She chose to attend Yale Law School when a Harvard law professor told her that they already "had enough women." She became a part of Walter Mondale's Subcommittee on Migratory Labor, researching the working conditions and lived experiences of migrant workers. She headed up George McGovern's campaign in the state of Texas. She refused Bill Clinton's repeated proposals of marriage. All before the age of twenty-five.

When she did agree to marry Clinton—after she'd moved to Arkansas, where he was preparing for a political campaign—she kept her maiden name. Her achievements continued to accumulate. In 1974, she became the second ever female faculty member of the University of Arkansas School of Law. In 1979, she became the first female partner at the nationally regarded Rose Law Firm. She added "Clinton" to her last name only after research showed that her maiden name, and all that it signified about her, was in part responsible for Bill Clinton losing the race for a second term as governor. And while she insisted that "Rodham" remain integral to her name, her stationery, and her identity, in 1982, Bill Clinton regained the governor's office. There were objections to Hillary's performance as First Lady of Arkansas—that she continued to work, for example, albeit at reduced hours—but they were slight compared with the scrutiny she would fall under, and the opprobrium she would incite, as First Lady of the United States.

This vitriol started early. In focus groups during the early stages of the campaign, Clinton's pollsters found that voters thought of Hillary as "being in the race 'for herself' and as 'going for the power.'" During the campaign, she was roundly criticized for her remarks on why she continued to work while her husband was governor of Arkansas. "I suppose I could have stayed home and baked cookies and had teas," she said. "But what I decided to do was fulfill my profession, which I entered before my husband was in public life."[3]

The quote was only made inflammatory, however, by excising the context of her answer: "I'm a big believer in women making choices that are right for them," Clinton had continued. "The work that I have done as a professional, as a public advocate, has been aimed at trying to assure that women can make the choices they should make—whether it's a full-time career, full time motherhood, or some combination . . ."[4]

But no matter: the first half of Clinton's answer was the ammunition that skeptics needed, and it helped force the Clintons to back away from a strategy of framing their campaign as a "buy one, get one free" sort of bargain. "She became a caricature of some people's worst fears about professional women," Susan Estrich, who'd served as Michael Dukakis's campaign manager, explained. "Americans are only willing to move so quickly in accepting the role of a career woman as [presidential] spouse."[5]

Hillary might have been more popular, favorability rating–wise, than Barbara Bush, but the plan for her to be a partner to Bill—instead of a helpmate—placed extra scrutiny on her performance of femininity. Shortly after Clinton won the presidency, Hillary gave a "symbolic" speech at the Children's Defense Fund, intended as "a first step in reconciling what will almost certainly be her active role in the new Administration with the public's longstanding uneasiness about first ladies who depart too much from the role provided them by history and tradition."[6]

That unease had been inflamed earlier in the week, when Bill told reporters that Hillary was participating in meetings with congressional leaders and advisers. "We just sort of sit down here around the table and talk," he said. "She's part of it. . . . She knew more than we did about some things. I think they would agree with that."[7] When the pair moved into the White House, Hillary's office was located not in the East Wing, where other First Ladies had limited their focus to social and domestic duties, but with Bill in the West Wing, where she would serve alongside other domestic advisers—and, according to a White House briefing, supervise the massive project of national health care reform.

That announcement came just three days after Clinton's inaugural fashions had been widely panned—a reaction that reportedly incited a behind-doors plea to a leading fashion mogul to help "make over" the First Lady. At that point, Clinton was best known for her no-fuss shoulder-length cut and simple lawyer-ready suits: "A woman," *The New York Times* wrote, "who bought dresses from sale racks and didn't give a fig for fashion."[8] A designer tasked with creating her campaign style told the *Los Angeles Times* that "there are more pressing things for her to do than dress up like *Vogue*."[9]

But it was *Vogue* that came to her "rescue," helping to blunt the impact of a First Lady who refused to resign herself to domestic duties. In February 1993, *Vogue* editor in chief Anna Wintour wrote to Clinton offering her services. While Clinton's acceptance thereof was never confirmed, she began appearing in (slightly) more fashionable outfits—like Donna Karan's "cold shoulder" dress, which had been worn by everyone from Liza Minnelli to Candice Bergen. Later that year, Clinton appeared in the pages of *Vogue*, this time wearing another Karan dress that was intended to be worn off-the-shoulders—but that Clinton insisted on pulling up like a turtleneck.

The spread, shot by Annie Leibovitz, incited a wide-reaching debate: Was it too sexy, too glossy, or just a purposeful ploy to soften the sharp edges of her image as the first First Lady since Eleanor Roosevelt to conceive of herself as a political force?

"Her admirers say that she has adroitly helped the country adjust to the notion of a First Lady sharing power with her husband by periodically doling out softer, more traditional images like hostess, mother and wife," Maureen Dowd explained in a lengthy piece meditating on the photos. "But some complain that her cascading images—changing hairstyles so many times, testifying on the Hill about health care one minute and chatting happily about Christmas baking the next, now adding Rodham to her name, now posing for fashion layouts—are dizzying and unsettling. 'It doesn't feel genuine,' said Sheila Tate, who worked as an aide to Nancy Reagan and George Bush."[10]

Of course the photos were calculated: perfectly timed to counter unrest at Clinton's work on "the Hill," as Dowd put it, agitating for health care reform. It was a role for which Clinton was particularly suited—back in Arkansas, she'd helped successfully revamp the educational system—but that was doomed to fail for reasons that had less to do with Hillary and more to do with the GOP's desire to retake congress in the 1994 elections. Similar to Obamacare today, it was dubbed "Hillarycare"; its eventual defeat, a ceremonious rebuke of her "professional" role.

So Clinton got a different sort of makeover: she receded from national view, traveling the world with daughter Chelsea and speaking about issues like women's rights and child welfare. Change in other countries was fine, so long as she didn't try to change America. She wrote a book about the role of community in child-rearing, and a children's book about Socks the cat. But the damage to Clinton's image was already done, and the rhetoric around her began to coalesce into a hard crust of unlikability—best exemplified by Henry Louis Gates's 1996 profile of Clinton, aptly titled "Hating Hillary." "Like horse-racing, Hillary-hating has become one of those national pastimes which unite the elite and the lumpen," Gates wrote. Journalist and DC insider Sally Quinn added that "there's just something about her that pisses people off." Some linked it to her refusal to schmooze: she simply didn't have the right people over for dinner enough. Hillary herself said, "I apparently remind some people of their mother-in-law or their boss or something."[11]

A mother-in-law, a critical boss, an ex-wife, a nagging wife, a nagging mother—all coded language for an undesirable woman who asks for something, who threatens dominance in some way. Gloria Steinem saw the threat as an overarching one, embodied not in Hillary so much as in the Clintons' relationship: "She and the President are presenting at a very high, visible level, a new paradigm of a male-female relationship. And that is very much resented."[12] Campaign consultant Mandy Grunwald believed women were threatened by the path Hillary had chosen: "They're looking at a woman who is close to their age and made totally different choices," she explained. Hillary "forces them to ask questions about themselves and the choices they've made that they don't necessarily want to ask."[13]

That *New Yorker* profile came out in 1996—right around when allegations of wide-scale mendacity on the part of both Clintons, as related to the Whitewater scandal, took center stage. And so the contours of Hillary's unlikable image began to settle: She lacked social graces. She was a harpy. She was, even back then, shrill. She didn't know her place. And she *lied*. That misdeed, like her handling of Benghazi, or her private e-mail server today, provided the shelter under which all the other sexist critique could fester: it didn't matter if one's rhetoric was sexist, after all, if the explicit complaint had nothing to do with her gender. Her popularity measured at just 43 percent—the lowest of any First Lady in modern history.

It wasn't just conservative men, after all, who thought Hillary was too shrill: there was a whole cadre of women, on both sides of the political spectrum, who found Clinton too strident, too homely, too abrasive—everything the postfeminist woman rejected. Even as Nora Ephron reminded the graduates at Wellesley that "every attack on Hillary Clinton for not knowing her place is an attack on you," there was a reticence to identify with her struggles. Postfeminism was in full and powerful effect: Why think about the overarching significance of sexist attacks on the First Lady, if you've been told the goals of feminism have already been achieved? Clinton's image, like so many signifiers of second-wave feminism, felt like a real drag.

But then Monica Lewinsky, and the subsequent scandal bomb that erupted around her, happened—and attitudes toward Clinton were thrown into flux. Hillary had dealt with questions of Bill's infidelity before: at the beginning of the presidential campaign, she had forcefully shut down questions about Gennifer Flowers by emphasizing that what happened in their personal life was between her and her husband. Yet when Clinton was impeached for lying under oath about his affair with Lewinsky, his and Hillary's personal life was rendered definitive public property.

Clinton had long refused the sentiment of "standing by your

man." In a *60 Minutes* interview during the 1992 buildup to the election, intended to confront initial rumors of infidelity, she declared, "I'm not sitting here, some little woman standing by my man like Tammy Wynette. I'm sitting here because I love him and I respect him." For her detractors, the quote became ammunition: proof that she looked down on housewives, traditional values, Tammy Wynette, or anyone who liked the song "Stand by Your Man." The backlash became so extreme that Clinton was forced to apologize to Wynette. Four years later, however, her steadfastness throughout the Lewinsky scandal endeared her to millions, including many on the right who had largely come to despise her. The more Clinton performed like a woman "standing by her man," the easier it was for America to like her.

In November 1998, Clinton appeared on the cover of *Vogue*—the first First Lady to do so, poised and exquisite in Oscar de la Renta. Anna Wintour declared it "a celebration of her, after the year she has had. A vindication of her beauty and her success as a woman."[14] The profile, like the photos that accompanied it, were, as *The New York Observer* explained, "an affirmation of the extraordinary and unexpected tidal wave of popularity that has engulfed the First Lady, initially in sympathy for her role during the Lewinsky scandal, and then beyond it."[15]

Clinton's popularity was not a result of her own actions, then, but her *reactions*. There were wide reports of Hillary's personal humiliation, but her proud public face endeared her to the public in a way that no number of achievements could have. She—and her advisers—saw an opportunity provided by that sympathy, and jumped at it, and in 2000, she handily defeated her Republican opponent to become the junior senator from New York.

Yet Clinton's approval ratings while campaigning declined—a manifestation of a phenomenon, demonstrated by data journalist Nate Silver, in which Clinton's approval drops every time she becomes explicitly political, just as it had with "Hillarycare." People could deal with Hillary Clinton as a resilient wife, or a stately woman on the cover of *Vogue*. It was when she grasped for actual power that the nation recoiled.

Clinton's time in the Senate has come to be viewed as her great compromise: she embraced the rhetoric of "family planning," moving away from her defense of abortion; she sought out Republican mentors; she fought flag-burners; she introduced legislation that would criminalize the selling of video games with adult content to minors. She became a religious attendee of the weekly prayer breakfast. She made, well, *friends*. "Clinton's curtseying was partly simply professionalism," political analyst Rebecca Traister explains. Yet "her reputation of being strident and chilly had been born mostly of sexist assumptions about powerful femininity, not reality. Expectations were upended easily when her archest of enemies actually worked with the woman most people agree is funny, warm, diligent, and immensely likable in person."[16] She was learning to govern—a process that slowly moved her to a more centrist set of politics.

Throughout Clinton's first term in Congress, her popularity ratings remained steady—in part because, as Silver points out, her favorability ratings have become a function "of the extent to which the other political party, and perhaps also the news media, feels as though they have license to criticize her."[17] Put differently, voters might have internalized sexism to direct at Clinton, but that sexism is not wholly activated until opponents and the media give it shape.

Which is precisely what happened when she declared her candidacy for president in 2007, and the old themes of the criticism from her time as First Lady were amplified exponentially. Not just by the Republicans and the media—but by her fellow Democrats as well.

There were the familiar nicknames of "Shillary" and "Shill Hill," but the Internet also metastasized the old sentiments into overarching misogyny: Facebook groups called "Stop Running for President and Make Me a Sandwich" and "Life's a Bitch So Don't Vote for One"; a YouTube video with a KFC bucket that read "Hillary Meal Deal: 2 Fat Thighs, 2 Small Breasts, and a Bunch of Left Wings." Her Wikipedia page was regularly graffitied with "slut" and "cuntbag"; two men showed up wearing "Iron my shirts!" T-shirts at a rally in New Hampshire. Shirts were emblazoned with "Fuck Hillary: God Knows She Needs It," "Even Bill Doesn't Want Me," "Stop Mad Cow," and "I Wish Hillary Had Married O.J." When a picture of a fatigued Hillary was posted on *The Drudge Report*, Rush Limbaugh asked listeners, "Will this country want to actually watch a woman get older before their eyes on a daily basis?"[18]

The sexism of such remarks is clear, but it also deserves some unpacking. Take "bitch": as communication scholar Karrin Vasby Anderson points out, the word connotes a "domestic animal that has gone wrong"—a woman who has betrayed her innate duty to the home, the private, the family.[19] Andi Zeisler, cofounder of *Bitch* magazine, explained "bitch" as a word "we use culturally to describe any woman who is strong, angry, uncompromising and, often, uninterested in pleasing men . . . We use it for the woman who has a better job than a man and doesn't apologize for it. We use it for a woman who doesn't back down from confrontation."[20]

Calling Clinton a bitch, then, is a way to shame and silence any woman who dares step out of line.

That image—as a highly capable and unapologetically powerful woman, as a *bitch*—was ascribed to her most powerfully in the media: by Christopher Hitchens, who called her "bitchy" on MSNBC's *The Tim Russert Show*; by Glenn Beck, who called her "a stereotypical bitch"; by Fox News anchor Neil Cavuto, who said she needed to distance herself from her "tough, kind of bitchy image." When a man at a John McCain rally asked "How can we beat the bitch?" the chief correspondent for *Politico* told CNN, "What Republican voter hasn't thought that? What voter in general hasn't thought that?"

There may have been plenty of reasons to object to Clinton's candidacy, but the one that shadowed them all, especially for these men in the media, was her gender. Clinton wasn't just a bitch, but a castrating one: there was the pantsuit-clad Hillary nutcracker, Tucker Carlson declaring that "when she comes on television, I involuntarily cross my legs," and Chris Matthews dubbing her male supporters "castratos in the eunuch chorus." The implication that Clinton would emasculate men was an anxiety-producing one, but it was also so bald-faced as to feel absurd: if we're past the age of sexism, after all, then men shouldn't feel threatened by powerful women. Comments about her castrating power underlined that neither theory was actually true.

It wasn't until Barack Obama emerged as a viable competitor for the Democratic nomination, however, that one of the most damaging strains of critique emerged. She wasn't just a nagging ex-wife or the unlikable bitch. She was something even worse, at least in contemporary politics: Hillary Clinton had no charisma.

The word "charisma" comes from the Greek *khárisma*: "favor freely given" or "gift of grace"—more specifically, from the gods or God. Someone who is touched, in other words, by good favor; a person whom everyone, even and especially God, just *likes*. Its contemporary usage, particularly when applied to politicians or movie stars, is a form of what theorist Max Weber described as "personality charisma": the means through which an individual is "set apart from ordinary men and treated as endowed with supernatural, superhuman, or at least specifically exceptional powers or qualities."[21]

It's on the basis of these qualities, Weber writes, that "the individual concerned is treated as a leader." Put differently, there's something about the person that makes us okay with him possessing power over us. In its biblical version, charisma manifests most vividly in the sermon; in politics, it's the speech. The ability to orate in a manner that makes people *feel* something— joy, sadness, patriotism, *hope*. It was a skill that Hillary Clinton's primary opponent, Barack Obama, had in spades.

Bill Clinton also had it in abundance; so did John F. Kennedy. George W. Bush had some form of it. Ronald Reagan, the former movie star, definitely had it. Charisma knows no party affiliation; it doesn't correlate to intelligence, or skill at governance. It makes people feel enthralled, devoted; it takes them out of their bodies. A good speech, like a good sermon, can feel almost sexual in its capacity to both charm and enrapture. But if charisma comes from the divine, it is divinity given almost uniquely to men—at least in political form.

Charisma has become the defining trait of the television-era campaign: the ability to make massive swaths of people believe that you deserve to lead them is more important than actual experience or leadership qualities. In 2008, as Clinton began stumping across the nation, it became increasingly clear that Hillary simply did not have it. In *Newsweek*, Jonathan Alter admitted that Clinton was "substantive and strong" and "a better debater so far than Obama."[22] She excelled in one-on-one conversations, and in offering cogent, straightforward descriptions of her policy positions. But she was still a woman: as Alter explained, "she lacks a critical asset. Male candidates can establish a magnetic and often sexual connection to women in the audience." Her speeches were measured and informative, but watching Obama speak felt like getting saved at church.

Acting on the advice of chief campaign strategist Mark Penn, Clinton had been riding the "masculine" ticket from the beginning of the campaign, hiding or camouflaging any behaviors (crying, being emotional, wearing frilly or hyper-feminine clothing) that could be perceived as weak or frivolous. In an early memo, Penn had declared that voters were not ready for a "first mama" but might be "open to the first father being a woman."[23] That was the conventional wisdom for how to "sneak" a woman into the presidency: make people forget that she was one altogether.

The strategy backfired. For the first half of the campaign, she effaced all feminine qualities, which made her seem unfeminine, and embraced "masculine" behaviors—yelling, being assertive, attempting charisma—and as a result, she was criticized, called shrill and worse. When a bit of softness and vulnerability did appear—in the infamous single tear that welled up in her eye as she talked about the toll of the campaign in New Hampshire—it was attacked as manipulative. And why wouldn't it be? She'd spent the last year attempting to convince voters she was a competent, genderless robot.

Something curious happened on the way to Clinton's defeat, however: women, even women firmly in support of Barack Obama, were noticing, articulating, and publicly discussing not just the sexism leveled at Clinton, but the suffocating double standards for a woman in the public eye. "I'm not a Clinton partisan," Rachel Maddow explained. "Yet in doing media appearances talking about politics I have become somebody who praises Hillary Clinton, if only because I feel like I'm up against this scrum against her . . . As a person who's not inclined toward Hillary Clinton's politics, I feel like somebody needs to defend her because it's such an onslaught of attacks on her."[24]

Clinton's treatment suggested a much larger cultural ill, one that had less to do with the specifics of her personality and more to do with the enduring structures of patriarchy—structures that had bearing on more than just the woman standing on the stage asking you to vote for her. It was one thing to dislike Clinton. It was quite another to ignore how her treatment was symptomatic of deep-seated, if often well-camouflaged, misogyny.

In mid-April 2008—three months after Obama became president—two feature-length pieces appeared online within four days of each other. The first, written by Amanda Fortini for *New York* magazine, was titled "The Feminist Reawakening: Hillary Clinton and the Fourth Wave."[25] The second, written by Traister published in *Salon* and titled "Hey, Obama Boys: Back Off Already!," discussed the ways in which young women were increasingly fatigued with the way men had taken to denigrating Hillary.[26] In the article, *Feministing* founder Jessica Valenti described her experiences talking with female students as she toured college campuses during the election: "'My friends or boyfriend or father are progressive guys,'" they'd tell her, "'but when they talk about Hillary, I feel like they're being sexist. But I can't put my finger on what it is.' Because their friends were not specifically sexist, or saying something that was tangibly misogynistic, they were having a hard time talking about the sexism of it."

Paired with an accumulating dissatisfaction with the realities of postfeminism, these young women were fueling a renewed embrace of feminism, which, in many circles, even in the late 2000s, still had the unglamorous, unbecoming connotations of "the f-word." "Clinton declared her candidacy, and the sexism in America, long lying dormant, like some feral, tranquilized animal, yawned and revealed itself," Fortini wrote. "Even those of us who didn't usually concern ourselves with gender-centric matters began to realize that when it comes to women, we are not post-anything."[27] Over the next eight years, the truth of that claim would become alarmingly clear: in renewed attempts to legislate women's reproductive health, in the explosion of online harassment of women, in the rhetoric that would continue to hover around Clinton's campaign for president, and in her defeat in 2016 by an outspoken misogynist who vows to roll back women's reproductive rights.

✦ ✦ ✦

After Obama's election in 2008, he appointed Clinton as secretary of state—a move described in some corners as a way to keep his enemies close; in others, as a savvy bit of strategy on Clinton's part to bolster her foreign policy experience. Her favorable ratings began to climb almost immediately, eventually reaching a rate of approval even higher than in the period immediately after the

Lewinsky scandal. Her rainbow of pantsuits became a meme; so did a photo of her checking her BlackBerry. It became cool, somehow, after all this time, to like Hillary—maybe, probably, almost certainly because she was doing what she does best: Working. Compromising. Not campaigning.

At the same time, feminism was percolating: not a wave so much as a mass, a visibility, a reclamation—and a wide-scale acknowledgment that feminism that was not intersectional was, well, bullshit. Which isn't to say that the divides that have long afflicted attempts at feminist coalition building had disappeared. Yet feminism in its myriad forms flourished, with figureheads old (Ruth Bader Ginsburg, Gloria Steinem, Elizabeth Warren, Clinton herself) and new (Beyoncé, Lena Dunham, Amy Schumer, Zendaya). That embrace, however, was born of necessity: legislation at the local and state levels threatened to take women's rights over their bodies back more than fifty years. Feminism felt not just important, or fashionable, but *essential*.

And this time, Clinton was ready to lean in—not just to the fact of her gender, but to the politics that accompanied it. She made the speech announcing her 2016 presidential candidacy in an open-air courtyard, referencing the literal lack of ceiling. She attacked Republicans who "shame and blame women, rather than respect our right to make our own reproductive health decisions."

Over the course of her campaign, she made women's issues— including affordable preschool and day care—fundamental planks of her platform. The attacks from both the left and the right returned with the predictability of a toxic tide, but this time, they were met with immediate, vocal response. In distinct contrast to both the 2008 campaign and the coverage of her early years in the White House, the mainstream press, bolstered by Twitter and the feminist blogosphere, suggested that this sort of sexist coverage was unacceptable.

When, in September 2015, Trump described Hillary as "very shrill" in a speech, *The New York Times* published a lengthy exploration of the ways in which the word has been wielded to describe women's voices, quoting a public-speaking expert who explained that "the tendency to yell on the campaign stump is not gender specific, but the public is much less accustomed to hearing a woman's voice in such settings."[28] When Bernie Sanders said that "all the shouting in the world" would never be a solution to the gun control debate, Clinton's response had feminist teeth: "Sometimes when a woman speaks out, some people think it's shouting"—a catchphrase she then used in e-mails to drum up support.

The *Pittsburgh Post-Gazette* reported on a luncheon, hosted by former CNN White House correspondent Jessica Yellin, in which she played recordings of all of the presidential candidates' voices and asked which one had been described as shrill. "That's coded language," Yellin told the meeting of female lawyers. "Applied to female candidates and other women in the public eye. The problem is, it becomes part of the narrative and gets repeated over and over."[29] CNN commentator Erica Jong explained that "we don't know how a female president should sound. We've never had one before . . . And men's voices are so much more familiar."[30] A blogger at *Linguistic Pulse* put it in even starker terms: "Women's voices are, on average, higher pitched than men's due to both anatomy and socialization."[31] When people describe Clinton's voice as "screeching" or "shrill," they're not actually talking about her voice, but about what the voice of a leader should sound like—a voice that remains, to most ears, incredibly masculine.

When interviewing opera diva Renée Fleming, the *Chicago Tribune* asked whether the criticism of Hillary's voice was sexist: "My daughter was a gender studies major," Fleming said. "So she'd say, 'yes, it's sexist.'" And while she admitted that Clinton's voice can sound, to her trained ear, "a little harsh," she also emphasized that "there's a sensitivity there with women."[32] And when journalist Bob Woodward told MSNBC that the dislike of Clinton "has to do with style and delivery" because there's "something unrelaxed about the way she is communicating," that, too, was met with a verdict of implicit sexism. "I was taken back to a moment in my career many years ago when a top CNN executive explained that for on-air delivery to resonate as authoritative and credible it should come in a low tone," CNN's Frida Ghitis explained. "In other words, only a man's voice sounds like it tells important truths."[33]

Meanwhile, the appellation "Bernie Bros" soon became shorthand for a section of the left blind to their sexist, patriarchal rhetoric. A Bernie Bro is ostensibly progressive—he hates the big banks, he's an environmentalist, he wants to reform the educational system—but he sees nothing wrong with calling Clinton a liar, a bitch, or worse. The work of Bernie Bros was most visible online— on Reddit, in the Facebook comments on Clinton's page and those of others who supported her, and on Twitter, where voicing any critique of Bernie, or support of Hillary, could incite immediate invective.

The menace was so real that many Clinton supporters retreated to hidden Facebook groups. But there was also a wide-scale acknowledgment of the problem: aides in the Sanders campaign reached out to both the Clinton campaign and users online, asking members of digital communities to police their own. In an interview with *Politico*, President Obama admitted that his staff and supporters had perhaps been "too huffy" when legitimate questions were raised about Clinton's treatment, admitting "there were times where I think the media probably was a little unfair to her."[34] Headlines like "Bernie Bros Made Me Finally Recognize Misogyny in America" and "The Bros Who Love Sanders Have Become a Sexist Mob" proliferated.

This election cycle, Clinton's sexist treatment wasn't just acknowledged—it became a centerpiece of her campaign, and an explicit means of leveraging support and identification. A *Washington Post* poll of Democratic women showed that those who'd been discriminated against because of gender, no matter their age, personal ideology, or income, were nearly 20 percentage points more likely to vote for her.[35] More *likely* to vote for her—not assured. Because as the election results underlined, the majority of white women—the very women some might expect to identify most strongly with Clinton—voted for Trump.

Back in the early stages of the campaign, however, the cumulative quotient of her treatment was resonating—so strongly that some believed Bernie Bros were a phantom creation, the work of Clinton staffers posing online. That idea was amplified by Bernie-supporting press. "The goal is to inherently delegitimize all critics of Hillary Clinton by accusing them of, or at least associating them with, sexism," Glenn Greenwald wrote, "thus distracting attention away from Clinton's policy views, funding, and political history and directing it toward the online behavior of anonymous, random, isolated people on the internet *claiming to be*

Sanders supporters. It's an effective weapon when wielded by Clinton operatives."[36] Clinton had been gaslighted about the sexism levied at her for decades. Now she was accused not only of exploiting it, but of creating it herself.

Many voters, especially on the left, didn't need to be told that Clinton had been treated with overt sexism: Trump alone had made that abundantly clear by suggesting that she couldn't "satisfy" America because she couldn't satisfy her husband, or that she played "the woman card" to ascend to her current place of power. But overt sexism, like overt racism and bigotry of all baldfaced forms, is easy to decry—even if you're not in the same political party as Clinton. What was harder to understand was how Clinton's lack of charisma, her unlikability, her general *badness* at campaigning, continued to serve such a powerful function in voter perception, often transmuted into vaguely sexist language.

As *Vox*'s Ezra Klein put it, "There is the Hillary Clinton I watch on the nightly news and that I read described in the press. She is careful, calculated, cautious. Her speeches can sound like executive summaries from a committee report, the product of too many authors, too many voids, and too much fear of offense." This is the Hillary whose jokes thud when she delivers them in debates; whom analysts chide for not smiling enough; who's earned the nickname "Hillary-bot." But there's another understanding of Clinton, gleaned from conversations with people who have worked with her for years. "Their Hillary Clinton is spoken of in superlatives: brilliant, funny, thoughtful, effective," Klein writes. "She inspires rare loyalty in ex-staff, and an unusual protectiveness even among former foes."[37]

Klein called the disconnect between campaign Hillary and

in-person Hillary "the gap"—and spent the entirety of his piece exploring exactly what it is, ultimately, that makes Hillary such an unlikable political candidate. Clinton, like most politicians, has inconsistencies, blind spots, and a history dotted with poor policy decisions, not to mention Benghazi, and the e-mails, and other not-insignificant questions about her trustworthiness. But none of those things could quite explain the hatred, or the plummeting poll numbers whenever she was on the campaign trail, contrasted with the skyrocketing ones when she was in office.

The answer was almost unsettling in its simplicity. Klein found that Clinton's flaw was *listening*: "Modern presidential campaigns are built to reward people who are really, really good at talking," he wrote. "So imagine what a campaign feels like if you're not entirely natural in front of big crowds. Imagine that you are constantly compared to your husband, one of the greatest campaign orators of all time; that you've been burned again and again for saying the wrong thing in public; that you've been told, for decades, that you come across as calculated and inauthentic on the stump. What would you do?" She started listening. Not just in theory, but in calculated, planned action—and to her supporters and adversaries alike. The capacity to listen and contemplate has rendered her a formidable legislator and statesman—yet, crucially, has done little to change her aptitude at campaigning. As Klein underlines, "presidential campaigns are built to showcase the stereotypically male trait of standing in front of a room speaking confidently."[38] When Clinton attempted to speak confidently in front of a room of people, she was called shrill and judged a failure. No matter of practice or training could change that.

A viral Facebook post, written by a normal guy, Michael

Arnovitz, from Portland, Oregon, arrived at a similar understanding. Arnovitz took an exhaustive look at Clinton's fluctuating popularity and its correlation to her time on the campaign trail, which echoed years of research on the reception of female candidates: "What's going on is what we all know, but mostly don't want to admit," he wrote. "Presidential campaigns favor men, and the men who campaign in them are rewarded for those traits perceived as being 'manly'—physical size, charisma, forceful personality, assertiveness, boldness and volume." When a woman fails, in essence, to be a man, she also fails as a candidate—if she tries to emulate masculine behaviors, she's too severe; if she leans in to feminine ones, she's simply unsuited for office.[39]

"There is simply no question that Hillary has for years been on the business end of an unrelenting double standard," Arnovitz argued. "And her battle with societal sexism isn't going to stop because of her success any more than Obama's battle with racism stopped once he was elected."[40]

The extent of introspection post-2008—by journalists and voters alike—was prompted by this nagging feeling: not that the system was rigged against Clinton, but that it was rigged against women. Clinton's supposed shrillness, her unlikability, her lack of charisma—so much of it was, and remains, the result of a paradigm constructed to favor and evaluate *men*. To call Clinton "too" anything is to authenticate and fortify power, broadly speaking, as the proper province of men.

But in the wake of the election, that seems to be the overwhelming opinion. The hatred that ultimately accumulated around Clinton can be attributed to many factors—to increased dissatisfaction with political insiders, or rage at the reality of globalism—but the underlying trigger is, at heart, her gender. It's not that Clinton's a soft woman, or even a shrill woman, so much as a sneaky woman. That's what is at the heart of the obsession with her private e-mail server, and the investigation of the Clinton Foundation; the suspicion that she, along with her confidante and personal aide Huma Abedin, have conspired to hide a grand, dark—yet ultimately undiscoverable—truth from the American people. For many, that's the real, if unconscious, fear: that women will take the reins of power, the keys to the system, the position of the presidency.

At the heart of all of this perceived duplicitousness, after all, is Clinton's unrepentant ambition. It's Clinton's defining character trait: her understanding of her worth is so strong that she's refused, at every point in her life and career, to let men define her. When her husband stood onstage at the Democratic National Convention, for example, and recounted when he "met a girl" in 1971, it was ultimately a story of a woman so driven and sure of her value that the former president, a man of similar ambition and intellect, had to find a way to fit into her life, not the other way around.

For Hillary supporters, this approach felt like a clarification of purpose: yes, many said, this is the type of woman, the type of boldness, the expansiveness of vision we desire. But that approach seems to have backfired, as the constant reminders of Clinton's intellect, ambition, experience, and self-worth served to stoke the fires burning her effigy. This country, after all, largely values such attributes only when they apply to men.

In the end, matriarchy isn't the fear. Rather, it's the idea that women will define their own value, and their own futures, on their own terms instead of by terms men have laid out—put differently, that each gender, and each individual, will have the power to determine their own destiny. To slightly modify the old bumper sticker, it's the radical notion that both men and women are people.

Clinton's candidacy has cast stark light on the deeply sexist expectations of female politicians, but it's also given those expectations oxygen. And while Clinton has demonstrated remarkable resilience, that doesn't mean that watching what she's had to endure will encourage other women to run for president. Think of the conversations women all over had with their daughters as they watched Trump interrupt Clinton over and over in the debates, or observed her calm, forced smile as he misrepresented her policies—interactions that suggested that no matter how skilled, contained, and intelligent a woman was, a man still had license to speak over her, to hover menacingly behind her, to criticize the moderators of the debate as unbalanced when they attempted to prevent him from interrupting her. Think of Clinton graciously conceding to a man so much less qualified than her. At this point, a young woman who's watched the election and *still* wants to enter politics risks being labeled a masochist.

Yet more women in politics—and vying for the presidency—is precisely what's necessary for the paradigm to actually shift. In a study conducted over the course of several decades in India, certain villages were assigned, at random, to be run by women. All the candidates for office were women; women were the only choice. At first, citizens still voiced a preference for male leadership—yet as with Clinton's time in office, their rating of women's competency, once they were in power, increased. Still, it was only after these villages were forced to have not just one female leader, but *two*, that their citizens demonstrated an increased willingness to vote for women in "open" elections.[41]

It will take more than just one election to alter the integral qualities of the "good president"—qualities that, once altered, have the potential to affect the way that all women, even those far from the political playing field, are evaluated in positions of power. But that doesn't mean that Clinton's loss is a step back. She punched the glass ceiling so hard that the task of shattering it has become far less formidable. There will certainly be backlash; it will again expose the ugliest, most enduringly misogynist aspects of our society. But such are the wages of change—the wreckage before the rebuilding. In her final e-mail to supporters, sent the day after the election, Clinton expressed deep pride and gratitude for the "diverse, creative, unruly, energized campaign" that had accumulated around her. And across America, the women who will complete the work Clinton started read those words and recognized themselves.

CHAPTER 8

TOO QUEER: CAITLYN JENNER

Caitlyn Jenner had the most glamorous of coming-out parties. On June 1, 2015, she appeared on the cover of *Vanity Fair* in a bustier, in a photo shot by Annie Leibovitz, with a simple headline: "Call Me Caitlyn." It was the first time that Caitlyn, formerly Bruce Jenner, had appeared in public, and anticipation was high: in April, 17 million people had watched Jenner announce her transition in a two-hour ABC special with Diane Sawyer. Since then, the paparazzi had been ravenous to capture an image, any image, of Jenner post-transition.

Production of the cover was shrouded in secrecy: Jenner was photographed at her new, isolated hilltop mansion, the images stored on a computer in a locked room unconnected to the *Vanity Fair* mainframe. In an age when secrecy of any kind is nearly impossible, Jenner's coming out was a grand reveal in the manner of the pre-digital age.

Seven months earlier, Jenner's stepdaughter Kim Kardashian

"broke the Internet" with nude pictures of her published in *Paper* magazine. This time it was Caitlyn's turn: her newly launched Twitter account beat President Obama's record for the quickest rise to more than 1 million followers; online, the article, with an accompanying photo spread, broke *Vanity Fair* traffic records, topping 6 million unique visitors.

There was the hyperbolic, and thus easily dismissed, backlash: an editorial in the *Pittsburgh Post-Gazette* likened Jenner to the "sadly celebrated" bearded lady of the twentieth century and declared that "for every person cheering your courage, there are others wishing you were a bit more of a coward."[1] There were the predictable anonymous comments on otherwise positive pieces ("By no stretch of the imagination, either Biblically or in Nature, is this in any way normal") and concern from the right that objecting to Jenner's transformation would make them look like bigots. Yet the dominant public posture was modeled by Jenner's family (daughter Kendall tweeted, "be free now pretty bird"; Kim exclaimed "How beautiful! Be happy, be proud, live life YOUR way!") and fellow celebrities. From Lady Gaga: "Caitlyn, thank u for being a part of all of our lives & using your platform to change people's minds"; From Ellen: "My hope for the world is that we can all be as brave as @Caitlyn_Jenner"; from Maria Shriver: "The women's empowerment space got a brave new voice in @Caitlyn_Jenner. Embrace your true self."

If you stayed in a specific section of the Internet and read the carefully worded think pieces within the mainstream media, you'd think the gender transition of a former Olympian—and paragon of masculinity—was something the nation had been anticipating for years. The year before, *Time* magazine had featured

Laverne Cox on its cover as a means of declaring the "trans tipping point"; that January, *Transparent* had won a Golden Globe for Best Series, and in 2014, Janet Mock's memoir, *Redefining Realness*, had made *The New York Times* bestseller list. You could easily argue there's nothing "too queer" about Caitlyn Jenner: sure, she's trans, but she's also highly feminine, precisely coiffed, and on the cover of the most glamorous magazine in the country—the opposite of unruly.

But that's a highly optimistic, and largely myopic, understanding of attitudes toward trans people today. Accepting the narrative that America has "tipped" over to generalized trans acceptance elides the current of transphobia that pervades not only the expected, hateful online spaces, but society at large—including the minds of many who've embraced Caitlyn Jenner.

* * *

Within the trans community, there's profound ambivalence around Jenner's emergence as its de facto spokesperson—because of her unique privilege, her inexperience with the breadth of trans experience, and her support of transphobic politicians, but also because Jenner's appearance and attitude manifest what's known as "transnormativity." Transnormativity can be loosely defined as the notion that a "successful" trans person is a person who *does not appear to be trans.* A transnormative person can "pass" in larger society as their preferred gender identity—and is able to do so because he or she so successfully embodies the norms of masculinity or femininity.

Yet embodying those norms requires capital—both cultural and monetary. As a result, the "most" transnormative individuals are generally those who are white, able-bodied, and upper-middle-class or higher. Trans people who had the most privilege in society before transition often become the ones with the most privilege post-transition: their ability to pass makes it easier to live and work in the world, to be "pretty" enough to deserve to be photographed, to live with less fear. There's a hierarchy of trans identity, and Caitlyn Jenner occupies its highest levels.

Passing also sustains the gender status quo—the notion that there are two genders, and each of those genders performs (sexually, culturally) in a way that matches that gender. A trans person in transition, or not fully transitioned, incites anxiety: in their persistent reminder that gender doesn't have to be binary, they trouble one of the defining structures of American society. In contrast, a fully passing trans person reinforces that structure.

Which isn't to critique Jenner so much as elucidate the tension that surrounds her celebrity. She became the most famous and visible trans person in history not because of her leadership skills or her knowledge of gender politics and trans history, but by default because of her already prominent position, both as a former Olympian and as a member of one of the most famous families in the United States.

More than anything, Jenner wants to pass as female. She believes that's the quickest way for her, and trans people in general, to become "the new normal." Looking at Jenner's past, that desire makes sense: she's spent the last thirty years terrified of what would happen if her true self were discovered. For Jenner and many other trans people, transnormativity is a way to escape the societal shame directed toward trans people—a way, at last, to fit in.

The problem, then, is that seeking transnormativity does

very little to actually address or dissipate transphobia. By making people *forget* that someone is trans, it also means they don't have to confront the anxiety, fear, or anger that arises when someone destabilizes the binary understanding of gender.

And even if grandmothers and conservatives all over the United States know who Caitlyn Jenner is, and might not even be offended by her, the overarching transphobia, manifest in everything from the tabloid covers of Jenner pre-transition to the hate speech found online, remains—and with very real ramifications, According to the Human Rights Campaign, a trans person is four times as likely to live in extreme poverty, 90 percent of trans people have been harassed on the job, and 2015 marked the highest number of trans homicides—at least twenty-two—in history.[2] In this way, Jenner's very *lack* of queerness reinforces the understanding that trans identity is a legitimate threat to society: one of the most dangerous unruly behaviors.

❖ ❖ ❖

Transnormativity is a cousin to the idea of homonormativity—defined by Lisa Duggan as "a politics that does contest dominant heteronormative assumptions and institutions, but upholds and sustains them, while promising the possibility of a demobilized gay constituency and a privatized, depoliticized gay culture anchored in domesticity and consumption."[3] Put simply, to be homonormative is to desire all the privileges and rights that straight people have—including marriage, the right to have children, the ability to be thought of as a consumer. Many of those desires have become cornerstones of the gay rights movement, but they've also incited criticism, as they do little to interrogate the systems (marriage, parenthood, capitalism) to which gays desire free entrance. Some believe there's little progress to be made in fighting for the right to join an oppressive, exclusionary institution instead of forcing that institution to change.

Nevertheless, homonormativity has become an ideal, especially in terms of representation: "successful" queer characters are always upper-middle-class achievers, engaged in committed relationships in which each partner takes a legible gender position (one more masculine, the other more feminine), sex is omitted entirely, and marriage and/or children have either been achieved or are the goal. Mitch and Cameron on *Modern Family* are the most vivid manifestation of contemporary homonormativity, but it also plays out in the celebrity images of Ellen DeGeneres and Neil Patrick Harris. Butch lesbians and effeminate gay men are either invisible or played for laughs, while bisexuals are almost entirely absent. The less a queer person challenges the gender binary, the more assimilated they are into straight behaviors and lifestyles, the more acceptable and palatable they become. As with trans people, the most socially acceptable way to be gay is for nothing, save the existence of your same-sex spouse, to betray your queerness.

Transnormativity shares many characteristics with homonormativity, but with a crucial difference. Gender dysphoria, like homosexuality, was long classified as a psychological disorder. Unlike homosexuality, however—whose defining attribute was a desire for the same sex—the medical establishment's understanding of transvestism and transsexuality was largely gleaned from the memoirs of Christine Jorgensen and Mario Martino, released in 1968 and 1977, respectively. As trans scholar Evan Vipond explains, Jorgensen "framed her transition as the medical correction of a mistake made by nature," and both included acknowledgment of the sentiment as a child, a feeling of "not being at home" in one's body, and a desire to fully transition from one gender to another.[4]

Even though many trans people might not experience dysphoria until a later age, or do not articulate alienation from their bodies, those tropes became the criteria through which medical professionals diagnosed trans patients. If a trans patient did not conform to those criteria, they would not be eligible for treatment, including hormones, surgery, and other services. As a result, many trans people co-opted the narratives of Jorgensen and Martino, regardless of how they actually matched their experience, simply to receive services—and in so doing, reinforced their standardization.

In this way, the medical understanding of the trans narrative reinforced a certain type of transnormativity—and within that type, there was simply no room for gender fluidity. This understanding plays out in filmic representations of trans women, which theorist Julia Serano divides into two overarching camps. There's the "deceptive" transsexual, a sort of femme fatale—because of their ability to pass as women, they "generally act as unexpected plot twists, or play the role of sexual predators who fool innocent straight guys into falling for other 'men.'" See: Jaye Davidson from *The Crying Game*, or, in the case of a trans man, Hilary Swank in *Boys Don't Cry*. Then there's the "pathetic" transsexual—one who can't pass, can't transition, can't integrate into society, and is thus "coded as harmless," as impotent, pitiable, a freak, a failure. See: Bree in *Transamerica*, Sophia in *Orange Is the New Black*. Female to male trans characters are largely invisible on-screen, as are trans women who don't fully embrace or desire hyper-femininity.[5]

Even though, as Serano explains, "there are as many types of trans women as there are women in general, most people believe that all trans women are on a quest to makes ourselves as pretty, pink and passive as possible."[6] The reasoning is straightforward: if the very existence of trans people compromises the status quo, the media offers up images, experiences, and plotlines that provide a salve for that anxiety. These images school audiences on what a "normal" trans person looks like—and, through the course of the narrative, suggest what does and should happen to those who fail to achieve that normality and thus pose a threat to the status quo. In short: abuse, alienation, death.

All of which contributes to the dominance of the transnormative, male-to-female, feminine character as the ideal (and disproportionately visible) trans individual—an ideal that Caitlyn Jenner both fulfills and reinscribes. The first and most essential way is through Jenner's race (white), class (born middle-class; now upper-), and ability (exceptional), all of which facilitated her rise to the position of American hero in the late 1970s—an avatar of American virility amidst the threat of Soviet dominance. As sportswriter Buzz Bissinger summarizes in the profile that accompanied Jenner's debut, "He adorned the front of the Wheaties box. He drank orange juice for Tropicana and took pictures for Minolta. He gave speeches about the 48 hours of his Olympic win all over the country to enthralled audiences. He was red, white, and blue. He was Mom and apple pie with a daub of vanilla ice cream for extra deliciousness in a country desperate for such an image. He had a tireless work ethic. He had beaten the Commie bastards. He was America."[7]

Which is another way of saying that Jenner's face and achievements felt so palatable, and signified so strongly the (white, straight) strength that America wanted/needed as its avatar, that major corporations elected to use Jenner's face to sell their products. Many men look masculine; others exude a look of Americanness. But Jenner became exemplary of both—a feeling bolstered by her virility (she had four children over the course of five years) and palatability.

Over the course of the 1980s, Jenner largely withdrew from society, grappling with depression as she tried to come to terms with her gender identity. That changed when she met Kris Kardashian, soon to be Jenner, in 1991. Kris reinvigorated Jenner's endorsement and speaking career—and, by extension, their fortune. As a result, when Jenner began to transition in 2014, it was from a place of phenomenal privilege: she had the resources not only to protect herself (in the form of a secluded home, assistants, and bodyguards) but also to easily acquire the surgeries, hormones, and post-transition wardrobe. Even if Jenner had been rejected by society, she'd still have a cushion of capital to insulate her from the harsh economic realities that face so many trans women.

Jenner's understanding of her trans identity follows the dominant transnormative narrative. In the Diane Sawyer special, the *Vanity Fair* profile, and various other interviews, Jenner recalls feeling like a girl at a young age: "When I was eight years old, I was running into my mom's closet, nobody would know," she told *Time*.[8] After the Olympics, she would don pantyhose and a bra under her suits when making public appearances. Jenner told both her first and second wives about her desire to be a woman, and attributes much of her inability to be a good parent to her first four children to a deep unhappiness in her body. "I never felt feminine," she explains in her reality television show *I Am Cait*, "but I always felt female."

Jenner also desired to fully embody the identity of a woman— and embrace all the characteristics, mannerisms, and attitudes that attend traditional femininity. Her fashion style is influenced by her daughters and stepdaughters, who've collectively cultivated a super-glam aesthetic. Her hair is voluminous; her lips are plump and glossed; her breasts are pushed up and emphasized in a wardrobe filled with low-V wrap dresses and towering heels. She loves the fashions sent to her by high-profile designers; she employs a full-time stylist and makeup artist.

Absent her trans identity, Jenner's particular mode of femininity is one of the tamest and most culturally compliant ways of existing as a woman in the world. Her *Vanity Fair* cover, in which she sits coyly in lingerie in a corner, is a textbook manifestation of the male gaze at work. As Jenner plays tennis in a short skirt with her sister in the premiere of *I Am Cait*, the camera pans up her legs, fetishizing her body as if she's in a music video. Later in the season, she revels in the idea that a man would open a door for her or carry her shopping bags.

This mode of gender performance has surrounded Caitlyn, literally living in her house, for decades. In the early episodes of season one, her femininity most resembles that of a teenage girl: she gleefully puts on blue and purple hair extensions brought to her by daughter Kylie; Kim tells her, "You're so skinny! You look like Kendall!" In other words: she has the physique of a twenty-year-old model. The spelling of her name—the inclusion of a "y" in particular—is not that of her generation, but her daughters'. She refers to herself and her trans female friends almost exclusively as "girls"—a perfect indication of the manner in which she views herself.

That idea is complicated, however, by Jenner's sexuality—which she herself admits she hasn't yet figured out. In most transnormative narratives, the trans woman desires to be with a man, ostensibly making the couple "straight," or at least able to pass as such. But Jenner says that if there's a hierarchy of things that mattered to her through the process of transitioning, sex was her lowest priority. She doesn't think she wants to be with women, but, at least at the close of season two, she had also never been with a man. In an appearance on *Ellen*, she jokes that she "already [has] too many children" and is now "in a different place in life," but would like to someday find a partner.

But reality television's primary engines are competition and romance, and absent competition, *I Am Cait* attempts to graft on a romance—in this case, inflating Jenner's relationship with trans actress Candis Cayne. Like an "ideal" gay relationship on television, this ideal trans one is all about the particulars of romance—flirting, crushes—absent the actual facts of sex. In season one, for example, Cayne invites Jenner for a sleepover, and Jenner spends five minutes with a stylist picking out appropriate lingerie. In a later episode, Jenner and Cayne's "date" to the ESPY Awards is framed like prom; in season two, Jenner and Cayne share a kiss that feels not unlike one prompted by a game of spin the bottle.

Within the narrative of *I Am Cait*, discussion of the romance always feels hackneyed. But its existence, especially as manifest in the gossip press, worked to wedge Jenner into a traditional narrative. In interviews, Cayne and Jenner chose their words carefully: Cayne denied rumors that they were spotted making out at a local hair salon, but told E! "We definitely have a connection!"; Jenner told Ellen DeGeneres that "Candis is backstage, but that's a whole other deal. Candis is great. We really have a lot of fun. She's a beautiful woman."

I Am Cait would probably have much higher ratings if Jenner did, indeed, fall in love. Instead, its tacked-on romance fails, on almost all levels, to distract from the larger drama of the show: Jenner's often clumsy reckoning with her own privilege and the multiplicity of trans experience, from her recoil at other women's histories with sex work to her disbelief that a trans woman wouldn't want to change the timbre of her voice to sound more "feminine." Such moments are just some of the ways that *I Am Cait* points to the difficulty of removing the politics of trans identity: when you're trans, at least in this cultural moment, the personal is always political.

✦ ✦ ✦

Nearly one in five trans people are victims of domestic abuse. Far more are cut off, alienated, or otherwise affected by transphobic members of their close circle. But that rejection is absent from the transnormative narrative, which generally depicts the family's reaction to transition as akin to getting a tattoo: surprise, maybe a little dismay, followed by acceptance. The trope of the accepting family is crucial: it suggests that trans people can and do integrate seamlessly into society (in school, in the workplace, in the family) and, in so doing, suggests that society doesn't need to change—trans people just need to fit into it.

Acceptance pervades all the major media texts of Jenner's transition. Jenner's eighty-nine-year-old mother, Esther, struggles to use correct pronouns for Caitlyn, yet her overarching attitude is one of understanding and love. When Esther first arrives to Jenner's house in the series premiere, Jenner reassures her, "It's okay!" to which Esther responds, "I knew it would be!" When Kim and Kanye West visit, West tells Jenner, "It's one of the strongest things that has happened in our existence as human beings that are so controlled by perception. . . . You couldn't have been up against more, like your daughter's a supermodel, you're a celebrity and every type of thing, and it was still like 'Fuck everybody, this is who I am.'" Jenner's four eldest children opt not to participate in the show, but come off, in both the Diane Sawyer interview and the *Vanity Fair* profile, as incredibly supportive— and eager to get to know a parent who had always been distant.

The only major frisson with the family happens because of Jenner's imprecise language in the *Vanity Fair* interview—the suggestion that his daughters with Kris Jenner were a "distraction," and a disagreement between Kris and Caitlyn as to Kris's awareness of the extent, and implications, of Caitlyn's desire to live as a woman. But even those tensions are played out for the camera with cathartic tears and concluding hugs. Later in the season, Kris Jenner comes for a heart-to-heart, but their conversation, like so many in the series, pivots not on the pain or discomfort of Jenner coming out, but of her *not* doing so for so long. Transitioning, in this light, isn't the trauma or the tragedy—*not* transitioning is.

Jenner alludes to friends who have kept their distance since the transition, but the majority are presented as accepting. It would be horrible press, after all, for a celebrity to come off as anything other than supportive and open-minded. Yet it's one thing to be okay with Jenner's particular and very public manifestation of trans identity, and quite another to be okay with those who don't fulfill that definition of transnormativity in one's own workplace, public spaces, classrooms—or bathrooms. As activist Jen Richards, a fixture in the first season of *I Am Cait*, explains,

"Cait's experience of coming out is singular. I don't think anyone's ever been so welcomed."

The inertia of Jenner's image is rooted in the central question: *Will she be able to pull off the identity of a cisgender person in time?* Will she achieve femininity in time to meet her family, to attend her first public speaking appearance at the ESPYs, to avoid getting caught by the paparazzi in the act of looking trans? Of course she will. According to trans scholar Caitlin Campisi, the ultimate sign of transnormativity for trans people is "an overall desire to be 'just like' their cisgender peers and view the resolution of their difference as a sign of success."[9] And Jenner is nothing if not a winner.

As Jenner puts it in episode two, "All I wanna do is just kinda slip into society"—an ethos she articulated in a December 2015 interview with *Time* magazine after being short-listed for the magazine's "Person of the Year." "I think it's much easier for a trans woman or a trans man who authentically kind of looks and plays the role," she explained. "So what I call my presentation. I try to take that seriously. I think it puts people at ease. If you're out there and, to be honest with you, if you look like a man in a dress, it makes people uncomfortable."

The reaction to Jenner's comments was swift. "Caitlyn's use of the word 'authentic' to qualify someone's appearance, and her reinforcement that trans people 'play a role' in their day-to-day lives, is a serious misunderstanding of what many in the community are still compelled to argue is a major reason behind their transitions," Alex Rees wrote in a scathing piece for *Cosmopolitan*. "Caitlyn still seems to be laboring under the impression that trans people owe mainstream society a debt, or an apology, for embracing their true selves—or at least that they must jump neatly back in one gender-normalized box having jumped out of another."[10] Rees is articulating one of the primary objections to transnormativity: sure, every trans person should embody their "authentic" self however they'd like, but that doesn't mean that each transition looks and functions exactly the same. There are larger stakes, too, when it takes place on such a massive and influential scale, held up as the image of what an "authentic" transition looks like.

Yet as cultural commenter Meredith Talusan points out, "the literal truth" of Jenner's statement is lost amidst the ire. "The fact is that trans people who look like cis people genuinely do have an easier time," Talusan explains, "since male-assigned people who don't conform to gender norms are easily the most despised and marginalized in US society within the transgender umbrella. Seen through a more forgiving lens, Jenner's comments are more easily read as candid rather than judgmental."[11] Candid, and also logical: if you keep reading Jenner's *Time* interview, it becomes clear that part of the reason she's so fixated on her appearance is because "When I go out, as Kim says, you've got to rock it because the paparazzi will be there."[12] The same paparazzi who, for the years leading up to her transition, catalogued every moment in which she failed to pass and then wielded it to shame her; who, when they discovered she'd had a tracheal shave, forced her to accelerate her transition; who, when they couldn't get a photo of her as a woman, cut and pasted her face onto another woman's body for the cover.

Jenner had seen what *not* passing felt like—and could visualize the national reaction that would follow if she continued to do so. Even outside of the pressures of the media, Jenner may have desired to embody womanhood the way that she does. But she was also surrounded by messages, explicit and implicit, from non-trans people and from the few "positive" trans representations in popular culture, that to pass, to fully integrate, was to succeed.

That's the difficulty of transvisibility in the twenty-first century: as *Feministing* writer Jos Truitt puts it, "trans women are disrespected and treated terribly when they don't pass, but if they do pass they're called out for upholding the gender binary and cis standards of beauty. It is an impossible bind."[13] And while Jenner hoped that her visibility would make things easier for her and all other trans people, violence against trans people, especially black or Latina, has actually increased since the so-called trans tipping point. At the same time, members of the right have used the trans desire to use bathrooms that correspond to their gender identity to incite a national panic on the right over the idea of perverted "men" in the same space as children.

Such panics are sensational, unwarranted, and often inflamed by politicians in an attempt to bolster support, but they're also a perfect example of the false equivalency between attention and acceptance. Ten years ago, trans people may have been largely ignored, at least in popular culture, or otherwise considered freaks. Yet with visibility comes hierarchies: of those who can be photographed by Annie Leibovitz for the cover of *Vanity Fair* and those whom no one wants to photograph; of those who can afford to disappear and return fully transitioned versus those who must wait for years; of those whose family, friends, and cultural and work spaces remain a support structure versus those whose are rejected; of those who desire to occupy the gender binary as compared with those who ignore or purposefully disrupt it.

Reina Gosset, activist-in-residence at Barnard College, puts the situation in stark terms: "So often, visibility uses the lens of respectability to determine who, even in the most vulnerable communities, should be seen and heard. I believe that, through the filter of visibility, those of us most at risk to state violence become even more vulnerable to that violence."[14]

Increased violence against trans people was not Jenner's intention. Neither was marginalization, or implicit hierarchies, or regimentation of what a "good" trans person would look like. But that doesn't mean that her visibility didn't amplify all of those things. Which is part of what makes *I Am Cait*, and its development from season one to two, so remarkable. It's a show that ostensibly focuses on Jenner and her embodiment of transnormativity—but in reality offers a persuasive counterpoint to it.

✦ ✦ ✦

Jenner might not be unruly, but the supporting characters of *I Am Cait* absolutely are. Their presence on the show—the literal places they take Jenner, the questions they force her to contemplate, and the diversity of trans experiences to which they expose her and, by extension, the audience—accomplishes the inverse of what you'd expect of a show named for the most famous trans woman in the world. Simply put: *I Am Cait* makes it impossible to conceive of trans experience as a monolith.

Jenner has surrounded herself with other trans women since the second episode of season one of the show. Jenny Boylan, a professor and bestselling author, had been communicating with Jenner for a year before her transition, and was originally signed on to *I Am Cait* as a consultant. The other participants were cast to provide varying perspectives: if Boylan offers the academic approach, unafraid to confront Jenner with the same sort of difficult questions that she would pose in the classroom, then Chandi Moore embodies the diversity of experiences and labor trans women endure to survive; Zackary Drucker shows that trans women can have healthy, loving relationships; Candis Cayne suggests how lonely it can still be for a "passing" woman who was out in Hollywood years before Jenner; Kate Bornstein takes the role of seen-some-shit, give-no-fucks auntie; and the eighteen-year-old Ella Giselle provides generational contrast.

Each has different ideas about the most pertinent issues facing the trans community, the importance of gender confirmation surgery, and the place or importance of drag or the word "tranny" in the trans community, and what it means to be a woman. They're periodically flabbergasted, annoyed, and dismayed by Jenner. But their continued presence radically de-centers the narrative from her: she may still have her name on the show, but as Boylan makes clear, "this show is not actually about her."

These women are central to season one, but it's not until season two—when they're forced together in a bus traveling across the United States—that the intensity of the conversations ratchets up. They force Jenner to come to terms with the irreconcilability of her Republican politics with the party's articulated stance toward the LGBT community—at one point, in Iowa to watch the Democratic National Convention, Jenner shakes hands with Hillary Clinton, later admitting that she has the strongest platform when it comes to trans rights and protections.

In Iowa, they visit Jenner's alma mater, a college loosely affiliated with the Mormon church, and meet with the only trans person in the town, who has braved existence there in order to show that "trans people are everywhere." They watch as Jenner is pick-eted at a luncheon in Chicago, and talk with Jenner about what it is about her identity that makes other trans people feel so vulner-able and angry. Chandi tells Cait about her past time not only in sex work, but as a white-collar criminal—for which she spent time in jail, and which now makes it difficult for her to do simple things like get a passport. They meet with Ella's father, and learn that even the next generation of kids, whose communities are the-oretically so accepting, still struggle with transphobia from within their families. They attend a Houston prayer service at the church of one of the pastors who led the movement to repeal the city's HERO Act (i.e., the Houston Equal Rights Ordinance, which pro-tects trans rights), one of whom Jenner confronts.

And when Jenner's interview with *Time* goes public—the same interview that prompted so much backlash from the trans community—they discuss it as a group: "When you refer to us as men in dresses you're validating all of these pastors and politi-cians that are using scare tactics against us," Candis says, to which Jenny adds, "People need to know you're fighting for ev-erybody, not just the pretty ones."

There's family drama interwoven in the show, but that, too, serves less as a distraction than a means to continually interro-gate Jenner's life and the way others have reacted to her: that Kris Jenner is still struggling to understand the last two decades of her life; that Scott Disick is still, like so many others, obsessed with anatomy questions. The questions are less about who's right and who's wrong, or who needs to bend to accept and who needs to integrate, and far more about dialogue.

Crucially, the end goal of this dialogue isn't to humiliate or belittle Jenner. Nor does it focus, like so much of reality television, on constructing a clear hero or villain. Instead, it renders Jenner, like every other trans person on the show, as a person with a story—and as Boylan says, "You can't hate someone whose story you know." You can disagree with them, you can have different goals, but it's far, far more difficult to hate them—and act, legislate, and speak in ways that are transphobic—if trans people are humanized on-screen.

I Am Cait provides not just one story, but half a dozen—some, like Jenner's, working to negotiate a "normal" space within the world of trans identity, others aggressively not. And while those other women would not have been given their own show on E!—in no small part because of that very unruliness—they have found themselves as the clustered, contradictory, complementary center of the most visible trans narrative in history.

✦ ✦ ✦

In July 2016, Jenner made headlines for declaring that it was more difficult to come out as a Republican than a trans person. She often shows, as Boylan puts it, that she has "a head like a rock." She's as problematic as a protagonist as she is as the de facto spokesperson for trans identities. But she's also demonstrated her willingness, over and over again, to try to change the way she's come to think about herself, her new community, and her place in the world. She might not be too queer, but she's used her visibility to introduce hundreds of thousands of people to those who are defiantly so.

When Jenner began discussing her hopes for season three, she could've chosen to recenter the show on herself—on her burgeoning friendship and affection for Candis, or her relationship with her far more famous Kardashian and Jenner family members. Instead, she said she wanted to focus on those who are gender nonconforming, either by choice or through lack of resources. Instead of avoiding the complexities of trans identity, she's wanted to lean in to them, committing herself to exploring the areas of her community that make people, including herself, feel uncomfortable. But in August 2016, E! announced the cancellation of *I Am Cait*, a "mutual agreement" with Jenner likely linked to the show's steady decline in ratings   or Jenner's refusal to mold the show around a traditional reality narrative. For all of Jenner's faults, *I Am Cait* forced viewers to reexamine not only their own presumptions about what it means to be trans, but the very fundamentals of gender and identity. The show's ratings, and its cancellation, should not diminish its achievements.

Take a step back and remind yourself: over the course of two years, a prized athlete and avatar of American masculinity became one of the most visible trans people (and, for that matter, women over sixty) in popular culture and then placed herself in situations that forced her to reconsider her world, to examine her various forms of privilege, to face the textured ways of life that are not her own. It's Jenner's openness, that inclination to seek empathy, even when it fails, that remains remarkable—not just in the world of reality television, but in the increasingly hostile world of American culture. Because when hate and fear become the status quo, the simple act of trying to understand others who don't live and act the same as you do—an attitude Jenner has now modeled for millions—becomes a profoundly unruly act.

CHAPTER 9

TOO LOUD:
JENNIFER WEINER

Football and sport are important, the buying of clothes, the worship of fashion, trivial.   —Virginia Woolf[1]

When women stop reading, the novel will be dead.
                                    —Ian McEwan[2]

I had some hope of actually reaching a male audience, and I've heard more than one reader in signing lines now in bookstores say, "You know, if I hadn't heard of you, I would've been put off by the fact that [*The Corrections*] is an Oprah pick. I figure those books are for women, and I'd never touch it." Those are male readers speaking.   —Jonathan Franzen[3]

There's a hierarchy within the world of books, deeply rooted in accumulated understandings of class, commerce, and gender. It goes something like this: The more popular, the more marketable, the more visible and readable a book is, the less worth it has within the cultural hierarchy. Crucially, those books—and the readers of them—are largely female: women who share them among friends, who check them out from the library, who buy them because Oprah or another book group tells them to.

Women make up around 80 percent of the fiction-buying public, making them an incredibly powerful market force.[4] They're just not buying the right books—at least according to a pervasive and problematic cultural assumption. The right books are "difficult": experimental, impenetrable, male. They get written up in prestigious book reviews; they win awards that place a tasteful gold stamp in their corner. Their authors don't blog or tweet about them, because they don't blog or tweet. They take decades to write. They're released in hardcover, the robust carapace of high literature. They occupy the rarefied air of high art. And the majority, but certainly not all, of the authors of these books are men.

On the other end of this hierarchy, there's the feminized, the commercially popular, the books reliant on tacky self-promotion. Their authors produce a book a year, if not more; each book cover looks vaguely like the one before. They're the books you buy at Target, the supermarket, the airport; the beach reads, the trash reads, the books people actually, well, read en masse. So here lies the publishing industry: the "accessible," commercial book at the bottom, necessary to the bottom line but not worthy of adulation; and in the rarefied air on top, there's the masculine, the artistic, and the reliant on cultural patronage. That's an exaggeration and simplification—but not by much. These attitudes dictate how we ascribe worth and value to artists and the work they create; they're also at the heart of the way we look at the books on someone's shelves, or the film posters on their wall, and make a judgment about their intelligence and class. Such judgments are deeply—if often subconsciously—gendered.

It's also something that Jennifer Weiner, the author of thirteen books, which have sold ten million copies, has spent the better part of a decade refusing to shut up about. Whether in her role launching the hashtag #Franzenfreude, her continued fight for coverage of "commercial" literature in *The New York Times Book Review*, or her defense of Twitter, Weiner has become the "unlikely feminist enforcer," as *The New Yorker* put it, for the effort to destabilize the hierarchies of the publishing world.[5]

In her refusal to stop talking, Weiner has been called strident, starved for attention, abrasive, and angry; her critiques of the industry have been characterized as tedious and misplaced. And while Weiner's approach has its faults, it's also been instrumental in creating quantifiable change: in the leadership and content of *The New York Times Book Review*, in the increased pressure on book sections to publish more writing by and reviews of work by women. But that success hasn't mitigated her image of unruliness, both as someone who doesn't know her place within established hierarchies, and as someone who's too loud and tactless in her efforts to change them.

As Weiner puts it, "Any woman who ever put pen to paper, or finger to laptop, has had to deal with sexism, discrimination and double standards, has had to fight harder than a man to get published, to get noticed, to get reviewed, to get profiled. I'm not saying that we all need to hold hands and sing Kumbaya, but I wish that there was some recognition of what the real problem is. Chick lit is not the problem."[6] The problem, of course, is entrenched, systemic, historic sexism: within the publishing industry, but also of the variety that stigmatizes someone like Weiner for speaking out about it.

And while even Franzen can admit that the issue "is important," he also believes Weiner is an "unfortunate person to have as a spokesperson."[7] Unfortunate because she writes stories that fulfill a specific psychological function for women living under postfeminism, unfortunate because her books are too commercial and their covers too pastel, unfortunate because she spends too much time on Twitter, unfortunate because she won't let Franzen off the hook for his deeply sexist understanding of how an author should present the labor and purpose of authorship. But mostly unfortunate because she doesn't know her place. And that, more than the request for the *Times* and other publications to devote more thoughtful energy to books like hers, is the ultimate in literary unruliness.

✦　✦　✦

Blame it on the refinement of the printing press and the rise of the middle class. The increased ease of printing, coupled with a rapidly expanding reading population, facilitated the rise of the eighteenth-century "women's novel," most famously, Samuel Richardson's *Pamela* and *Clarissa*, but also hundreds of other books, largely written by women, long forgotten or excluded from literary history. These books sold like crazy, but their focus on the lives of women and the concerns of the domestic sphere automatically degraded them, and the form of the novel altogether, within the literary hierarchy. The "real" literature of the time took the form of treatises, satires, essays, and poetry; the novel was a diversion, not art.

Female authors in particular became targets of the established and venerated authors of the time, in part because they "disrupted" the marketplace that had theretofore been dominated by men: Alexander Pope made fun of Eliza Haywood, one of the most prolific and popular authors of the eighteenth century, for being *too* desired by publishers; an 1818 review of Mary Wollstonecraft Shelley's *Frankenstein* explained, "The writer of it is, we understand, female . . . we shall therefore dismiss the novel without further comment." In 1855, Nathaniel Hawthorne famously referred to female writers as the "damned mob of scribbling women." Scribbling, like children; mob, as in unruly: a distraction and a disturbance.[8]

As the written word became a form of mass culture, books written by women were denigrated for their commercialism and perceived frivolity. This understanding was internalized by female authors themselves: Mary Ann Evans, who would later adopt the pseudonym George Eliot, roundly criticized the genre in the essay "Silly Novels by Lady Novelists," describing them as frothy, prosy, pious, and pedantic.[9] In many ways, Evans, writing as Eliot, would go on to model her own style of writing, and image as a writer, *against* that of the female novelist—which is precisely why she was able to gain legitimacy.

The sheer success of the novel as art introduced questions of "literary legitimacy," with the established male arbiters of the literary scene: the men whose work sold very little, yet survived through the patronage of well-off benefactors on one side, and the women who had become the dominant consumers of books (just not the "right" ones) on the other. And as their position as arbiters came into question, they became defensive, tightening the boundaries between what, and who, is worthy—and what, and who, is not.

Those boundaries were tightened once again in the late nineteenth and early twentieth centuries, when the burgeoning women's movements, the increased circulation of women in the public sphere, and advances of the Industrial Revolution made it easier than ever for the work of women to reach large audiences—and for women to in turn make livings to support themselves. As cultural theorist Andreas Huyssen explains, with the continued spread of mass culture (magazines, novels, early motion pictures, what we often refer to as pop culture), myriad forces labored to ensure that it was "associated with women while real, authentic culture remain[ed] the prerogative of men."[10]

In Dwight Macdonald's highly influential work on taste hierarchies, *Masscult and Midcult*, he defines mass culture as "offer[ing] its customers neither an emotional catharsis nor an aesthetic experience, for these demand effort." Masscult follows the rules of genre; its pleasures are predictable. "The production line grinds out a uniform product whose humble aim is not even entertainment, for this too implies life and hence effort, but merely distraction," Macdonald writes. "It may be stimulating or narcotic, but it must be easy to assimilate. It asks nothing of its audience . . . And it gives nothing."[11]

"Authentic culture," by contrast, was most potently manifest in the work of the avant-garde: the modernists working to invert the expectations of literature, architecture, dance, drama, and music, distinguished by the "expression of feelings, ideas, tastes, visions that are idiosyncratic and the audience similarly responds to them as individuals." If mass culture dulled the senses, the avant-garde electrified them; if mass culture was a broadly palatable commercial product, the Hershey's chocolate of the arts, then avant-garde was red chili pepper–infused chocolate with 60 percent cacao. One was an escape from work; the other work itself.

The rigor, complexity, and alienation that attend the avant-garde ensure that only a certain sort of person, with a certain set of class privileges, will like it—which effectively reinforces its exclusivity and importance. This understanding of mass versus high culture also pivots on the *experience* of consumption: it doesn't matter what the actual *content* is so much as the attitude, and reaction, one has to it. You approach a movie like *National Treasure* or a novel like *The Da Vinci Code* with the understanding that you'll "get it"—its humor, its pathos, its purpose—and everyone else will "get it" in a similar manner. Going to a Mahler symphony or watching an experimental film, by contrast, requires a posture of possibility. You must strive to understand; your understanding may not match anyone else's.

Macdonald thought masscult an unfortunate and very American result of the spread of industrialization and the porous boundaries between classes. But what really galled him and other cultural critics was the rise of "midcult," which "has the essential qualities of Masscult—the formula, the built-in reaction, the lack of any standard except popularity—but it decently covers them with a cultural figleaf. In Masscult the trick is plain—to please the crowd by any means. But Midcult has it both ways: it pretends to respect the standards of High Culture while in fact it waters them down and vulgarizes them."[12]

Anything that makes you *feel* like you're doing something smart, but you're still pretty comfortable or unchallenged doing it, that's midcult. *Time* magazine is midcult, as is *Game of Thrones*. *Portlandia* is midcult; *Downton Abbey* is midcult. So is NPR and orchestras playing Led Zeppelin and *The Old Man and the Sea* and nature shows narrated by David Attenborough. Macdonald describes a midcult success as something that "has been praised by critics who should know better, and has been popular not so much with the masses as with the educated classes."

These taste hierarchies are foundational to Western society, calcified and reified to the point of status quo. *Of course* complexity is better than simplicity; *of course* you should qualify your enjoyment of anything that is not on the highest rung as a "guilty pleasure"—as if you were momentarily afflicted with bad taste and, as such, risk outing yourself as not just less intelligent, but less deserving of your own class.

While there are notable differences in the complexity, nuance, allusion, artistic innovation and experimentation found in mass, mid, and high culture, the argument that one is intrinsically *more valuable* than the others is, of course, fundamentally elitist. It's no accident that this sort of cultural work—by Macdonald and others—is often the pet project of men, generally with vested interests in maintaining hierarchies calibrated to their particular and exclusive definitions, which delegitimize culture that provides pleasure and meaning to audiences largely composed of women. If we authenticate and declare our worth and class in no small part through the objects we consume, then labeling the objects consumed by women as "less than" effectively delegitimizes and devalues women's place in the world.

Which is why midcult is such an anxious, self-conscious designation: it's always striving to differentiate itself from masscult while also aligning itself with the avant-garde, through either aesthetics or packaging or presumed audience. That's why a novclist like Jonathan Franzen got itchy when his work was selected as part of one of midcult's most formidable manifestations: Oprah's Book Club.

The Corrections is filled with complex, contradictory characters; it's beautifully, enthrallingly written. And while it's neither formally nor narratively innovative, it's also relentlessly abrasive, resisting the production of the "uniform" reaction ascribed to mass- and midcult. Yet Franzen didn't want it grouped with the mix of mass- and midcult books that, in 2001, filled the club's roster. "She's picked some good books," he told Powells.com, "but she's picked enough schmaltzy, one-dimensional ones that I cringe, myself." Oprah's pick of *Beloved*, he could get behind; Wally Lamb's *She's Come Undone*, he needed to define himself, and his book, against.[13]

Franzen told one reporter that *The Corrections* would be a "hard book for that audience"; he chafed at the commercial implications of the "Oprah's Book Club" logo on its cover, or having it sold, as a result of its designation, in masscult locations like Wal-Mart and Costco, fearing that appearing on Oprah's show would be out of step with "the high-art literary tradition" of which he considered himself a part.[14] While Franzen later softened his remarks—"Mistake, mistake, mistake to use the word 'high,'" he told *The New York Times*—he was clearly suffering from a case of taste anxiety. Intentionally or not, he articulated that the makeup of the readership, coupled with its commercial success, would change the value of his work.[15]

Franzen decided not to go on Oprah's show—television, after all, was a decisively masscult medium which, in a famous 1996 essay for *Harper's*, he had railed against—but *The Corrections* remained part of the book club, prompting his publisher to print an additional 500,000 copies. Franzen would go on to receive an estimated $1.5 million in royalties: for all of his kvetching about losing readers, he'd gained hundreds of thousands.[16] Yet his critics were everywhere: even academic Harold Bloom, one of the holders of the old flame of literary elitism, said he would've been "honored" to be invited by Oprah. "It does seem a little invidious of [Franzen] to want to have it both ways," Bloom said. "To want the benefits of it and not jeopardize his high aesthetic standing."[17]

Critics decried Franzen in all corners of the mainstream (mass- and midcult) establishment—including *The Philadelphia Inquirer*, where a young journalist named Jennifer Weiner took him to task. In 2001, she'd been writing for the paper for several years, covering everything from pop culture to the latest Philly cultural events. But Franzen's anxiety about Oprah's Book Club set her off: "Could anyone be more ungrateful, snobby and sexist—and, in the end, more harmful to the fortunes of [his publisher] Farrar?" she wrote. "Franzen's future works will wind up with precisely the audience he is seeking—smart, male, and extremely small."[18] Weiner's prediction was wrong, in part because Franzen's anti-publicity move was, of course, very good publicity, but the sentiment behind it—and the raw anger with elitism—had been culturally gestating for some time.

Weiner grew up in the suburbs of Connecticut, a self-professed weird kid with few friends who always felt alone—for being larger than the other girls in her class, for being the only Jew on the block, for having a broken family. Her parents told her she'd find her people when she went to college at Princeton, but that didn't really work, either: she found the students there just as snobby, and spent a significant amount of time successfully lobbying against the all-male, centuries-old "Eating Clubs." As she later recalled, "I think I have always had a willingness to point at something and say, 'This is wrong,' even if I got grief for it."

Upon graduating, Weiner worked for a smattering of local papers before landing at the *Inquirer*, where she began writing her first book, *Good in Bed*, at night and on weekends. The novel was largely based on the events of her own life—her struggle to fit in and feel valuable in a society that cherishes thinness, her difficulties with her parents' divorce and her mother coming out as a lesbian, her quest to find love with a man who valued her. All the domestic and emotional concerns that had devalued women's writing for centuries.

Weiner had a steady job at a major paper and had attended an Ivy League School, but she was still firmly outside the literary establishment: she lived in Philadelphia, not New York; she didn't spend her post-college years interning at literary magazines or getting an MFA, but stringing at local papers; she couldn't devote herself full-time to writing her book, so she wrote it in the pauses of her life; she didn't know how to find an agent, so she sent her manuscript to twenty agents.[19]

When *Good in Bed* was released, Weiner had no idea it was "chick lit," in part because most people didn't know that "chick lit" existed. The designation is now widely used to describe a type of masscult book that isn't Harlequin romances, but focuses, in some way, on women—and often features romance, shopping, and other activities women do. Yet the term's genesis can be traced to the mid-1990s, when editors Cris Mazza and Jeffrey DeShell published a collection of female writers with the goal, as

Mazza explained in a 2005 essay looking back on the origination of the term, of determining how "women's experiments with form and language were distinct from men's."[20]

They chose the title of *Chick-Lit: Postfeminist Fiction* as a sort of "sardonic joke," aiming "not to embrace an old, frivolous, or coquettish image of women," as "chick" implied, but to take responsibility for our part in the damaging, lingering stereotype. Put differently, they wanted to reclaim the pejorative of "chick" by pairing it with writing that challenged the understanding of what those "chicks" were like. A year later, James Wolcott used the term to describe Maureen Dowd's columns in *The New York Times*, but it wasn't until the enormous success of Helen Fielding's *Bridget Jones's Diary*, and a slew of similar novels that followed—including Melissa Bank's *The Girls' Guide to Hunting and Fishing*, Sophie Kinsella's *Confessions of a Shopaholic*, Candace Bushnell's *Sex and the City*, and Weiner's *Good in Bed*—that the term became au courant.[21]

It's not as if this type of novel hadn't existed before—it used to be referred to, especially in the British context, as the "shopping and fucking" novel. Its central tenets have been described in many ways, some vapid ("it's often about the quest of a young woman who's lost a bad boyfriend, or is looking for a good boyfriend, or maybe she's lost a lot of good boyfriends and has found a lot of bad boyfriends," as one female literary agent put it), others academic (exploring the "conflict between relishing one's independence vs. wanting a safety net or emotional security that a partner can provide").[22] But it was best described by the manager of a San Francisco bookstore: "It's like pornography: I can't define it, but I know it when I see it."[23]

Part of that sight recognition could be attributed to the way the books were marketed: the cover design was either in red, white, and black or in a wash of pastels, often featured the back of a woman (full body or just head), a beach, a shopping bag, and/or, as one reviewer put it, "toe cleavage." It was a clever marketing tool: a way for booksellers to readily signify what *kind* of read they were in for, if not the precise content. They weren't trash, but they also weren't quite Oprah's Book Club, either, even if many of the women who participated in a book club, Oprah's or otherwise, were the target audience.

Chick lit had become a genuine literary phenomenon, with sales in the millions. Still, it was roundly belittled and dismissed: even as publishing houses were creating new imprints to handle the demand, Booker Prize nominee Beryl Bainbridge called it "a froth sort of thing"; an anonymous chick lit editor argued that it "harms America"; a writer in *The New York Times* called it "the literary equivalent of a tract-house development."[24] These are the same elitist, reductive arguments employed by Macdonald, just tailored around the feminine contours of the twenty-first-century "women's novel."

This derision was crystallized in a collection appropriately titled *This Is Not Chick Lit*, which declared the genre an opiate to the masses: "Chick lit's formula numbs our senses," the collection's editor, Elizabeth Merrick, wrote. "Literature, by contrast, grants us access to countless new cultures, places, and inner lives. Where chick lit reduces the complexity of human experience, literature increases our awareness of other perspectives and paths. Literature employs carefully crafted language to expand our reality, instead of beating us over the head with cliches that promote narrow world views. Chick lit shuts down our consciousness. Literature expands our imaginations."[25]

By saying what it wasn't, the collection hoped to communicate what it *was*: namely, literature, or as the subtitle proclaimed, "Original Stories by America's Best Women Writers (No Heels Required)." The writing featured within, ranging from Chimamanda Ngozi Adichie to Jennifer Egan, may have been more diverse than the early (highly white, largely straight) manifestations of chick lit, but the authors also straddled the same position as Franzen: somewhere self-conscious and anxious between midcult and high culture.

Of course, few artists want to be associated with any genre that's denigrated in the popular cultural imagination, even if it makes them massive amounts of money. Which is why ambivalence is all over interviews with authors whose work had been ascribed the "chick lit" label: Elise Juska, author of *Getting Over Jack Wagner*, explained, "I wanted my book to be funny not fluffy, and I know that 'fluffy' can be the perception of Chick Lit."[26] Erica Jong disliked being written off as "nothing more than the contemporary version of the 'How to Get Married Novel.'"[27] Alison Jameson found that because her novel was marketed as chick lit, the press tour became an opportunity for interviewers to ask questions about her love life, and Plum Sykes, commenting on the term, explained, "I think a man might have invented it. I don't think girls would label themselves that way."[28]

Weiner was no different. She found the term "aggravating" and spoke openly about it in interviews and at speaking engagements.[29] "People use the term 'chick lit' to dismiss women writers," she said in 2005. "Any book with a young heroine dealing with a dysfunctional family, romantic issues or family trauma, any book with autobiographical components," gets designated as chick lit. "It's not fair. When Jonathan Safran Foer's first book came out, you know, it was about him, but I feel like the tone of pieces written about him was much more respectful, and much more, *oooh*, fancy writer. But when women's books come out, it's like, oh, you're not a real *writer*, you're just publishing your diary."[30]

Of course, Jhumpa Lahiri, Alice Munro, Marilynne Robinson, and Zadie Smith all write, in some capacity, about women's interior lives—and evade the chick lit label. But they're only able to do so by virtue of their awards and generous reviews. Which gets to the heart of Weiner's frustration: absent recognition by national awards organizations or review sections like *The New York Times*'s, there's no way for a woman, writing about women's lives, to unyoke herself from a classification as chick lit, mass culture, less-than, not literature.

The sales realities of the publishing industry offered some solace "The thing I try to tell myself is that readers do not care," Weiner admitted. "Ninety-nine percent of the people in a bookstore don't really know the term 'chick-lit'—or they think it's a [type of] gum."[31] But as her financial footing within the industry became more secure, she became increasingly explicit in decrying her classification. "The chick-lit label is sexist, dismissive, and comes with the built-in implication that what you've written is a piece of beach-trash fluff," she explained in 2009, "with as much heft and heart as a mouthful of pink-cotton candy that doesn't deal with anything other than boys and shoes."[32]

Ultimately, sales figures could not stave Weiner's quest for legitimation. She secretly harbored a desire "for a review in the paper I'd read for my entire life, the *New York Times*." "The *Times* is the holy grail for most writers," she explains in 2016's memoir

Hungry Heart. "Being reviewed in the paper means you've really, truly made it—or, at least that's how it felt to me." But *The New York Times* book critics "mostly ignored popular fiction and stuck to capital-L literature . . . Unless they were reviewing the popular fiction that men read."[33] No matter that the *Times*'s "music critics wrote about opera and Top 40; TV critics covered sitcoms as well as PBS's twelve-part series on slavery; restaurant critics reviewed Per Se, and the under-twenty-five-dollar-a-head ethnic eateries in the boroughs." When it came to culture, the paper of record covered mass, mid, and high culture. Except, to Weiner's great annoyance, in books—where the only mass-culture fare was the likes of John Grisham.

For Weiner, *The New York Times Book Review* crystallized all the most offensive, antiquated, and fundamentally sexist attitudes toward chick lit. Which is why, when Franzen's next book, *Freedom*, was released in 2011—and the *Times* reviewed it twice and *Time* put Franzen on the cover with the caption "Great American Novelist," she went *in*. The catalyst came in the form of a tweet from Jodi Picoult, whose books might not be considered strictly under the rubric of "chick lit," but who was definitely commercial and outside the then-coverage of the *Times Book Review*.

"Is anyone shocked?" Picoult tweeted. "Would love to see the NYT rave about authors who aren't male literary darlings." Weiner's addition was a variation on the idea she'd been articulating for years—"When a man writes about family and feelings, it's literature with a capital L, but when a woman considers the same subjects, it's romance, or a beach book."

When the *Times*'s Lizzie Skurnick called Weiner to ask her what to name this dissatisfaction with the adulation afforded

Franzen and other white male literary darlings, she replied, "Franzenfreude," and a hashtag was born. It was a particularly midcult thing to do: "schadenfreude," like so many non-English nouns incorporated into the vernacular of the college-educated, is one of those words we use to telegraph our intelligence and sophistication. Weiner was decrying Franzen's elitism, while also being careful to refine her own elevation within the hierarchy. And yet: "schadenfreude" describes taking joy (*freude*) in others' misfortune (*schaden*). Weiner's off-the-cuff amalgam didn't, as she intended, suggest anger at Franzen's fortune, but rather, taking joy in Franzen.

Franzen, coincidentally, is fluent in German. But the vast majority of people who contributed to the hashtag never cared nor commented: to criticize the German of someone's hashtag is precisely the sort of elitism they were rallying against. That support ballooned after Weiner and Picoult outlined their grievances at length, which ultimately had less to do with Franzen and more to do with the coverage of "commercial" books written by women. As Weiner told *The Huffington Post*, "Do I think I should be getting all the attention that Jonathan 'Genius' Franzen gets? Nope. Would I like to be taken at least as seriously as a Jonathan Tropper or a Nick Hornby? Absolutely."[34]

In a different era, Weiner's and Picoult's observations may have drawn attention, but would've likely failed to gain traction. Weiner, however, refused to stop talking about it—especially after *Slate*'s *DoubleX* blog published a study showing just how skewed the *The New York Times Book Review*'s coverage had been over the previous two years: 545 fiction books were reviewed in the *Times* between June 2008 and August 2010, and only 38 percent of those fiction books had been written by women. Of the 101 books that had received *two* reviews (one in the weekly *Times*, another in the Sunday *Book Review*), 29 percent were written by women.[35]

Soon after, an organization called VIDA started surveying both the content of literary-oriented magazines *and* the books reviewed, further underlining the gender imbalance within the literary world: over the course of 2010, *The New Yorker*, for example, published 449 short stories and articles written by men, but only 163 written by women.[36] And the percentages only got worse the more highbrow you went: in *The New York Review of Books*, a venerated bimonthly not to be confused with *The New York Times Book Review*, 88 percent of its articles were written by men. This wasn't just a bunch of bitter women making noise on Twitter. The problem was real, the evidence irrefutable.

Weiner's initial complaint was the treatment of her genre, but her argument began to point toward a greater problem within culture at large—one in which the thoughts of men, either in the books they write or in the articles they write about other ideas or books, take precedence over the ideas of women. But Weiner wasn't satisfied with simple visibility. Through Twitter and her blog, she drew attention to the small ways that books like hers continued to receive sexist treatment: when Pulitzer Prize winner Jennifer Egan said her advice to young female writers "would be to shoot high and not cower" instead of modeling their work after "very derivative, banal stuff"; when Meg Wolitzer decried a "disturbing trend" of "fiction about and by women who the reader is meant to feel 'comfortable' around—what I call slumber party fiction—as though the characters are stand-ins for your best friends"; when Lena Dunham declared she doesn't "have a taste for airport chick lit, even in a guilty pleasure way" or "any book that is motored by the search for a husband and/or good pair of heels."[37]

Weiner oscillated between petty and measured in her critiques, calling Egan out for her "chummy NYT podcasts" and averring that *A Visit from the Goon Squad* wasn't "any fun." But after Egan apologized for the wording of her remarks, Weiner emphasized, "I don't want to turn this into a big thing between me and Egan. Of course, women writers can have opinions, of course they can talk about what they like and don't like. But there's a time and a place for that critique. I had a hard time finding a male author who took the occasion of 'I have won a big prize and I'm going to take this platform to talk about work I don't like.' What if Philip Roth won a prize and said 'Suck it, James Patterson?'"[38]

Still, Weiner was criticized for her aggressiveness—and her refusal to let the issue die. While *The Wall Street Journal* called her the "conscience" of modern fiction, an article in *The Daily Dot* declared she'd become known for her "feuds," which the *Daily Telegraph* called "feisty social-media spats."[39] She was "strident"; her complaints may have been "so urgent to women writers," yet felt "so tedious to male editors and pundits." In *Salon*, Daniel D'Addario compiled a list of her adversaries, claiming that her recent issues with Claire Messud weren't "the first time that Weiner has cannily tilted a conversation on its axis to ensure her issues—and sometimes her books—are the center of a debate."[40] A piece in *Philadelphia* magazine, written by another chick lit author, simply declared, "Jennifer Weiner, Shut Up."[41] Even her fans were fatigued: in *The Week*, an article headlined "I Love Jennifer Weiner, but She Needs to Back Off" denounced Weiner's attack on other women as "going over the line."[42]

Weiner had admitted her own attacks sometimes went over the top: "Everyone wants to believe he or she is the hero of his or her own story," she wrote in a 2013 essay on *Salon*. "I'm no exception. I never thought I was being obnoxious or pushy or shrill—just determined, and fighting for something that mattered. . . . Were there things I could have said more thoughtfully, times I should have waited (and checked my German) before hitting the 'publish tweet' button, unnecessarily caustic comments I made about other books and other writers? Yes."[43]

But she also pointed to the reason she'd become the locus of attack: "If you don't want the status quo to change—if you are an agent or an editor or an author who's been well served by the paper covering what it covers—it's easier to attack the person pushing for change than it is to refute her argument . . . And I gave the status quo'ers a big, juicy target."[44]

❖ ❖ ❖

In 2013, Franzen reemerged from his literary writing cave to promote a collection of essays, written by early twentieth-century Austrian intellectual Karl Kraus, that he'd helped to translate, edit, and annotate. He wasn't peeved that Weiner had accomplished the goals of her campaign. Rather, he was annoyed with *how* she'd gone about it. An excerpt, titled "What's Wrong with the Modern World," explored the work of the writer and thinker at length, and took an explicit dig at "Jennifer Weiner–ish self-promotion," condemning a vision of the artistic world in which "the work of yakkers and tweeters and braggers, and of people with the money to pay somebody to churn out hundreds of five-star reviews for them," will flourish. He questions: "But what happens to the people who became writers *because* yakking and tweeting and bragging felt to them like intolerably shallow forms of social engagement?"[45]

Naturally, Weiner penned a response—"What Jonathan Franzen Misunderstands About Me"—pointing to the long lineage of writers who've preferred "yakking and bragging to quiet and permanence," including Oscar Wilde and Truman Capote, and the hypocrisy of making those claims in an excerpt to promote his own work. "From his privileged perch," she writes, "he can pick and choose, deciding which British newspaper gets the honor of running his 5600-word condemnation of self-promotion that ends with an unironic hyperlinked invitation to buy his new book."

This skirmish, like Weiner's criticism of Franzen's *Times* coverage, was again rooted in gendered issues of taste culture. In his essay, Franzen advocates for the sort of solitary self-contemplation that has long been the provenance not just of the wealthy, but of men in particular. To retreat with your own thoughts and words is a privilege that few women, no matter their class, can afford—even if, like Weiner, they're paid millions for their books.[46]

Franzen's understanding of the ideal author is also rooted in the century-old model of authorship put forth by Kraus and his fellow European intellectuals: that the work was not for financial gain, but pure and exalted triumph of the mind, and thus should not be tainted by concerns of capital. To be worried about financial success, or readership numbers, is to declare yourself midcult, if not worse. But women's relation to writing has long been shaped by different forces: for many, if not most, part of the joy of writing was how its profits enabled, and continue to enable, women to determine their own destiny—untethered to a man.

Writing, in other words, as a form of metaphorical and financial independence.

Women's writing first became accessible through the novel, but it took the Internet to make it ubiquitous: message boards, blogs, and social media have amplified the capacity for "yakking" (a way of speaking generally attributed to women) and "bragging" (something women are admonished for doing). Weiner, who's been blogging since before most people knew what the word meant, has long understood the Internet's potential—both for someone like her and for her readers. Instead of a top-down power structure, it's far more democratic: a conversation, not a lecture. As Beth Driscoll points out, "For Franzen, mass media is a kind of noise that interferes with legitimate literary practices. It is also a mechanism for the dilution of literary quality." He's nostalgic for "the days when cultural gatekeeping occurred out of sight, away from the public forums of the internet and Twitter."[47] The hierarchy Franzen desires is maintained largely because of its exclusion of people like Weiner and her readers: of *course* he'd think Twitter, and the amplification of Weiner's arguments about taste culture, was "intolerably shallow."

For Weiner, Twitter has become a place where she talks to readers to "remind them of my existence between books—a common hustle for a commercial female author who can't count on the *New York Times* to do that job."[48] It's also where she's cultivated a massive following live-tweeting *The Bachelor*, which, as she writes in *Hungry Heart*, she sees as a way to "love and hate the show at the same time, to be entertained by its boy-meets-crowd-of-girls, boy-culls-crowd-of-girls, girls-get-dumped-and-cry, while also recognizing and shining a disinfecting light on its narrow beauty standards, its relentless heteronormativity, its frustrating lack of diversity, what it says about desire versus the performance of desire; about true love and, with ever-recurring declarations about 'journeys' and 'fairy tales,' the propagation of old, punitive myths about how happy endings work and who deserves to get them."[49] Put differently, Weiner derives cutting cultural analysis from the seemingly insignificant and feminized products of pop culture—analysis available to hundreds of thousands of women who might not otherwise seek it out.

Twitter is also where she objected to the sexism of *New York Times* interviewer Andrew Goldman questioning Tippi Hedren on whether she'd relied on the "casting couch" to get ahead, and called out Goldman's suggestion that she was just bitter that she hadn't had the opportunity to do so herself—an insult that contributed to his eventual dismissal from the *Times*. It's where she vocalized her support and experience with Planned Parenthood, and helped position the shaming of readers of YA and *Fifty Shades* within a long history of denigrating books not written by men or produced with men in mind. Weiner herself admits there are tweets she wishes she could delete, soften, or modify: ones that went too far, where she said too much. But that's the hallmark of unruliness: by surpassing the boundaries of respectability, she was able to yak and tweet and brag loud enough, about topics and ideas in which women have a real stake, for others to hear it.

In the end, all Weiner's kvetching, along with pressure from other men and women in- and outside of literary structures, somehow worked. In April 2013, the *Times Book Review* hired a female editor in chief, and launched a section that would regularly feature roundups and commentary by and on commercial writers—including women. A literary author—Rebecca Mead—profiled Weiner for *The New Yorker*. Weiner herself started writing a regular column for the *Times*. Not in the book review, but in opinion, where her commentary ranges from "When Can Women Stop Trying to Look Perfect?" to "Miss America, My Guilty Pleasure."

The loud, nerdy girl had, in a way, won—or at least demonstrated that change was possible, even if more was needed. After a March 2016 piece about commercial fiction featured only three female authors (out of fifteen discussed), Weiner penned a letter to the editor: "It may be true, as Rivka Galchen writes, that commercial books are like Doritos—delicious and disposable and, in the end, unimproving. But as long as publications continue to pay more attention to commercial fiction by men, some Doritos will always be more equal than others."[50]

✦ ✦ ✦

In a column from June 2016, Weiner discusses her insecurity about attending her Princeton reunion—Princeton, after all, was home to Jeffrey Eugenides, who'd complained that he didn't know what Picoult was "bellyaching" about, and the alma mater of a *Huffington Post* critic who'd compared popular fiction to Hot Pockets. But after attending the reunion, and feeling none of the elitism or snobbery she'd expected, Weiner admitted that she might be mapping her own insecurity onto others: "The overall pleasant evening has led me to the painful realization that I've spent 15 years insisting that books like mine deserve a place on the shelf, and maybe I don't entirely believe it myself. Why else was I so willing to give credence to the naysayers and have trouble hearing the readers who said my books gave them comfort, kept them entertained, made them feel less alone?"[51]

Weiner has confronted the dismissal of her work and its importance for so long, from such respected arbiters of pop culture—it's only natural she had internalized it. It took more than a decade of bestsellers, and an unmitigated willingness to fight against those who would disparage them, for Weiner to actually experience the acceptance, cultural or otherwise, for which she'd fought so arduously. It's one thing to argue that you belong—it's another thing to actually believe it. As Weiner's experience makes clear, part of the difficult, essential work of unruliness is shaking the status quo so thoroughly, so persistently, so loudly that everyone—even the very women behind that agitation, many of whom have internalized the understandings they fight so tirelessly against—can see their value within it.

CHAPTER 10

TOO NAKED: LENA DUNHAM

No matter where you first saw Lena Dunham, chances are she or her body was acting out. By posting photos to social media that are unflattering and bizarre; by wearing clothes that purposefully don't fit her; by writing frankly about her sexual assault; by writing and playing characters who have unfortunate sex in public places. When others have criticized Dunham—for a lack of diversity on her show, for her privilege, for her too-tight clothes and too-off-color humor—she's responded not with silence, but with more talk. She's the Internet's favorite punching bag, and she's amassed a veritable army of trolls commenting upon her every move as a result. *New Yorker* television critic Emily Nussbaum calls her "our era's op-ed magnet."[1] She can seemingly do no right, and yet she's one of the most powerful young women working in Hollywood today.

The magnitude and strength of reactions to Dunham are prompted by a cluster of intersecting unruly behaviors, but it's her willingness to take off her clothes that inflames people the most. There's an entire blog devoted simply to the idea of *Put Your Clothes On, Lena Dunham.* An article dedicated to "14 Tatted, Topless & Unapologetic Pics of Lena Dunham Naked" positions her "the queen of nudity." Howard Stern said, "It's a little fat girl who kinda looks like Jonah Hill and she keeps taking her clothes off and it kind of feels like rape. . . . I don't want to see that." Joan Rivers declared, "You are sending a message out to people saying 'It's okay! Stay fat! Get diabetes! Everybody die!'" At the end of 2013, *The Atlantic* published a list of "Ideas That Have Outlived Their Usefulness" that included "Zombies," "Brooklyn," and "Lena Dunham, naked, on your TV screen."[2]

The impulse behind these statements is the same: Dunham's unclothed body is not what we typically see represented for our viewing pleasure. Instead, it's a way to communicate character—and illuminate our unspoken understanding of which bodies are allowed to be naked in front of others and which ones should remain clothed.

But the underlying reason Dunham's body has become so inflammatory is that it's not nude—it's naked. That might sound like semantics, but the words have precise connotations. The naked body is raw, without pretense, bare; the nude is nakedness refined: smoothed, proportional, pleasing. The naked body *becomes* nude as it's filtered through the eye of the artist—an eye that, for the history of Western culture, has almost always been male. In addition to controlling the way her body is filmed, Dunham also refuses to heed the ideological imperatives of slimness, which compels shame for anyone whose body isn't toned or otherwise tightly regimented. Dunham becomes "too naked," then, when she refuses to turn herself into a nude, insisting on showcasing her body exactly as it appears.

As the director of her own nakedness, Dunham has helped create a different aesthetic of the unclothed body in popular culture, asserting that women's bodies are worthy even when they are not arranged, distorted, or otherwise represented through and for the gaze of men. Yet the sheer ferocity of emotions that have accumulated around Dunham and her work make it abundantly clear: few things enrage, confuse, and repulse audiences more than the suggestion that the primary visual purpose of a woman's body is not the pleasure of men.

+ + +

The word "naked" comes from the Anglo-Saxon family tree of the English language. "Nude" comes from the French side. Today, the terms are often used interchangeably—but as art historian Kenneth Clark famously explained in 1954, the naked body is "no more than a point of departure for the nude." People *say* that the naked body is one of the most naturally beautiful things in the world, but that's not actually true: Clark argues that unlike a tiger, or a snowy landscape, which becomes art simply by being depicted as faithfully as possible, nakedness "does not move us to empathy, but to disillusion and dismay." Nakedness, in other words, is ugly: "We are immediately disturbed by wrinkles, pouches, and other small imperfections," Clark declared. Which is why the artist does not "wish to imitate" the naked figure, but to "perfect" it.[3]

Think of the smooth marble of the sculpted nude, or the supple roundness of the Venus de Milo: those proportions might not be the same ones exalted today, but to viewers of the time, the flesh, like the body itself, was perfect. A portrait can thus be judged by its adherence to the ideals of proportion: its skill in transforming the naked body into a creation that's pleasing to the eye. Clark contrasts the Venus de Milo's proportions with those of Hans Memling's painting of Adam and Eve, dated to 1485. In it, Eve is presented with an elongated belly and small breasts: "the basic pattern of the female body is still an oval, surmounted by two spheres, but here the oval has grown incredibly long, the spheres distressingly small." It's a description that could readily apply to photos of Dunham, whose stomach is often referred to, even by herself, as a "potbelly"; her breasts "small-ish." In their negligence of "proper" proportionality, both the painting of Eve and a picture of Dunham "fail" as nudes.[4] They're just naked—and, as such, shameful.

In *Carnal Knowing*, religious scholar Margaret R. Miles traces the evolution of the representation of the female nude in Western art, noting that the moment that the naked body was "re-formed" and perfected was also the moment it ceased to express anything unique.[5] Or, as art critic John Berger puts it, "To be naked is to be oneself. To be nude is to be seen by others and not recognized for oneself."[6] The process of representation is from subject to object—and, nearly without exception, through the brush, hands, or eyes of men.

The nude was all over the Christian art tradition, from depictions of the Virgin Mary to those of Mary Magdalene. These nudes were replete with symbolism—meaningful, beautiful, didactic, commonplace, moral. The American understanding of nudity was and remains highly influenced by Puritan ideology, which conceived of exposed flesh as the gateway to sin. This was especially visible in the rhetoric of the Hays Code, drafted in 1930 by Will H.

Hays and several film studio heads as a means of circumventing censorship on the part of the national government. If the studios censored themselves, the understanding went, they could keep the government (which might also start looking into their monopolistic business practices) at a distance. The Hays Code issued thirteen "Don'ts" (including bans on profanity and the depiction of drug trafficking) and thirty-one "Be Carefuls," demanding caution in the depiction of marriage, the flag, "first night scenes," sedition, sympathy for criminals, and more.

The Code is generally recognized as a means of curbing depictions of violence and suggestions of sex, but almost all of its prohibitions were related to bolstering white, straight, American patriarchy increasingly under threat. For the first few years of its existence, the code was largely for show, but as fears of boycotts grew in the early 1930s, the code's "Don'ts and Be Carefuls" list, enforced by William Hays and his deputy, Joseph Breen, effectively became the moral guidelines of the moving image.[7]

Take the Code's opinion on nudity, the dire effect of which, even in "semi-nudity" form, "has been honestly recognized by all lawmakers and moralists." "The nude or semi-nude body may be beautiful," the Code averred, but that "does not make its use in the films moral." The nude body's intrinsic immorality sprang from its effect on "immature" audiences, but also from its endorsement of behaviors that occasioned a female character taking off her clothes; that is, exercising or taking control of her own sexuality.[8]

The prohibitions of the Code were gradually loosened in the 1950s and '60s, disassembled by joint pressure from the Supreme Court, which ruled against the direct censoring of films in 1952, and the studios themselves, which were struggling to attract audiences as their customers moved to the suburbs and, increasingly, stayed home with the comforts of television. As a result, explicit, "adult" content (very, very slowly) began showing up on-screen: in 1963, Jayne Mansfield appeared nude, with pubic area carefully out of sight, in *Promises! Promises!*; since then, simulated sex and nude breasts have become a near-standard feature of R-rated cinema.

Which doesn't change the fact that for nearly half a century, representing the nude body was an act of immorality. That understanding has been gradually softened, but only to a certain extent, and with far more leniency when it comes to the depiction of *female* nudity. There are certainly mainstream films in which a woman's undress contributes to the narrative, yet in general, nudity functions, like a car crash or a musical montage, as spectacle. Alternately, nudeness could underline dependency or some other weakness. In the torture porn genre of the 2000s (*Turistas*, *Hostel*, etc.), semi-nudity was mixed with actual violence against women, underscoring their ultimate vulnerability. If a female character had demonstrated power or independence, a nude scene was a subtle way to render her passive: a means for the subject to be reminded of her status as secondary, superfluous object.

Because network television is broadcast over airwaves owned by the American government, it is also subject to regulation by the government through the Federal Communications Commission, or FCC. Like other regulatory and/or censoring organizations, the FCC gets to decide what's obscene and what's not—a slippery and highly subjective definition. Back in the 1960s, you couldn't say "tits" or show Jeannie's belly button on *I Dream of*

Jeannie; today, you can show partial nudity so long as it's after 10:00 P.M. With time, other restrictions have loosened: from 2005 to 2010, the use of expletives (not "fuck," but words like "ass," "boobs," "butt," "douche," "balls") went up 69 percent.

Still, there are limitations, even in basic and extended cable, on what a program can show, suggest, or say—limitations from which some showrunners cower. The general understanding is that putting limits on content also limits artistic and narrative expression. Take away those limits, and the content becomes more realistic, freer, *better*. It's one of the ways that HBO, whose status as "premium cable" exempts the channel from FCC regulations, has cultivated its reputation as "quality television." For much of HBO's early existence, that freedom was generally used to produce titillating late-night fare like *Real Sex* and *Taxicab Confessions*. It wasn't until the launch of *The Sopranos*, *Sex and the City*, and *Oz* in the late 1990s—what is generally regarded as the beginning of "the third golden age of television"—that the liberty to show boobs and butts on-screen became integral to the understanding of narrative excellence.

In many of HBO's most significant, expensive, celebrated, and long-running shows—*The Sopranos*, *Rome*, *Deadwood*, *Boardwalk Empire*, and *Game of Thrones*—female nudity has been deployed in two overarching ways: first, as a form of "sexposition," in which women's bodies are employed as backdrop for a scene in which characters discuss or otherwise telegraph the goings-on of the plot (see especially: *Game of Thrones*); second, as victims of violence, sexual or physical or both. Both of these uses point to women's primary value as objects, decorative or disposable.[9]

Sex and the City, *Looking*, even *True Blood* deploy nudity to different ends—including male nudity—but it's generally that: nudity, not nakedness. The bodies are beautiful and unclothed exclusively during or leading up to a sex act. There's nakedness in *Six Feet Under*, but often only for those who've already died; other shows, including *Treme* and *Getting On*, have a more nuanced approach to nudity, but their audiences were several million in magnitude below the masculine powerhouses that have made HBO one of the most profitable enterprises on television.

Which is all to say that on the standard bearer in terms of "quality" television—a channel run almost entirely by men, its most popular shows conceived and produced, down to the person, by men—the dominant understanding of an unclothed body is that of *nude* beauty. Depictions are almost always female, almost always perfected, and almost always deployed in sexual or violent ways.

That was the paradigm into which *Girls* premiered in the fall of 2010. For Dunham, nakedness was nothing new. As she describes in her memoir, *Not That Kind Of Girl*, she'd always been interested in the rules for who gets to get naked: when she realized, as an elementary-schooler, that her male friend got to take his shirt off while they biked around in the woods, she took hers off, too. When she got to Oberlin, she used her naked body as "a tool to tell a story. . . . Pressed for actors who embodied the spirit of sexual despair I was looking to cultivate," she writes, "I cast myself."[10]

In the most famous video of Dunham from that time, she isn't actually naked, but nearly so: in "The Fountain," Dunham wears a bikini as she brushes her teeth and goes through other daily ablutions in a massive campus water fountain. As in all of Dunham's unclothed appearances, it is done without shame. "There were just pages of YouTube comments about how fat I was, or how not fat I was," she recalled. She removed the video because she didn't want her first Google result to be "a debate about whether my breasts are misshapen," but it was the first of a number of productions that engage in the debate that, as Dunham explains, interested her the most: "Who got to be naked, and why?"[11]

In her feature film *Tiny Furniture* and the six seasons of *Girls* that would follow, Dunham's body was not nude, but often naked. The difference was both Dunham's *type* of body and what she did with it. As Rebecca Mead put it in a 2010 profile for *The New Yorker*, Dunham "does not have the body of a Girl Gone Wild." She has "pale, ample thighs and a generous belly; greenish tattoos spiderweb her arms and back."[12] She is disproportional; imperfect; unsmooth—her body, represented on-screen, a "failed" piece of art.

That "failure" largely derives from her refusal to reduce, shape, and otherwise tone her body to look like others on-screen. In the indispensable *Unbearable Weight: Feminism, Western Culture, and the Body*, Susan Bordo lays out the ways in which the imperative toward slimness became a guiding force of Western culture. It wasn't until the late nineteeth century that "those who could afford to eat well began systematically to deny themselves food in pursuit of an aesthetic ideal." While fasting had been employed, within religious contexts, for centuries, it was always in terms of regimenting the desires of the soul, not attempting to modify the body. But for the middle class of the late nineteenth century, "fat, not appetite or desires became the declared enemy."[13]

While some of the middle class used their growing bellies as a gauche means of demonstrating their wealth, that practice went out of fashion by the turn of the twentieth century, as the effortlessly slim body came to signify status: gaining weight to signify status became something only the tacky bourgeois did. Effortless slimness says, "I have no desires, not even food"—and that's the height of power. Satisfaction and satiation thus became the aspirational ideal for the middle class. "Social power had come to be less dependent on the sheer accumulation of material wealth," Bordo writes, "and more connected to the ability to control and manage the labor and resources of others."[14]

This ideal was internalized most powerfully by women, whose presence and appearance remained a means for their husbands or fathers to demonstrate their wealth and class. Combine that imperative with the ingrained understanding of women's duty in life to nurture and feed and care for others, and you have a heady ideological mix of self-control and self-surveillance. As Bordo explains, "the control of female appetite for food is merely the most concrete expression of the general rule governing the construction of femininity: that female hunger—for public power, for independence, for sexual gratification—be contained, and the public space that women be allowed to take up be circumscribed, limited." Put differently, hunger has become the antithesis of "good" femininity: to eat, to desire, to be unsatisfied is to be a "bad woman." The most vivid manifestation of that badness, that *unruliness*, is fat on one's body, implying a lack of control, a lack of respect toward social mores.

But Dunham is not *fat*—a few sizes up from the *Girls Gone Wild* body, sure, but not *fat*, at least not in the way ascribed to Melissa McCarthy. The objection to her body has something to do with those ten to fifteen pounds, but even more with their distribution. As Bordo demonstrates, the obsession, approximately since the 1980s, has less to do with the *size* of the body so much as its tautness. For much of the twentieth century, the hook of weight-loss advertisements was the ability to get rid of excess weight: to "reduce." Yet over the past thirty years, the rhetoric has shifted to eliminating "bulge, fat, or flab."[15]

Today, we see that attitude manifest in the obsession with Michelle Obama arms, the Beyoncé butt; it's the impulse behind the waist trainer and the smoothing lines of Spanx. It has far less to do with actually losing weight and far more to do with the quest for what Bordo calls "firm bodily margins." Such successfully "normalized" bodies can vary somewhat in the size of the ass, the legs, or the breasts, but their beauty is rooted in their discipline, through either exercise or surgery.

The toned body, after all, requires even more work than the skinny one: it's about constant self-improvement. And while women can and do take real enjoyment from the act of exercise, the maintenance of that body requires an incredible amount of time and labor—psychological and physical. It is, as Bordo puts it, "an amazingly durable and flexible strategy of social control."[16]

Women can consider themselves free, feminist, and liberated in so many ways—yet still be controlled by the notion of an ideal body of which their own continually falls short.

An untoned body, by this logic, indicates a woman who is either a failure—unable to discipline herself thoroughly—or someone who flaunts that imperative entirely, without a regard for the standards that dictate goodness or wellness. For her willingness to put her "imperfect," untoned body on-screen, not obscured with lighting or touched up in postproduction, Dunham falls squarely in the second camp.

The dedication to imperfection begins when Dunham's character, Hannah, is clothed: her body always seems to be overfilling her wardrobe, testing its boundaries, willfully neglecting the imperative toward smoothness. As *Girls* costume designer Jennifer Rogien explains, they were assiduous in cultivating a look that would highlight just how unruly and uncompliant Hannah's body was. They deliberately tailored clothes to make her look worse; if an outfit had a belt that would highlight her waist, they threw it out.[17]

It was, as Rogien put it, "all part of our efforts to make Hannah look like she didn't have it together," a "together"-ness that extended to control of her body.[18] Unlike those of Marnie or Shoshanna, whose bodies are exemplars of the toned, slender imperative, and who select clothes to flatter them, Hannah's clothes were fitted with Spanx, then worn without them: the imperfect flesh visible not through nakedness, but through the resistance to the clothes that attempt and fail to cover it.

This understanding of the naked body is only possible because of Dunham's overarching control of *Girls*. The show is executive produced by Judd Apatow (whose name and power helped procure HBO funding), and Dunham regularly cedes directorial control to others. Yet the vision of the show, and how Hannah's body will be clothed and filmed, can safely be attributed to her. It's why she was able to cast herself in the lead role when women with her look, verve, and body usually get cast as sidekicks; it's how she's able to persist in her project, as a college boyfriend put it in one of her early short films, of being "naked in front of people who don't really want to see you naked."[19]

222

✦ ✦ ✦

Dunham does more than just get naked: she gets naked in markedly public spaces. In one of the most notable episodes of *Girls*'s second season, Hannah trades shirts with a guy in the middle of a dance floor. She wears his yellow mesh top, which displays her braless breasts, as she roams the city for the rest of the night. Much was made about the "believability" of a woman's near-nakedness in and around a SoHo club: "As much coked out–ness as I've been around in my years in NYC, I've never witnessed this," one recapper explained. "This is a Hannah-specific situation. That she continues to feel like the sexiest person is believable because of the coke."[20]

But that's the point: the audience sees Hannah's breasts as the world sees Hannah's breasts: imperfect, inappropriate, unsexy. But Hannah, especially Hannah-on-coke, doesn't see her body the way the world does: to her, the mesh shirt and her loose breasts are deliciously sexy; her look could not be more perfect; she conceives of herself as an immaculate nude for all to gaze upon. The reason the episode angered, frustrated, or flabbergasted audiences, then, was because they couldn't see Hannah the way she saw herself. Why should she be this naked, the refrain went—what purpose does it serve? A clear one: the disconnect between the way others view Hannah and the way Hannah views herself is, in many ways, the driving narrative of the show.

The same principle applies to a now infamous scene of Hannah eating a cupcake in the tub with Marnie: *Who would bathe with their friend in the same room?* viewers of the pilot episode of *Girls* questioned (answer: best friends who share one bathroom); *Who would eat a cupcake, for breakfast, in the shower?* they asked (someone with a complicated relationship to her body and controlling it).

Consider the scene before: when Marnie's boyfriend, Charlie, exclaims that Hannah and Marnie looked like "angels" cuddled together in bed, Hannah replies, "Victoria's Secret angel," as she points to Marnie, then "Fat baby angel" as she points to herself. Charlie responds, "No way, you look awesome these days!" to which Hannah, pulling the cupcake from the fridge, says, "Please avert your eyes." In the bathroom, Hannah sits inside the tub, her upper torso leaning over the side so as to better eat her cupcake, while Marnie, perched on the side, shaves her legs. Their exchange is telling:

> HANNAH: Are you gonna leave your towel on? You know I never see you naked and you always see me naked and it should actually be the other way around.
> MARNIE: You are beautiful, shut up.
> HANNAH: I don't need that, I need to see your boobs.
> MARNIE: You don't get to, I'm sorry. I only show my boobs to people I'm having sex with.
> HANNAH: You literally slept in my bed to avoid [sex with Charlie].

The scene accomplishes a tremendous amount of character work, crystallizing each woman's attitude toward nakedness and, by extension, intimacy. Hannah conceives of herself as the "fat baby angel," and knows that she "should" be ashamed of eating a cupcake, in the tub, for breakfast ("Please avert your eyes"). She also understands nakedness as a privilege that shouldn't be allotted to her: looking at the outline of Marnie's slender legs, she understands that "it should be the other way around." When she says "I need to see your boobs," however, it's also a plea for intimacy: she wants Marnie to be as vulnerable to her as she is to Marnie. But Marnie reserves that "privilege"—to see her perfected self—for men who desire her sexually. She only wants to be nude—viewed through the prism of heterosexual desire—not naked.

It's a clear portrait of Marnie's conformist tendencies, and how she conceives of the value of her body in relationship to men—even if, as the subsequent conversation makes clear, she doesn't desire them in return. Hannah, by contrast, is hungry: for the cupcake in front of her, for intimacy. She both knows she should be ashamed of that hunger—she has internalized that, in some capacity, like all women—but she acts upon it anyway. It's why Hannah's in the bathtub and Marnie's perched above her, shaving her legs and, by extension, performing the labor of compulsory femininity. The blocking provides an unsubtle suggestion of which woman (and body) has more power and worth: "What does it feel like to be loved that much?" Hannah asks.

The scene isn't played for laughs, but for the tease of abjection. As with so many instances of nakedness in *Girls*, Dunham is essentially daring the audience to find it gross—and then examine that reaction. How would the scene be viewed differently if the positions were switched? Could Marnie eat a cupcake for breakfast because her body suggests she's otherwise skilled at self-denial and regimentation? And if this nakedness, so effective in its construction of character, is "unnecessary," what kind of nakedness *is* necessary?

Even when Hannah gets naked in scenarios that demand it—say, during sex—it remains objectionable. Take "Another Man's Trash": the episode, halfway through season two, that incited the most heated debate of the series to date. Most of the ire centered on whether or not it was plausible that Hannah would spend two hazy sex-filled days in the brownstone of a handsome older doctor played by Patrick Wilson.

Even before she gets naked in the episode, Hannah flaunts her body in public: she's wearing an ill-fitted romper with a cutout where her stomach pokes through; as she climbs the steps of Joshua's brownstone, the camera shows the fabric of the romper riding up the back of her thighs, exposing slightly dimpled flesh. She's been dumping the trash from the coffee shop where she works in Joshua's garbage can—first out of necessity, and then because she liked the feel of it—and after confessing as much, she moves to kiss him, which leads to sex, which leads to two days together before the haze of desire fades and they disappear from each other's lives.

In the time in between, the camera seems to deliberately present moments that Joshua—and, by extension, the audience—should find objectionable: Hannah's stomach pouring over the waistband of her romper as she attempts to put it back on; Hannah awkwardly playing Ping-Pong dressed only in a pair of boy shorts, intercut with images of Joshua's tanned, smooth, muscled torso and, momentarily, a shot of them having sex on the Ping-Pong table. The narrative also resists any opportunity to shift its register to pity: Hannah makes Joshua clearly articulate his desire for her to stay, then requires that he make her come first. She claims a position of power not usually afforded her, and is thrilled when his actions affirm it.

The nakedness of the Ping-Pong game can be read as a reflection of the rapidness of their intimacy. But it also provokes the viewer, in a way a completely clothed, or strategically, artfully nude scene between the two actors could not—in part because we've been so thoroughly conditioned to react to a pairing like Hannah and Joshua with confusion and disgust. Which is why some critics argued that the episode was actually just *a dream*: no matter that the series hasn't engaged in anything close to magical realism; there has to be *some* narrative explanation for this pairing.

Joshua's emotional fragility, post-separation from his wife, is explanation enough for why he'd want someone to colonize his life for two days. But the real reason for the pairing is far simpler: they each desired the other. And by preserving Dunham's body in its naked form, Dunham uncouples the notion of desirability from its perfected nude representation.

For Dunham, the outlines of desire are endlessly mutable and dynamic—and, as a result, have far less legislating control over women's bodies. And that idea—even more than the radical notion that a man who looks like a Ken doll wouldn't desire his female equivalent—is truly discombobulating. Imagine the liberation: in stead of spending time degrading ourselves for falling short of the very narrow understanding of what types of bodies are worthy of desire—and, by extension, value—we could be thinking about things that make us feel good, or anything at all, really, that isn't rooted in shame at how our bodies don't look like someone else's.

✦ ✦ ✦

In *Not That Kind of Girl*, Dunham recalls a series of naked selfies her mother, Laurie Simmons, started taking in the 1970s. "My mother is slim," Dunham writes. "A long torso, loose arms, and a collarbone sheer as a rock face. But the camera clung to her imperfections—the ripple of fat below her butt, the sharp knob of her knee, the massive birthmark on her forearm that she had

227

removed as a fortieth-birthday present to herself. I think of her developing these images, sloshing them around in the photo solution with a pair of salad tongs. Waiting, as they blushed gray, then appeared in full contrast, to see what she really looked like."[21]

These images presented what Dunham's mother "really looked like" not because the camera is a tool of realism, but because they were taken by Simmons herself. "My mother understood, implicitly, the power of it. See these hips, these teeth, these eyebrows, these stockings that bunch and sag at the ankles? They're worth capturing, holding on to forever. I'll never be this young again. Or this lonely. Or this hairy. Come one, come all, to my private show."[22]

Dunham's images of her naked self possess a similar power. She's cognizant, even in the earliest stages of her art, of the power of presenting oneself, especially as it's magnified: first to the thousands who watched her early short films on YouTube, then the hundreds of thousands who saw *Tiny Furniture*, and now the millions who follow her Instagram account, where, through the control of the camera and caption, she directs and recontours the gaze. Instead of perfecting her body, she underlines the power of not doing so.

Which is precisely why Dunham's attracted so many trolls, so many think pieces, such incessant questioning of her qualifications and the quality of her work, all of them articulating, in various shades of profanity and erudition, the same essential question: Why am I so offended by this woman's body, and how has she remained so resilient in the face of my offense?

The answer, I'd argue, is that Dunham has long understood her body in utilitarian ways—in part because of the way her mother treated her body in her own art, in part because her own body's utility, especially when it comes to her struggle with endometriosis, has long besieged her. But also because she simply understands the power of representation.

Miles claims that representations of the unclothed female body have long been a means of manifesting "male frustration and limitation"—what man desires and what he cannot have have been inscribed, throughout the history of the Western world, in terms of sin, sex, and death. That's how a woman saw herself presented, and that was how she was taught to conceive of herself. As the last twenty years of HBO and the vast majority of popular films attest, those three themes remain dominant. And women have continued to internalize that conception—evidenced most powerfully through our own repulsion at our bodies and the accompanying compulsion to modify them.

Dunham's nudity isn't "brave," because, as Dunham herself explains, for it to be brave she would have to be afraid. What she demands, instead, is bravery from others. To look at the naked body and react not in shock, or in shame, but with a willingness to look deeper: to men's monopoly on the representation of women's bodies and the suffering that has sprung from it, and to just how narrow a slice of existence remains, defined by women contending with one another to find happiness or value. Look *inward*, Dunham suggests—and realize there's another way.

CONCLUSION

Questions of representation—who controls it, and who says where and at what point it becomes "too much" in any capacity—have served as the foundation of this book, whose premise is predicated on the small yet significant ways that women have either resisted or wrested control of the way that men have represented them. All of these women have inverted and exceeded expectations; they've produced their own narratives or rebelled against ones that constrain or displease them.

Which isn't to say that they always succeed: the imperative against unruliness might be largely created by men, but as these chapters have shown, it's often enforced by women, whether in the form of mothers, best friends, peers, producers, or women reproducing judgment on unruly celebrities. At some point, every single one of these women has "failed"—or, perhaps more generously, presented inconsistencies—in her resistance. Those moments shouldn't be read as failures, however, so much as testaments to the sheer tenacity of the ideologies of femininity that shame, alien-ate, and expel those who refuse them.

Yet those retreats to conformity are also the reason these women remain represented in the first place. Put differently, something about each of the women in this book has permitted her not only to exist, but also to obtain and wield power within spheres dominated by men. Each has been able to challenge the ways women are represented—and, in turn, how we think of the sheer expansiveness of female behavior—because she hasn't been thrown out of the business entirely. Which isn't to be celebrated so much as persistently acknowledged: even in this moment of unruliness, each of these women's power has a ceiling. Some of them have touched its limits and retreated; others have simply been students of what happened to their unrulier antecedents and peers and have shaped their images to avoid a similar fate.

If spending this much time becoming deeply acquainted with these women's work and reception has taught me one thing, it's just how difficult and deeply disheartening it can be to be a woman in the public eye. All of these women are as imperfect as you or me, but when they say or do the wrong thing—or even say or do the *right* thing—the backlash can be swift, exacting, and cruel. To be an unruly woman in the public eye is to always be inviting criticism—and constantly fortifying yourself against it. Each woman in this book is a workaholic and a perfectionist, in part because anything less than that amount of labor and precise atten-tion to detail could be her downfall. Unruliness can be liberating, but within our current cultural climate, it is also endlessly ex-hausting.

To be an unruly woman today is to oscillate between the

postures of fearlessness and self-doubt, between listening to the voices that tell a woman she is *too much* and one's own, whispering and yelling *I am already enough, and always have been.* It is terrifying and liberating; it is lucrative and it is career-destroying; it is fashionable and it is gauche; it is shameful and it is redemptive. But it is also a mode of being that is endlessly electric. To refuse others' understanding of yourself and your capabilities doesn't just feel like self-determination: it's moving from being the object in someone else's narrative to the subject of one's own.

This book has worked to account for the ways in which unruliness has been historically censored, and the ways in which it is more necessary than ever. But it also telegraphs, with great and necessary hope, a future in which the term and concept have ceased to hold meaning: a woman only becomes unruly, after all, when she crosses a societally prescribed line of what "proper" femininity looks like. And while every society, no matter how utopian, will always produce norms, and censor and shame those who fail or refuse them, these women's prominence, economic prowess, and control may help accelerate the long historical march toward women wresting control of those norms, and expanding them to better reflect the ways of being that they find satisfying, nourishing, expansive, and radically inclusive.

A backlash, however, is coming. One has accompanied every period of feminist and unruly advance, and harbingers of the next one are already here for all to see: most vividly in the misogynist rhetoric of supporters of Donald Trump and the move to curtail women's control over their reproductive rights, but also in the anger over "ruining" male childhoods by rebooting a movie with a female cast, the victimhood running through Gamergate, and the general hysteria over "PC culture," which so precisely mirrors the feminist backlash of the 1990s. From our current vantage point, that backlash is so easy to disavow. But its currents are strong, capable of cloaking themselves with the sort of persuasiveness that even the most enlightened among us begin to heed. Historically, it has taken very little to turn women against one another and even less to turn men, so anxious about the maintenance of power, against women who attempt to seize some modicum of it for themselves.

This book is a celebration, but it's also a warning: right now, it's cool to be unruly and, by extension, easy to understand both its appeal and its progressive power. But the best way to honor and accelerate the project of unruliness is to refuse to participate in its demonization, even when—*especially when*—the cultural tide threatens to turn against it. Because unruliness isn't a single, easily disavowed decision, or an article of clothing one can take off and discard with the season. It's an attitude shared by so many women of history, so many women of this book, and so many others reading it: a hope that someday, the only rules a woman will have to abide by are those she sets for herself.

ACKNOWLEDGMENTS

Thanks are due to: Kathleen Karlyn, my first graduate professor, whose conception of unruliness is the foundation on which this book is built; my patient editors at BuzzFeed, who allowed me the space to write this book, and my even more patient editor at Penguin, Kate Napolitano, who shepherded this book from a kernel of an idea to a finished product; my ever-loyal and encouraging agent Allison Hunter, who's been with me since the beginning; Jenna Weiss-Berman, Julie Gerstein, Meredith Talusan, Charlie Petersen, Russell Meeuf, and hundreds of members of my Facebook group, who provided research guidance and/or read drafts and made them better; Alaina Smith Fuld, Beth Irwin Randall, Anna Pepper, Jeff and Robin Warzel, and Laura Bracken and Ed Miller, all of whom gave me a place to write in peace but also in good company; and Charlie Warzel, who read every word, made space for this enormous undertaking in our lives, and has always loved the unruliest parts of me the most.

Notes

Introduction

1. Kathleen Rowe Karlyn, *The Unruly Woman: Gender and the Genres of Laughter* (Austin: University of Texas Press, 1995).

2. Ibid.

3. Dominic Patten, "Bruce Jenner Interview Ratings Hits Newsmag Demo Record in Live+3," *Deadline Hollywood*, April 29, 2015, http://deadline.com/2015/04/bruce-jenner-interview-ratings -diane-sawyer-20-20-1201416149/.

4. Natalie Robehmed, "Kim Kardashian West's Earnings: $51 Million in 2016," *Forbes*, November 16, 2016, http://www.forbes.com /sites/natalierobehmed/2016/11/16/kim-kardashian-wests -earnings-51-million-in-2016/#dde6ff524754.

1. Too Strong: Serena Williams

1. Joy Duckett Cain and Tamala Edwards, "At the Top of Their Game," *Essence*, August 1998.

2. Ibid.

3. Vicki Michaelis, "Fame, Fortune Can Wait, Father of Two Teenage Tennis Phenoms Maintains," *Ottawa Citizen*, March 20, 1994.

4. Ibid.

5. Ibid.

6. Todd Holcomb, "Net Results," *The Atlanta Journal-Constitution*, March 25, 1998.

7. Ibid.

8. Michaelis, "Fame, Fortune Can Wait."

9. Richard Williams with Bart Davis, *Black and White: The Way I See It* (New York: Atria Books, 2014).

10. Frederick C. Klein, "Will Father Watch the Open?," *The Wall Street Journal*, August 31, 1998, http://www.wsj.com/articles/SB90451 589180108500.

11. "Double Trouble," *Women's Sports & Fitness*, November/December 1998.

12. Ibid.

13. Ibid.

14. Robin Finn, "A Family Tradition at Age 14," *The New York Times*, October 31, 1995.

15. "Williamses Display Big Power in a Victory and a Tough Loss," St. Paul *Pioneer Press*, June 1, 1998.

16. Lynn Zinser, "Benefiting from Workload, Serena Williams Has No Plans of Slowing," *The New York Times*, September 10, 2013.

17. Selena Roberts, "Richard Williams Raises Issues with WTA," *The New York Times*, November 14, 2000.

18. Michael Silver, "Serena's at Peace with Herself," *Sports Illustrated*,

March 22, 1999, www.si.com/vault/1999/03/22/257834/serenas at
-peace-with-herself-after-back-to-back-titles-serena-williams
-has-no-doubt-she-can-win-big.

19. Mike Walters, "Venus Takes Sis Serena to Court" and "Tennis: Australian Open—Venus Williams to Meet Sister Serena," *The Mirror*,
   January 20, 1998.

20. "Williams's Dad Alleges Racism," *The Washington Post*, March 27,
   2001, https://www.washingtonpost.com/archive/sports/2001/03
   /27/williamss-dad-alleges-racism/63720e58-1ae9-48e7-8577
   -da4d4b55dd39/?utm_term=6dc9f3687034.

21. Ibid.

22. Caryl Phillips, "Ignored, Resented, Jeered and Mocked—A Young-
   est Sister Moves Coolly to Greatness," *The Guardian*, December
   21, 2002.

23. Ginia Bellafante, "Shopping With: Serena Williams; Game, Set,
   Dress Me in Leather," *The New York Times*, October 17, 1999.

24. Ibid.

25. "Serena Reveals and Revels in Her Catsuit: 'It Is Really Sexy. I
   Love It,'" *National Post* (Canada), August 28, 2002.

26. M. Gibson, "Advantage Prats," *Sunday Telegraph* (Sydney, Australia), September 1, 2002. Retrieved April 7, 2003, from the Lexis-
   Nexis database. Cited in http://www.csub.edu/~rdugan2/soc
   %20477%20culture%20readings/serena%20and%20cat%20suit
   .pdf; Jaime Schultz, "Reading the Catsuit: Serena Williams and
   the Production of Blackness at the 2002 U.S. Open," *Journal of
   Sport & Social Issues* 29, no. 3 (August 2005): 338–57.

27. Elena Bergeron, "How Serena Williams Became the G.O.A.T.,"
   Fader, October 4, 2016, http://www.thefader.com/2016/10/04
   /serena-williams-interview-cover-story.

28. Robin Givhan, "A Tight Squeeze at the U.S. Open," *The Washington Post*, August 30, 2002, https://www.washingtonpost.com/archive/lifestyle/2002/08/30/a-tight-squeeze-at-the-us-open/791ff3f9-9fe2-4dc6-8f47-e34c03d52aa3/.

29. Quoted in "Serena Williams's Dress Stole Show," *The Gazette* (Montreal), July 26, 2003.

30. Nigel Clarke, "Serena Models Herself on J-Lo," *The Express*, May 26, 2003.

31. Nicole Lampert, "Courting Attention, Serena and a Beach Bikini," *Daily Mail*, December 29, 2004.

32. "Sexy . . . or Scary? Serena Sets Off Hot Debate," *Daily Mirror*, July 18, 2003.

33. Vivek Chaudhary, "I Can Beat the Men, Says Serena; The Younger Williams Sister Revives the Court Battle of the Sexes," *The Guardian*, October 8, 1999.

34. Ibid.

35. Kevin Garside, "Wimbledon 2003 Week 2: Muscles v Brussels; Women's Semi-Finals," *The Mirror*, July 3, 2003.

36. Eben Harrell, "Quiet, Please: Will Tennis Pros Give Up the Grunt?," *Time*, June 22, 2009, http://content.time.com/time/arts/article/0,8599,1905782,00.html.

37. Simon Hattenstone, "Serena's Triumph over Tragedy a Weepy Classic," *The Guardian*, January 31, 2007.

38. Mark Stevens, "You Weight and See; Size Up Serena at Your Own Risk," *Herald Sun* (Australia), January 12, 2006.

39. Matthew Norman, "Serena's Loyal Supporters," *The Telegraph*, January 22, 2006.

40. Brittney C. Cooper, "Refereeing Serena: Racism, Anger, and U.S. (Women's) Tennis," Crunk Feminist Collective, September 12, 2011,

http://www.crunkfeministcollective.com/2011/09/12/refereeing
serena racism anger and u s womens tennis/.

41. Clare Raymond, "Female Hulk with a Bum to Match," *The Mirror*,
July 18, 2003; and Jason Whitlock, "Serena Could Be the Best Ever,
But . . . ," Fox Sports, July 9, 2009, https://web.archive.org/web
/20090709162516/http://msn.foxsports.com/tennis/story
/9757816/Serena-could-be-the-best-ever,-but-.

42. "Bikini Confessions," *People*, June 27, 2011, http://people.com
/archive/bikini-confessions-vol-75-no-25/.

43. Howie Kahn, "Serena Williams, Wonder Woman, Is Our September
Cover Star," *Self*, August 1, 2016, http://www.self.com/story/serena
-williams-september-cover-interview.

44. "Bikini Confessions."

45. Rebecca Johnson, "Why Serena Williams Is Best Friends with
Her Fiercest Competitor," *Vogue*, March 21, 2015.

46. Stephen Rodrick, "Serena Williams: The Great One," *Rolling
Stone*, June 18, 2013.

47. Amar Singh, "Gamesmanship Set and Match," *London Evening
Standard*, July 3, 2007.

48. "Double Trouble," *Women's Sports & Fitness*, November/December
1998.

49. Lisa Dillman, "Sanchez Vicario Eludes Serena Williams in 3
Sets," *Los Angeles Times*, June 1, 1998.

50. David Jones, "Can Serena Save Herself?," *Daily Mail*, June 21, 2003.

51. Ibid.

52. Douglas Robson, "Serena Shows Renewed Resolve," *USA Today*,
June 1, 2004.

53. Alison Kervin, "Tearful Serena Bows Out," *Sunday Times*, June 26,
2005.

54. Barney Ronay, "Welcome Back Serena Williams," *Sportblog, The Guardian*, June 8, 2011.

55. Jo Anne Simon, letter to the editor, *The New York Times*, September 20, 2009, http://query.nytimes.com/gst/fullpage.html?res=9B01 E6DB1439F933A1575AC0A96F9C8B63.

56. Carl Maultsby, letter to the editor, *The New York Times*, http://query .nytimes.com/gst/fullpage.html?res=9B01E6DB1439F933A1575A C0A96F9C8B63.

57. Kerry Howley, "Serena Williams Is Eyeing a Fashionable Post-Court Life, but First She's Got Tennis History to Make," *New York*, August 9, 2015.

58. Cooper, "Refereeing Serena."

59. Diane Pucin, "Serena Williams Advances to Third Round but Is Upset with Court Assignment," *Los Angeles Times*, June 23, 2011.

60. Kevin Mitchell, "Wimbledon 2011: Serena Williams Deserves Respect. She Should Demand It," *Sportblog, The Guardian*, June 24, 2011.

61. Ibid.

62. Rodrick, "Serena Williams: The Great One."

63. William D. Friedman, letter to the editor, *The New York Times*, September 17, 2011, http://www.nytimes.com/2011/09/18/sports /letters-to-the-editor.html.

64. Jim Fitzpatrick and Roy Hegarty, letters to the editor, September 17, 2011, http://www.nytimes.com/2011/09/18/sports/letters-to -the-editor.html.

65. Johnson, "Why Serena Williams Is Best Friends with Her Fiercest Competitor."

66. Ibid.

67. Deirdre Edgar, "Sportsperson of the Year Debate Draws Its Own Backlash," *Los Angeles Times*, December 14, 2015.

68. Claudia Rankine, *Citizen: An American Lyric* (Minneapolis: Graywolf Press, 2014).

69. Claudia Rankine, "The Meaning of Serena Williams," *The New York Times Magazine*, August 25, 2015.

70. Bergeron, "How Serena Williams Became the G.O.A.T."

2. Too Fat: Melissa McCarthy

1. Rex Reed, "Declined: In *Identity Thief*, Bateman's Bankable Billing Can't Lift This Flick Out of the Red," *The Observer*, February 5, 2013.

2. Quoted in Debbie Rodan, Katie Ellis, and Pia Lebeck, *Disability, Obesity and Ageing: Popular Media Identifications* (Farnham, UK: Ashgate, 2014).

3. Hadley Freeman, "Melissa McCarthy: I Love a Woman Who Doesn't Play by the Rules," *The Guardian*, May 28, 2016.

4. Erik Hedegaard, "Riot Girl," *Rolling Stone*, July 3, 2014; and Rhys Blakely, "Plus-sized, Outspoken and Over 40, Melissa McCarthy Is Not Your Average A-list Actress," *The Times* (London), May 30, 2015.

5. Blakely, "Plus-sized, Outspoken and Over 40."

6. Hedegaard, "Riot Girl."

7. "Big Love of a Different Sort," *Toronto Star*, October 23, 2010.

8. Hedegaard, "Riot Girl."

9. Lacey Rose, "Melissa McCarthy Is Having Her Moment," *The Hollywood Reporter*, September 28, 2011.

10. Ibid.

11. Ibid.

12. Mo Ryan, "*Mike & Molly* Just Regular People," *Chicago Tribune*, August 4, 2010.

13. Maureen Elizabeth Johnson, "*Mike & Molly*—An Other World," master's thesis, Marshall University, ProQuest Dissertations Publishing, 2013.

14. Brian Lowry, "Review: *Mike & Molly*," *Variety*, September 19, 2010.

15. June Thompson, "Mike and Molly Aren't Afraid to Laugh as They Battle the Bulge," *The Gazette* (Montreal), October 12, 2010.

16. Alex Strachan, "Dispelling the Myth TV Is Only About the Skinny; Plus-Sized Partners Out Real-Life Problems on the Funny *Mike & Molly*," *Edmonton Journal*, March 20, 2011.

17. Ryan, "*Mike & Molly* Just Regular People."

18. Strachan, "Dispelling the Myth."

19. Ibid.

20. "Melissa McCarthy," *Daily Variety*, June 9, 2011.

21. Karen Valby, "All I Want for Mother's Day Is for 'Bridesmaids' Melissa McCarthy to Be a Movie Star," *Entertainment Weekly*, May 7, 2011.

22. Rose, "Melissa McCarthy Is Having Her Moment."

23. Ibid.

24. Ibid.

25. Hedegaard, "Riot Girl."

26. Ibid.

27. Darryn King, "It's Not That Women Aren't Funny. It's That the Characters Stink—Interview, Melissa McCarthy, Actor, Comedian, Feminist," *The Sydney Morning Herald*, May 2, 2015.

28. Ibid.

29. Brandon Voss, "The A-List Interview: Melissa McCarthy," *The Advocate*, May 16, 2014.

30. Robbie Collins, "*Bridesmaids* Star Melissa McCarthy Tells Robbie Collins About Her New Film, *Identity Thief*, and Breaking into the Hollywood Boys Club of Comedy," *The Daily Telegraph*, March 22, 2013.

31. King, "It's Not That Women Aren't Funny."

32. Blakely, "Plus-sized, Outspoken and Over 40."

33. Judith Newman, "Melissa McCarthy Shares Her Ultimate Secret to Happiness in *Redbook*'s April Issue," *Redbook*, March 8, 2016, http://www.redbookmag.com/life/interviews/a42962/melissa-mccarthy-redbook-april-2016-cover-star/.

34. Ramin Setoodeh, "*Tammy*'s Melissa McCarthy and Ben Falcone Build a Comedy Empire One Rauchy Joke at a Time," *Variety*, June 24, 2014.

35. David A. Keeps, "Funny Girl: Exclusive Interview with Melissa McCarthy," *Good Housekeeping*, November 6, 2012; and Hedegaard, "Riot Girl.

36. Blakely, "Plus-sized, Outspoken and Over 40."

37. King, "It's Not That Women Aren't Funny"; and Joseph Lamour, "Melissa McCarthy Confronted a Critic Who Said Actresses Should Always Be Pretty in Movies," Upworthy, May 20, 2015, http://www.upworthy.com/melissa-mccarthy-confronted-a-critic-who-said-actresses-should-always-be-pretty-in-movies.

38. Keeps, "Funny Girl."

39. Rose, "Melissa McCarthy Is Having Her Moment."; Dave Itzkoff, "Melissa McCarthy Goes Over the Top," *The New York Times*,

June 13, 2013; and "Melissa McCarthy: I'm Too Friendly for LA," *Belfast Telegraph*, June 21, 2013.

40. King, "It's Not That Women Aren't Funny"; "Melissa McCarthy: The Art of Living Fearlessly," *More*, June 2015; and Kate Coyne, "Melissa McCarthy: Love the Way You Look!," *People*, September 21, 2015, 94–99.

41. Kimberly Nordyke, "Melissa McCarthy Named Brand Spokesman for Ivory Soap," *Pret-a-Reporter*, November 7, 2011.

42. Coyne, "Melissa McCarthy: Love the Way You Look!"

43. Ibid.

44. "Melissa McCarthy and the Comedy Issue: This Week's Cover," *Entertainment Weekly*, October 27, 2011, http://www.ew.com /article/2011/10/27/melissa-mccarthy-comedy-issue-this-weeks -cover.

45. Keeps, "Funny Girl."

46. Itzkoff, "Melissa McCarthy Goes Over the Top."

47. Keeps, "Funny Girl"; and Connie Wang, "Melissa McCarthy Is Not a Fan of the Term 'Plus-Size' for Some Very Legit Reasons," *Refinery29*, August 17, 2015.

48. Edward Barsamian, "Exclusive! Melissa McCarthy Launches Her Fashion Label," *Vogue*, July 29, 2015.

49. Coyne, "Melissa McCarthy: Love the Way You Look!"

50. Ibid.

51. Wang, "Melissa McCarthy Is Not a Fan of the Term 'Plus-Size.'"

52. Mark Harris, "Why Does Hollywood Keep Disrespecting Melissa McCarthy?," *Vulture*, New York, April 15, 2016.

53. Rebecca Ford, "How Melissa McCarthy Became the New Adam Sandler," *The Hollywood Reporter*, April 10, 2016.

54. Ted Scheinman, "Bang! Zoom! Straight to the Moon! Melissa McCarthy and the New Female Slapstick," *Los Angeles Review of Books*, February 20, 2013.

55. Harris, "Why Does Hollywood Keep Disrespecting Melissa McCarthy?"

3. Too Gross: Abbi Jacobson and Ilana Glazer

1. Rebecca Traister, "The Single American Woman," *The Cut, New York*, http://nymag.com/thecut/2016/02/political-power-single -women-c-v-r.html.

2. Ibid.

3. Nick Paumgarten, "Id Girls: The Comedy Couple Behind 'Broad City,'" *The New Yorker*, June 23, 2014, http://www.newyorker .com/magazine/2014/06/23/id-girls.

4. Ibid.

5. Ted Simmons, "Amy Poehler Talks 'Broad City' Roots and Weirdly Specific 'Street-Level Feel,'" *The Hollywood Reporter*, November 10, 2014, http://www.hollywoodreporter.com/news /new-york-comedy-fest-2014-747925.

6. Jon Weisman, "Amy Poehler to Produce Comedy Central Series," *Variety*, October 8, 2012, http://variety.com/2012/tv/news/amy -poehler-to-produce-comedy-central-series-1118060430/.

7. Gabby Bess, "Coming Out as a #Stonergirl Online: The Emergence of the Female Pot Smoker," *Paper*, June 3, 2014, http:// www.papermag.com/coming-out-as-a-stonergirl-online-the -emergence-of-the-female-pot-smok-1427309514.html

8. Ari Spool, "Toke Like a Girl," *The Stranger*, August 16, 2007.

9. Anna Brain, "Seth and the City," *The Daily Telegraph*, January 14, 2015.

10. Willa Paskin, *"Broad City," Slate*, January 22, 2014, http://www
.slate.com/articles/arts/television/2014/01/broad_city_star
ring_ilana_glazer_and_abbi_jacobson_reviewed.html.

11. Megan Angelo, "Adrift in New York, Web Comics Seek a Larger
Audience," *The New York Times*, http://www.nytimes.com/2012
/04/15/arts/television/young-comics-adapting-broad-city-from
-web-to-fx.html; Alessandra Stanley, *"Broad City* Brings a Female
Twist to Failure," *The New York Times*, January 21, 2014; and Sam
Adams, *"Broad City* Season Two," *Indiewire*, January 14, 2015,
http://www.indiewire.com/2015/01/broad-city-season-2-reviews
-abbi-and-ilanna-are-back-as-raunchy-and-right-on-as-ever
-125104/.

12. Lacey Rose, "The 'Broad City' Stars Q&A: Young Jewesses Are
Really Hot Right Now," *The Hollywood Reporter*, April 6, 2016,
http://www.hollywoodreporter.com/features/yas-queen-broad
-city-stars-880082.

13. Jada Yuan, "The *Broad City* Hustle," *New York*, March 10, 2015.

14. Sara Stewart, *"Broad City* Stars Dish on Marijuana and NYC,"
New York Post, October 31, 2014.

15. Maureen Halushak, *"Broad City*'s Abbi and Ilana: 'The Best
F-cking Interview,'" *Flare*, December 21, 2015; Chuck Barney, "Tonight's TV Picks," *The Mercury News* (San Jose), January 20, 2014,
http://www.mercurynews.com/2014/01/20/tonights-tv-picks
-outbreak-on-revolution-premonition-on-american-horror-story
-coven/; "Six Degrees No Bacon," *Jewish Press of Tampa*, http://
jewishpressoftampa.our-hometown.com/news/2014-04-11/Cul
ture/6_degrees_no_Bacon.html; Chuck Barney, "Tina Fey, Amy
Poehler Bring Funny Back to Golden Globe Awards," *The Mercury
News* (San Jose), January 5, 2015, http://www.mercurynews.com
/2015/01/05/tina-fey-amy-poehler-bring-funny-back-to-golden
-globe-awards/; and Memphis Barker, "Love Friends but Want

Something More Feminist, Racially Diverse, and Risqué? Then Watch *Broad City*," *The Independent*, March 10, 2015.

16. Mike Albo, "How *Broad City* Became the Greatest Show on Television," *Out*, February 2, 2016.

17. Simmons, "Amy Poehler Talks 'Broad City' Roots."

18. Paumgarten, "Id Girls."

19. Albo, "How *Broad City* Became the Greatest Show on Television."

20. Paskin, "*Broad City*."

21. Phillip Maciak, "Theses on the Dance Moves of Ilana Glazer," *Los Angeles Review of Books*, April 2, 2014, https://lareviewofbooks.org/article/unruly-stoner-girl-makes-broad-city-radical/.

22. Halushak, "*Broad City*'s Abbi and Ilana."

23. Yuan, "The *Broad City* Hustle."

24. Amanda Erickson, "Abbi Jacobson Has Always Wanted to Meet Darren Star. So We Got Them Together," *The Washington Post*, August 27, 2015.

25. John Wenzel, "*Broad City* Stars Ilana Glazer and Abbi Jacobson Talk Touring, Fans," *The Denver Post*, November 19, 2014.

26. Kayla Epstein, "*Broad City* Stars: 'Comparing Us to Girls Is Reductive,'" *The Guardian*, May 19, 2015.

27. Nell Scovell, "*Broad City*'s Abbi Jacobson and Ilana Glazer Play Broad and Real Simultaneously," *Vanity Fair*, January 2015.

28. Rachel Syme, "The Broad Strokes," *Grantland*, January 14, 2015, https://grantland.com/features/broad-city-season-2-comedy-central-abbi-jacobson-ilana-glazer/.

29. Halushak, "*Broad City*'s Abbi and Ilana."

30. Stewart, "*Broad City* Stars Dish on Marijuana and NYC."

31. Jonah Weiner, "The Other Girls," *Rolling Stone*, January 29, 2015.

32. Kyla Wazana Tompkins and Rebecca Wanzo, "Brown Broads, White TV," *Los Angeles Review of Books*, March 16, 2015, https://lareviewofbooks.org/article/brown-broads-white-tv/.

33. Emily Nussbaum, "Laverne and Curly," *The New Yorker*, March 7, 2016.

34. Ibid.

4. Too Slutty: Nicki Minaj

1. Chuck Creekmur, "Dear Nicki Minaj: An Open Letter from a Father," *MadameNoire*, July 25, 2014, http://madamenoire.com/565169/dear-nicki-minaj-an-open-letter-from-a-father/.

2. Lauren Nostro, "The Real Her," *Complex*, December 2014/January 2015.

3. bell hooks, "Selling Hot Pussy: Representations of Black Female Sexuality in the Cultural Marketplace," in *Black Looks: Race and Representation* (Boston: South End Press, 1992).

4. Teresa Jusino, "Nicki Minaj and Miley Cyrus at the VMAs: A Case Study in Intersectional Feminism," *The Mary Sue*, September 2, 2015.

5. Touré, "Challenging Hip-Hop's Masculine Ideal," *The New York Times*, December 23, 2011.

6. Nikki Lane, "Black Women Queering the Mic: Missy Elliott Disturbing the Boundaries of Racialized Sexuality and Gender," *Journal of Homosexuality* 58 (2011).

7. Savannah Shange, "A King Named Nicki: Strategic Queerness and the Black Femmecee," *Women & Performance: A Journal of Feminist Theory* 24, no. 1 (2014): 29–45.

8. Julianne Escobedo Shepherd, "Nicki Minaj Assumes Control," *Fader*, March 11, 2010.

9. Siobhan O'Connor, "Character Study: Just How Real Is Nicki Minaj?," *Vibe*, June/July 2010.

10. Nostro, "The Real Her."

11. Shepherd, "Nicki Minaj Assumes Control."

12. Uri McMillan, "Nicki-Aesthetics: The Camp Performance of Nicki Minaj," *Women & Performance: A Journal of Feminist Theory* 24, no. 1 (2014): 79–87.

13. Marquita R. Smith, "'Or a Real, Real Bad Lesbian': Nicki Minaj and the Acknowledgement of Queer Desire in Hip-Hop Culture," *Popular Music and Society* 37, no. 3 (2014): 360–70.

14. Caryn Ganz, "The Curious Case of Nicki Minaj," *Out*, September 12, 2010.

15. Smith, "'Or a Real, Real Bad Lesbian.'"

16. Ibid.

17. Ganz, "The Curious Case of Nicki Minaj."

18. Jonah Weiner, "Nicki Minaj," *Rolling Stone*, October 14, 2010.

19. Ibid.

20. Nostro, "The Real Her."

21. Ann Powers, "Fractured Femmes: Madonna and Nicki Minaj Man Up," *The Record*, NPR.org, April 5, 2012.

22. Jody Rosen, "Review: Nicki Minaj: *Pink Friday: Roman Reloaded*," *Rolling Stone*, April 6, 2012.

23. Shepherd, "Nicki Minaj Assumes Control."

24. Taffy Brodesser-Akner, "Nicki Minaj: Cheeky Genius," *GQ*, October 19, 2014.

25. Jonah Weiner, "Darling Nicki," *Rolling Stone*, January 15, 2015.

26. Knox Robinson, "The Rise and Rise of Nicki Minaj," *V Magazine*, January 24, 2013, http://vmagazine.com/article/the-rise-and-rise-of-nicki-minaj/.

27. Carrie Battan, "Cover Story: Nicki Minaj," *Fader*, August/September 2014.

28. Brodesser-Akner, "Nicki Minaj: Cheeky Genius."

29. Sophie Kleeman, "Nicki Minaj's New 'Anaconda' Video Is Here—and It's a Huge Letdown," *Mic*, August 20, 2014.

30. Creekmur, "Dear Nicki Minaj."

31. Nostro, "The Real Her."

32. Weiner, "Darling Nicki."

33. Mychal Denzel Smith, "Nicki Minaj's Butt and the Politics of Black Women's Sexuality," *Feministing*, July 29, 2014, http://feministing.com/2014/07/29/nicki-minajs-butt-and-the-politics-of-black-womens-sexuality/.

34. Julianne Escobedo Shepherd, "Hustle & Glow," *Nylon*, March 2016.

35. Sydney Lace, "Hip-hop Rumors: Nicki Minaj Goes HAM on the Breakfast Club!," AllHipHop.com, November 23, 2012, http://allhiphop.com/2012/11/23/hip-hop-rumors-nicki-minaj-goes-ham-on-the-breakfast-club-calls-them-dck-riders/.

36. Weiner, "Darling Nicki."

37. Vanessa Grigoriadis, "The Passion of Nicki Minaj," *The New York Times Magazine*, October 7, 2015.

38. Mark Anthony Green, "Nicki Minaj and Meek Mill on How to Deal with Haters," *GQ*, September 22, 2015.

5. Too Old: Madonna

1. Susan Sontag, "The Double Standard of Aging," in *Essays of the 1960s & 70s*, ed. David Rieff (New York: Library of America, 2013).

2. Ibid.

3. Vanessa Barnett, "Drake and Madonna Kiss . . . and It's Super Gross!" *HipHollywood*, April 13, 2015.

4. Deborah Jermyn and Su Holmes, eds., *Women, Celebrity & Cultures of Ageing: Freeze Frame* (Basingstoke, UK: Palgrave Macmillan, 2015).

5. Steven Anderson, "Forgive Me Father," *The Village Voice*, April 4, 1989, 67–68.

6. Lucy O'Brien, "Madonna: Like a Crone," in *"Rock On": Women, Ageing and Popular Music*, ed. Abigail Gardner (Burlington, VT: Routledge, 2016).

7. Ibid.

8. Ibid.

9. D. J. Conway, *Maiden, Mother, Crone: The Myth & Reality of the Triple Goddess* (Minneapolis: Llewellyn Publications, 1997).

10. R. Simpson, "Even with Muscles Like These . . . ," *Daily Mail*, June 26, 2006; "Madonna's Lawyers: Guy Ritchie Said She Looked Like a 'Granny'; Accuse Him of Verbal Abuse," New York *Daily News*, October 19, 2008, http://www.nydailynews.com/entertainment/gossip/madonna-lawyers-guy-ritchie-granny-accuse-verbal-abuse-article-1.302692; http://www.dailymail.co.uk/tvshowbiz/article-1121343/As-Madonna-poses-ANOTHER-raunchy-album-picture-doing-70.html.

11. Austin Scaggs, "Madonna Looks Back: The Rolling Stone Interview," *Rolling Stone*, October 29, 2009.

12. Lindy West, "Madonna, What Are You Doing," *Jezebel*, January 27, 2014.

13. Julia Baird, "What Happened to Madonna," *The Sydney Morning Herald*, April 1, 2012.

14. Brian Hiatt, "Madonna," *Rolling Stone*, February 25, 2015

15. "Are you supposed to just DIE?" is from television interview Jonathan Ross in 1992 to promote *Erotica*.

16. Marlow Stern, "Shirley Manson of Garbage on Brexit, Taylor Swift, and How the Scots Have 'Disowned' Trump," *The Daily Beast*, June 26, 2016.

6. Too Pregnant: Kim Kardashian

1. Madeleine Davies, "Kim Kardashian Calls Pregnancy 'The Worst Experience of My Life,'" *Jezebel*, October 5, 2015, http://jezebel.com/kim-kardashian-calls-pregnancy-the-worst-experience-of-1734798586.

2. Bettijane Levine, "Demi Moore Exposes New Mood on Motherhood," *Los Angeles Times*. July 15, 1991.

3. Susan Heller Anderson, "Demi Moore, Uncovered on *Vanity Fair*'s Cover," *The New York Times*, July 11, 1991, B20.

4. Levine, "Demi Moore Exposes New Mood on Motherhood."

5. Ibid.

6. Molly Jong-Fast, "View: Out of Step and Having a Baby," *The New York Times*, October 5, 2003.

7. Jane M. Ussher, *Managing the Monstrous Feminine: Regulating the Reproductive Body* (New York: Routledge, 2006).

8. Quoted in Robyn Longhurst, "Breaking Corporeal Boundaries: Pregnant Bodies in Public Places," in *Contested Bodies*, ed. John Hassard and Ruth Holliday (New York: Routledge, 2003).

9. Renée Ann Cramer, *Pregnant with the Stars: Watching and Wanting the Celebrity Baby Bump* (Stanford, CA: Stanford University Press, 2015).

10. Janice Min, *How to Look Hot in a Minivan: A Real Woman's Guide to Losing Weight, Looking Great, and Dressing Chic in the Age of the Celebrity Mom* (New York: St. Martin's Press, 2012).

11. Imogen Tyler, "Pregnant Beauty: Material Femininities Under Neoliberalism," in *New Femininities: Postfeminism, Neoliberalism, and Subjectivity*, ed. Rosalind Gill and Christina Scharff (New York: Springer, 2013).

12. Min, *How to Look Hot in a Minivan*.

13. Veronica Bridget Ward, "Eating Disorders in Pregnancy," *The BMJ* 336 (January 2008): 93–96, https://www.ncbi.nlm.nih.gov/pmc/articles/PMC2190274/.

14. Claire Zillman, "This Startup's Perk for Pregnant Employees? A $2000 Maternity Clothes Shopping Spree," *Fortune*, October 23, 2015.

15. Cover image, *New York Post*, March 27, 2013.

16. Rose Walano, "Kim Kardashian's Pregnancy Style: Look Back at Her Best Looks the First Time Around!," *Stylish* (blog), *Us Weekly*, June 1, 2015, http://www.usmagazine.com/celebrity-style/news/kim-kardashians-first-pregnancy-style-photos-201516; and Shanelle Rein-Olowokere, "Oh, Mama! Kim Kardashian's Super-Trendy Maternity Style," June 15, 2013, http://people.com/babies/kim-kardashian-maternity-style-trends-photos/.

17. Tia Williams, "Kim Kardashian's Maternity Style Evolution: Kiki, or Heather Locklear on *Melrose Place*?," VH1.com, May 21, 2013, http://www.vh1.com/news/84850/kim-kardashians-maternity-style-3/.

18. Rein-Olowokere, "Oh, Mama!"; Cameron Wolf, "An Obsessive Comparison of Kim Kardashian's Pregnancy Styles," *Racked*, November 12, 2015, http://www.racked.com/2015/11/12/9703198/kim-kardashian-pregnancy-style; and nsolofsky, "The Best and Worst of Kim Kardashian's Maternity Style," OKMagazine.com, June 18, 2013, http://okmagazine.com/photos/best-and-worst-kim-kardashians-maternity-style/.

19. Hilary Mantel, "Royal Bodies," *London Review of Books*, February 21, 2013.

20. Maureen Brewster, "Bump Watch: Fashioning Celebrity Pregnancy as Performance and Product," master's thesis, the New School, 2014.

21. Cramer, *Pregnant with the Stars*.

22. Allison Takeda, "Kim Kardashian Flaunts Pregnant Bikini Body on Vacation in Greece: Picture," *Us Weekly*, May 8, 2013, http://www.usmagazine.com/celebrity-body/news/kim-kardashian-flaunts-pregnant-bikini-body-on-family-vacation-in-greece-picture-201385.

23. Cramer, *Pregnant with the Stars*.

7. Too Shrill: Hillary Clinton

1. Tom Junod, "You Think You Know Hillary Clinton, But You Have No Idea," *Esquire*, February 2016.

2. Hillary Rodham, "The Class of '69," *Life*, June 20, 1969.

3. Gwen Ifill, "The 1992 Campaign: Hillary Clinton Defends Her Conduct in Law Firm," *The New York Times*, March 17, 1992, https://www.nytimes.com/2016/10/16/magazine/how-hillary-clinton-became-hillary.html?_r=0.

4. Quoted in Rebecca Traister, *Big Girls Don't Cry: The Election That Changed Everything for American Women* (New York: Simon & Schuster, 2011).

5. David Lauter and Karen Tumulty, "Hillary Clinton Speech May Signal More Active Role," *Los Angeles Times*, November 18, 1992.

6. Ibid.

7. David Broder, "What Role Should Hillary Clinton Play?," *The Washington Post*, November 29, 1992.

8. Maureen Dowd, "Hillary Rodham Clinton Strikes a New Pose and Multiplies Her Image," *The New York Times*, December 12, 1993.

9. Jill Gerston, "A Closetful of Classics," *Los Angeles Times*, November 20, 1992.

10. Dowd, "Hillary Rodham Clinton Strikes a New Pose."

11. Henry Louis Gates, Jr., "Hating Hillary," *The New Yorker*, February 26, 1996.

12. Ibid.

13. Ibid.

14. Anna Wintour, "Editor's Note," *Vogue*, November 1998.

15. Ed Vulliamy, "White House in Vogue," *The New York Observer*, November 22, 1998.

16. Traister, "Big Girls Don't Cry."

17. Nate Silver, "Why Hillary Clinton Would Be Strong in 2016 (It's Not Her Favorability Ratings)," *The New York Times*, December 11, 2012.

18. Margaret Talbot, "2016's Manifest Misogyny," *The New Yorker*, October 24, 2016.

19. Karrin Vasby Anderson, "'Rhymes with Rich': 'Bitch' as a Tool of Containment in Contemporary American Politics," *Rhetoric and Public Affairs* 22, no. 4 (1999): 599–623.

20. Andi Zeisler, "The B-Word? You Betcha," *The Washington Post*, November 18, 2007.

21. Max Weber, *On Charisma and Institution Building* (Chicago: University of Chicago Press, 1968).

22. Jonathan Alter, *Between the Lines: A View Inside American Politics, People and Culture* (State Street Press, 2008).

23. Joshua Green, "The Hillary Clinton Memos," *The Atlantic*, September 2008.

24. Quoted in Traister, *Big Girls Don't Cry*.

25. Amanda Fortini, "The Feminist Reawakening: Hillary Clinton and the Fourth Wave," *New York*, April 13, 2008.

26. Rebecca Traister, "Hey, Obama Boys: Back Off Already!," *Salon*, April 14, 2008.

27. Fortini, "The Feminist Reawakening."

28. Amy Chozick, "Hillary Clinton Raises Her Voice, and a Debate over Speech and Sexism Rages," *The New York Times*, February 4, 2016.

29. Kim Lyons, "How Will a Woman Running for President in 2016 Be Portrayed?" *Pittsburgh Post-Gazette*, April 26, 2015.

30. Erica Jong, "Why I Trust Hillary Clinton," CNN.com, May 26, 2016.

31. Nic Subtirelu, "Bashing Hillary Clinton's Coice: 'Screeching,' 'Shrieking,' and 'Shrill,'" *Linguistic Pulse*, February 8, 2016.

32. Kim Janssen, "Soprano Renee Fleming 'Would Love To' Work on Hillary's Voice," *Chicago Tribune*, June 10, 2016.

33. Frida Ghitis, "The 'Shrill' Smear Against Hillary Clinton," CNN
.com, February 8, 2016.

34. Glenn Thrush, "Obama on Iowa, Clinton, Sanders and 2016," *Politico*, January 25, 2016.

35. Lori Poloni-Staudinger, J. Cherie Strachan, and Brian Schaffner,
"In 6 Graphs, Here's Why Young Women Don't Support Hillary
Clinton as Much as Older Women Do," *The Washington Post*, April
11, 2016.

36. Glenn Greenwald, "The 'Bernie Bros' Narrative: A Cheap Campaign Tactic Masquerading as Journalism and Social Activism,"
The Intercept, January 31, 2016.

37. Ezra Klein, "Understanding Hillary," *Vox*, July 11, 2016.

38. Ibid.

39. Available at "The Most Thorough, Profound and Moving Defense
of Hillary Clinton I Have Ever Seen," *Daily Kos*, June 11, 2016.

40. Ibid.

41. Lori Beaman, Raghabendra Chattopadhyay, Esther Duflo, Rohini
Pande, and Petia Topalova, "Perceptions of Female Leaders in
India," Abdul Latif Jameel Poverty Action Lab, Massachusetts
Institute of Technology, 2009, https://www.povertyactionlab.org
/evaluation/perceptions-female-leaders-india.

8. Too Queer: Caitlyn Jenner

1. Jennifer Graham, "Caitlyn Is Still a Mister," *Pittsburgh Post-Gazette*, June 4, 2015.

2. Human Rights Campaign and Trans People of Color Coalition,
"Addressing Anti-Transgender Violence," http://hrc-assets.s3-web
site-us-east-1.amazonaws.com//files/assets/resources/HRC
-AntiTransgenderViolence-0519.pdf.

3. Lisa Duggan, *The Twilight of Equality? Neoliberalism, Cultural Politics, and the Attack On Democracy* (Boston: Beacon Press, 2003).

4. Evan Vipond, "Resisting Transnormativity: Challenging the Medicalization and Regulation of Trans Bodies," *Theory in Action* 8, no. 2 (April 2015): 21–45.

5. Julia Serano, *Whipping Girl: A Transsexual Woman on Sexism and the Scapegoating of Femininity* (Emeryville, CA: Seal Press, 2016).

6. Ibid.

7. Buzz Bissinger, "Caitlyn Jenner: The Full Story," *Vanity Fair*, July 2015.

8. Katy Steinmetz, "Caitlyn Jenner on Privilege, Reality TV and Deciding to Come Out," *Time*, December 9, 2015.

9. Caitlin Campisi, "Homonationalism on TV? A Critical Discourse Analysis of Queer and Trans* Youth Representation on Mainstream Teen Television Shows," master's thesis, University of Ottawa, 2013.

10. Alex Rees, "Caitlyn Jenner Tells *Time* Magazine That 'If You Look Like a Man in a Dress, It Makes People Uncomfortable,'" *Cosmopolitan*, December 10, 2015.

11. Meredith Talusan, "The Problem with Caitlyn Jenner Is Bigger than Beauty Standards," *BuzzFeed*, December 19, 2015.

12. Steinmetz, "Caitlyn Jenner on Privilege, Reality TV and Deciding to Come Out."

13. Jos Truitt, "On Jill Soloway, Caitlyn Jenner, and the Trans Representation the Media Wants," *Feministing*, December 21, 2016.

14. Jos Truitt, "Transgender People Are More Visible Than Ever. So Why Is There More Anti-Trans Legislation Than Ever, Too?," *The Nation*, March 4, 2016.

9. Too Loud: Jennifer Weiner

1. Virginia Woolf, *A Room of One's Own* (London: Hogarth Press, 1929).

2. Ian McEwan, "Hello, Would You Like a Free Book?," *The Guardian*, September 20, 2005.

3. Jonathan Franzen, interviewed by Terry Gross, *Fresh Air*, October 15, 2001, http://www.npr.org/templates/story/story.php?storyId =1131456.

4. Trip Gabriel, "Women Buy Fiction in Bulk and Publishers Take Notice," *The New York Times*, March 17, 1997.

5. Rebecca Mead, "Written Off," *The New Yorker*, January 13, 2014.

6. Jane Mulkerrins, "Jennifer Weiner: Why I'm Waging War on Literary Snobbery," *The Telegraph*, August 17, 2014.

7. Susan Lerner, "A Conversation with Jonathan Franzen," *Booth: A Journal*, February 13, 2015, http://booth.butler.edu/2015/02 /13/a-conversation-with-jonathan-franzen/.

8. Aja Romano, "Why Jonathan Franzen's Social Media Fear Indicts the Entire Publishing Industry," *The Daily Dot*, September 22, 2013; and Stephanie Harzewski, *Chick Lit and Postfeminism* (Charlottesville: University of Virginia Press, 2011).

9. Nathan Sheppard, *The Essays of George Eliot* (New York: Funk & Wagnalls, 1883).

10. Andreas Huyssen, "Mass Culture as Woman: Modernism's Other," *After the Great Divide: Modernism, Mass Culture, Postmodernism* (Bloomington: Indiana University Press, 1987).

11. Dwight Macdonald, *Masscult and Midcult: Essays Against the American Grain* (New York: New York Review of Books Classics, 2011).

12. Ibid.

13. Quoted in Kathleen Rooney, *Reading with Oprah: The Book Club That Changed America* (Fayetteville: University of Arkansas Press, 2005).

14. Beth Driscoll, *The New Literary Middlebrow: Tastemakers and Reading in the Twenty-First Century* (New York: Palgrave Macmillan, 2014).

15. David D. Kirkpatrick, "Oprah Gaffe by Franzen Draws Ire and Sales," *The New York Times*, October 29, 2001.

16. Jonathan Franzen, "Perchance to Dream," *Harper's*, April 1996; and ibid.

17. Kirkpatrick, "Oprah Gaffe by Franzen Draws Ire and Sales."

18. Jennifer Weiner, "Oprah Meets Chutzpah," *The Philadelphia Inquirer*, October 27, 2001.

19. Mulkerrins, "Jennifer Weiner: Why I'm Waging War on Literary Snobbery."

20. Cris Mazza, "Imperative: Chick Lit and the Perversion of a Genre," *Poets & Writers*, January/February 2005.

21. James Wolcott, "Hear Me Purr," *The New Yorker*, May 20, 1996.

22. Leslie Gray Streeter, "The 'Chick-Lit' Label: Demeaning or Empowering?," *The Palm Beach Post* (Florida), October 4, 2005.

23. Mazza, "Imperative: Chick Lit and the Perversion of a Genre."

24. Natalie Danford, "The Chick Lit Question," *Publishers Weekly*, October 20, 2003; quoted in Tania Modleski, *Loving with a Vengeance: Mass Produced Fantasies for Women* (New York: Routledge, 2008); and Whitney Otto, "Unoriginal Sins," *The New York Times*, May 12, 2006.

25. Elizabeth Merrick, *This Is Not Chick Lit: Original Stories by America's Best Women Writers (No Heels Required)* (New York: Random House, 2006).

26. Tanya Barrientos, "Sassy, Kicky 'Chick Lit' Is the Hottest Trend in Publishing," *The Philadelphia Inquirer*, May 25, 2003.

27. Jessica Pressler, "Miss Popularity," *Phildelphia* magazine, October 1, 2005.

28. Pavel Barter, "Woman of Substance," *The Sunday Times* (London), July 29, 2007; and Aileen Jacobson, "Gender Bias," *Chicago Tribune*, May 17, 2004.

29. Streeter, "The 'Chick-Lit' Label."

30. Pressler, "Miss Popularity."

31. Streeter, "The 'Chick-Lit' Label."

32. Lucy Clark, "One Smart Chick Can Save the Lit," *The Sunday Telegraph* (Australia), August 9, 2009.

33. Jennifer Weiner, *Hungry Heart: Adventures in Love, Life, and Writing* (New York: Simon & Schuster, 2016).

34. Jason Pinter, "Jodi Picoult and Jennifer Weiner Speak Out on Franzen Feud," *The Huffington Post*, August 26, 2010.

35. "Fact-Checking the Franzenfreude," *DoubleX*, *Slate*, September 2, 2010.

36. "The Count 2010," *VIDA: Women in Literary Arts*, May 16, 2011, http://www.vidaweb.org/the-count-2010/.

37. Julie Steinberg, "Jennifer Egan on Winning the 2011 Pulitzer Prize for Fiction," *The Wall Street Journal*, April 18, 2011; Edra Ziesk, "Meg Wolitzer: Men Won't Read Books About Women," *Salon*, April 9, 2013; and "Lena Dunham: The Creator of HBO's *Girls* Shares Her Reading Habits," *The New York Times*, April 19, 2012.

38. Julie Steinberg, "Jennifer Weiner Talks 'Good in Bed,' Chick Lit and Cheating Husbands," *The Wall Street Journal*, May 24, 2011.

39. Ibid.; Aja Romano, "Why Jonathan Franzen's Social Media Fear Indicts the Entire Publishing Industry"; and Jane Mulkerrins, "Jenny & the Chick-Lit Factory," *The Sunday Telegraph*, August 17, 2014.

40. Daniel D'Addario, "A Brief History of Jennifer Weiner's Literary Fights," *Salon*, May 24, 2013.

41. Sandy Hingston, "Jennifer Weiner, Shut Up," *Philadelphia* magazine, September 13, 2010.

42. Emily Shire, "I Love Jennifer Weiner, but She Needs to Back Off," *The Week*, January 8, 2014.

43. Jennifer Weiner, "I'm Glad the NYT Is Finally Covering Commercial Fiction, and Sorry If I Went Too Far," *Salon*, September 10, 2013.

44. Ibid.

45. Jonathan Franzen and Karl Kraus, *The Kraus Project: Essays by Karl Kraus* (New York: Farrar, Straus and Giroux, 2013).

46. Jennifer Weiner, "What Jonathan Franzen Misunderstands About Me," *The New Republic*, September 18, 2013.

47. Beth Driscoll, *The New Literary Middlebrow*.

48. Weiner, *Hungry Heart*.

49. Ibid.

50. "Letters," March 2, 2016, *The New York Times Book Review*, http://www.nytimes.com/2016/03/06/books/review/letters -lit-up.html.

51. Jennifer Weiner, "The Snobs and Me," *The New York Times*, June 10, 2016.

10. Too Naked: Lena Dunham

1. Emily Nussbaum, "The Little Tramp," *The New Yorker*, May 11, 2015.

2. "Ideas That Have Outlived Their Usefulness," *The Atlantic*, July/August 2013.

3. Kenneth Clark, *The Nude: A Study in Ideal Form* (first published 1956; Princeton, NJ: Princeton University Press, 1972).

4. Ibid.

5. Margaret R. Miles, *Carnal Knowing: Female Nakedness and Religious Meaning in the Christian West* (Eugene, OR: Wipf and Stock, 2006).

6. John Berger, *Ways of Seeing* (New York: Penguin Books, 2008).

7. For more on the institution of the Hays Code, see Thomas Doherty, *Pre-Code Hollywood: Sex, Immorality, and Insurrection in American Cinema, 1930–1934*, second edition (New York: Columbia University Press, 1999).

8. Specifics of "Don'ts and Be Carefuls" available in ibid.

9. For more on "sexposition," see Myles McNutt, "Game of Thrones—'You Win or You Die,'" *Cultural Learnings*, May 29, 2011.

10. Lena Dunham, *Not That Kind of Girl: A Young Woman Tells You What She's "Learned"* (New York: Random House, 2015).

11. Rebecca Mead, "Downtown's Daughter," *The New Yorker*, November 15, 2010.

12. Ibid.

13. Susan Bordo, *Unbearable Weight: Feminism, Western Culture, and the Body*, tenth anniversary edition (Berkeley: University of California Press, 2004).

14. Ibid.

15. Ibid.

16. Ibid.

17. Lizzie Crocker, "How Lena Dunham Gets Dressed for 'Girls,'" *The Daily Beast*, January 11, 2015.

18. Ibid.

19. Quoted in "The Fountain," short film directed by Lena Dunham, 2007.

20. Dhani Mau, "*Girls* Fashion Recap," *Fashionista*, January 28, 2013.

21. Dunham, *Not That Kind of Girl*.

22. Ibid.